Representations of Animals on Greek and Roman Engraved Gems

Representations of Animals on Greek and Roman Engraved Gems

Meanings and interpretations

Idit Sagiv

Archaeopress Publishing Ltd
Summertown Pavilion
18-24 Middle Way
Summertown
Oxford OX2 7LG

www.archaeopress.com

ISBN 978 1 78491 869 9
ISBN 978 1 78491 870 5 (e-Pdf)

This book is available direct from Archaeopress or from our website www.archaeopress.com

In memory of my beloved inspiring mother, Osnat (Sabina) Sagiv

Contents

List of figures

Acknowledgements

This publication is based upon my doctoral thesis, which was accepted for the degree of PhD at the University of Tel-Aviv in 2015.

First of all I whould like to thank Dr Talila Michaeli for her helpful advice. I have had the privilege of having Dr Michaeli as my PhD supervisor whose keen observations and kind support have provided invaluable assistance during the years I have spent in research.

I especially wish to thank Revd Dr Martin Henig who generously gave me his expert advice. My thanks are also due to him for encouragement and help with this work.

I am indebted to Dr Silvia Rozenberg, former Senior Curator of Classical Archaeology, The Israel Museum Jerusalem for her kind permission to study the gems for my thesis research.

I am grateful to Ms Galit Bennett-Dahan, Curator of Classical Archaeology, The Israel Museum Jerusalem for her help and approving the publication of the photos.

Finally, I wish to thank Dr David Davison and Dr Rajka Makjanic, directors of Archaeopress for their courtesy and kind editorial support and for Gerry Brisch for editing the text.

Introduction

Engraved gems are precious stones, usually semi-precious, that were processed and polished so that the top surface of the stone featured the design or motif desired by the artist. Gem engraving is a miniature art form whose charm combines the grace of colourful stones and their brilliance with the beauty of the image depicted on them. Engraved gems are divided into two main types: intaglio refers to carving with the design cut into the flat background of the stone; while cameo refers to relief carvings, with the design projecting out from the background, usually using two different colour layers of the same stone. Most of the gems are small in dimension, ranging from several millimetres to a few centimetres. It should be noted however, that there are unique examples, most of them cameos, which are of considerable size, such as the 'Gemma Augustea' kept in Vienna, or the 'Great Cameo of France' (Le Grand Camée de France) kept in the Cabinet des médailles, Paris.[1] The origin of this art lies in the carving of cylinder seals that were common in Mesopotamia from as early as the 4th millennium BC and which spread throughout the Middle and Near East. Minoan and Mycenaean artists learned the intricate technique of engraving gemstones from Eastern artists and produced seal stones until the collapse of the Mycenaean civilization, around 1100 BC. The revival of the art of carving gems and seals occurred in Greece only at the end of the 8th century BC. The artists there were inspired by Egypt and the Near East and borrowed several forms (from Egypt the Greek artists borrowed the scarab form) and materials, but the themes and styles were adapted to the tastes and preferences of Greece. Greek designs were varied, and instead of rulers and representations of mythical beasts, so common in Eastern carving, gods and heroes were now selected, as well as mythological and everyday scenes. Greek artists explored the natural world, thus gradually freeing themselves from earlier conventions (Richter 1968: I). On the gems were engraved various images that included not only deities and

---

[1] 'The Gemma Augustea' – h: 19cm, w: 23cm; 'The Great Cameo of France' – h: 31cm, w: 26.5cm.

mythological themes, but also animals, famous sculptures, astrological signs, portraits and various objects. The art of carving gems reached its peak in the era between the end of Archaic and the end of Hellenistic times. With the rise of Rome, Greek engravers migrated there and during the end of the Republic and the early Empire periods they excelled in carving portraits and symbolic mythological scenes. From the time of Augustus onwards, gemstones, which were once exclusive to the wealthy and affluent ruling classes, became more widely available, and, as a result, the art of gem engraving lost the previous high quality that typified it (Richter 1956: XV–XVI).

Gems ceased to be prevalent in the middle of the 3rd century AD, or slightly later, at the beginning of the 4th century AD. The reasons for the decline of the art of gem engraving are not clear. A certain continuation of the tradition of seal rings can be seen in the Sassanian seals that continued to be manufactured until the Arab conquest (Henig 1997: 93).

In their own time, the depictions on gems were both meaningful and also often symbolic. Many of the images are no longer familiar to us, and research, based on ancient literary sources, is required in order to interpret their meanings (Plantzos 1999: 98). The images depicted on seal rings bore a magical meaning of threat and warning. Anyone who dared to break the seal knew that he risked a terrible punishment for this crime, so the effectiveness of the seal was based on the fear of what might befall with the subsequently discovery (Plantzos 1999: 22). When analyzing the symbols that appear on gems, we find elements borrowed from ancient mythologies, such as Babylonian (Chaldean) and, especially, Egyptian, including cults relating to Serapis-Asclepius, Isis, Harpokrates, Mithras and elements taken from the books of Zarathustra, the Bible and Kabbalistic writings (Babelon, s.v. 'Gemmae', Daremberg and Saglio (eds), *DAGR*, t. 2.2: 1481). According to ancient writers, the devices shown on the seal rings were meaningful for the wearer (Richter 1971: vol.1, 4). For example, it is known that Pompeius chose a depiction of a lion holding a sword (Plutarch, *Lives*, vol. v, *Pompey* LXXX: 5); Julius Caesar chose that of an armed Aphrodite, seeing himself as a descendant of the goddess through Aeneas (Dio Cassius, *Roman History*, vol. iv, XLIII: 43), while Augustus had three rings: the first featured a sphinx (Pliny, *Natural History*: XXXVII.Iv.10); the second a portrait of Alexander; and the third his own portrait made by Dioskourides (Pliny, *Natural History*: XXXVII.iv.10; Suetonius, *De vita caesarum, Augustus/Octavian*, L: 4; Dio Cassius, *Roman History*, vol. vi, LI: 3, 4 ff). According to Martin Henig, Vollenweider also assigns meanings to animal representations on gems, based on *Anthologia Graeca* epigrams depicting engraved gems, as well as a fragment from Heliodorus' *Aethiopica* (Henig 1997: 45; *Anthologia Graeca* IX: 746–747, 750, 752; Héliodore, *Les Éthiopiques*, t. 2, livre V: 13–14).

The subject of this study, based on my thesis, is animal representations and their meanings on Greek and Roman engraved gems. Animal depictions on gems have not been studied iconographically and stylistically and technically as one division. In addition, no comparison has been made between animal depictions on gemstones and their representations in other media. No research has examined to what extent gemstone artists based their work on artistic models depicting animals which developed in a particular region or were common in the Greco-Roman world from a given time onwards, and/or the degree of their independence. In addition, the beliefs expressed in animal depictions on gems have not been sufficiently examined by analogy with the beliefs associated with the subject as reflected in ancient texts.

Until the second half of the 19th century, interest in engraved gems, including scarabs, scarabaeus, intaglios and cameos, was essentially, to use the words of Henig, 'a recreation practiced by dilettanti' (Henig 1978: xxxi). The gems bearing animal depictions that were published at the time were treated in the same way as other carved stones: they were documented by etching or drawing with minimal text, which in most cases was inaccurate. At the end of the 19th and beginning of the 20th centuries, scientific research methods began to be practised in the field of Greco-Roman engraved gems. The most important and comprehensive work among these publications is the monumental three-volume work by Furtwängler (Furtwängler 1900). In this study, and in most of the other catalogues in this literary-research category, the gems are photographed and these comprise a good basis for research. Furtwängler placed the stones in their historical context, i.e. in dating them to centuries and half-centuries, and by assigning them to the different regions and production centres in the Greco-Roman world. He analyzed the gems stylistically and tried to determine the interactions between carving styles and production areas, and also to understand their meanings. His work serves as a foundation and infrastructure for contemporary scholars of ancient gems. However research has progressed greatly over the past century and his conclusions must be re-examined, regarding both the delineation of engraving styles in time and space and his iconographic interpretations.

Furtwängler's research, and most of the other catalogues published in the last thirty years of the 19th and early 20th centuries, do not include technical details, i.e. the dimensions of the stone, and there is almost no reference to the variety of carving techniques, types of drills, etc. The dimensions of the stones in the photographs are small, so it is difficult to understand the details of the carving techniques of each gem. Therefore the conclusions regarding style, technique, and dating (when given) are sometimes erroneous, or unspecified, as is currently accepted for the study of gems. In the catalogues of Furtwängler and others –

such as those of Babelon (1897), Middleton (1891) and Walters (1926) – there are a great many gems bearing animal depictions. These gems do not appear in these publications as a separate division. In most of them the descriptions of the animals are minimal and not accompanied by stylistic or technical analyses, some of which include very general dating (for example 'Hellenistic', 'Roman', 'Etruscan', etc.), while in others the dating is more specific (i.e. '1st–2nd century AD'). In most of these catalogues, no systematic comparison was made to other media depicting animals.

The artistic and aesthetic value of the engraved gems and their technical and stylistic aspects began to be discussed in a more profound and comprehensive manner from the 1950s. In catalogues and articles dealing with engraved gems there is also an attempt to compare them with other media of Greco-Roman art, and to use these comparisons both for dating and to establish the time-span of characteristic styles. This attempt was especially applied to large cameos and the highest quality gems, to the few gemstones on which the artist's name is engraved, and to those types that could be compared to famous statues and common types appearing also on coins. The studies of both Richter (1956) and Vermeule (1957) are among the most prominent in this research direction.

Only in recent decades have studies been published dealing with sorting and classification according to engraving styles, types of gemstones and iconographic analyses. These studies have promoted the research of gems, and as a result it is now possible to associate a large number of the gems which were not included in this literature to stylistic divisions defined and limited in time. The most important contribution lies in the researches of Henig (1978; 1994; 2004), Boardman (1970; 2003), Boardman and Vollenweider (1978), Maaskant-Kleibrink (1978), Zazoff (1983), and Zwierlein-Diehl (1969; 1973) and many more.

While Henig concentrated on the meaning of animal images on Greek and Roman gems as a whole, and suggested a range of likely explanations (1997: 45–53), few studies have otherwise dealt specifically with animal representations. Other articles published on the subject of animal depictions on gems deal with a specific theme, but not as a group, such as Maaskant-Kleibrink's article (1999: 19–27) dealing with 'Leda' on ancient gems, Nagy's paper dealing with the image of an eagle on a specific Imperial gem (1992: 99–108), Ward's study investigating the cow suckling a calf motif on scarabs (1992: 67–81), and Henig's research on animals emerging from a sea-shell as represented on gems (1984: 243–247).

This present research focuses on a group of about 70 gems (intaglios only) kept in the Israel Museum, Jerusalem, and which has not yet been published. This group will serve as a test group for the broader subject of animal representations on Greek and Roman gems. The group in question is of a very high quality, which allows us to explore and study them closely, with close-up photography to see all the details, and conduct stylistic research in an unmediated manner. John Boardman found that the theme of animal depictions is the most common on the Archaic, Classical and Greco-Persian gems (1980: 104, 108, 109), yet there is still no complete corpus that encompasses all the scarabs, scarabaeus, and Greco-Roman gems depicting animal images. Gisela Richter indicates that the images engraved on gems possessed special meanings for their owners, based on ancient literary sources (1971: 4–5). However not all scholars agree that animal portrayals on gems possess symbolic value. Boardman himself believes that most of the gems were used as jewellery rather than as seals, and bases his argument on the almost total absence of recording the name of the wearer, the repetition of nearly identical themes, and the almost total absence of personal subjects. However he does admit that we know from ancient sources that there was such use, and therefore he believes that such use was reserved exclusively for metal rings.

This research seeks to study those gems with images of animals from the Israel Museum, and for this purpose comparison will be made with other gems kept in international collections. The characteristics and meanings of animal depictions in the ancient world will be examined within various media, such as sculpture, mosaics and vases, in order to examine the changes in their representations on a miniature medium – gemstones. In this study I will discuss whether the miniature medium allowed for the selection of symbols that did not appear in the larger media, and if so what are the reasons for this, for example whether the changes were due to the fact that the gems were intended for a particular population. The question of what happened when the depictions of animals were transferred to other media and whether the gems convey other meanings is a weighty methodological question. The study seeks to examine what was the uniqueness of animal imagery on ancient gems compared to other media, and what is the significance of this distinction.

The engraved gems presented here for the first time will be depicted in detail while learning the motifs and studying the iconographic and stylistic sources of animal images on gems. The meanings of specific animal representations that appear on the gems will be examined while attempting to provide interpretation. In addition, an attempt will be made to address the question of whether there is a connection between the choice of a certain gemstone and the image portrayed on it.

Of particular importance is the attempt to date the gems, bearing in mind always that their archaeological context is unknown. Therefore dating is based on the carving style and engraving technique, the material and the shape of the gemstones, as well as the choice of subjects. In addition, there was a need to identify the material from which each gem is made, using the relevant literature and with the co-operation of a gemmologist. And, finally, the research includes identification of the historical, cultural and religious concepts behind the themes depicted on the engraved gems.

Engraved gems: a survey

1. The Uses of Engraved Gems

Three main uses are known for engraved gems in Greek and Roman times: as seals, jewellery, and amulets (Babelon, s.v. 'Gemmae', Daremberg and Saglio (eds), *DAGR*, t. 2.2: 1460; Richter, *Engraved Gems of the Greeks, Etruscans and Romans*, vol.1, 1).

A. *Engraved Gems as Seals*

The main purpose of an engraved gem (intaglio) was to be used for sealing. The device was stamped on a soft material, such as wax or clay, and was used as a personal signature, when signing letters, documents, contracts and wills. This fact assigns a special interest to gems research, since apart from their artistic and historical value they also testify to the private life of ancient people. The seals were used in ancient times to secure property, letters and contracts, as identification of the wearer, a ritual act and also as official seals of the authorities (Plantzos 1999: 118–122; Richter 1956: XVI). The images carved on the gems bore a meaning, a threat and a warning, and thus the seals constituted symbolic locks. Whoever broke the seal risked a terrible fear of punishment for this crime (Brodrick 1972: 99).

Mesopotamian cylinder seals, as well as seals carved in various regions of Greece during the Minoan and Mycenaean period, were worn around the wrist or hung on necklaces and sewn into clothing. On the other hand, Greek and Etruscan gems, starting from the Archaic era, were usually embedded in rings (Boardman 1980: 107). The Romans, as the heirs of Etruscan and Hellenistic culture, adopted the custom of seal rings (Henig 1978: 55–70).

The Greek owner embedded his seal on the doors of the rooms, closets and basements where he kept his supplies (for example, wine, food and drinks), and also on the boxes where he kept his valuables, such as his secret papers and jewellery, as a means of protection from theft. In other words, seals can be regarded as the equivalent of modern locks or other security devices. Ancient writers often refer to this custom. For example, when Agamemnon returned from Troy, Clytemnestra sent him a message that he would find the treasures intact, without any broken seal (Aeschylus, *Agamemnon*: 609 ff). The women of Athens were angry, according to Aristophanes, with this custom of their husbands, and on the first occasion they found a way to break the seals (Aristophanes, *Women at the Thesmophoria*, vol. III: 414–416, 425). In exceptional events, such as reconciliation in *Lysistrata*, the landlord agreed that the seals would be removed from his boxes and the hoarded refreshments would be offered for everyone (Aristophanes, *Lysistrata*, vol. III: 1198).

Latin literature also tells of the practice of keeping valuables by using stamps. For example, Pliny the Younger, who sent letters from Nicomedia to Trajan, wrote him in one of them that he is sending a lump of raw gold from a quarry in Parthia together with the letter, and that the parcel is sealed with his signet ring, bearing the sign of a quadriga (Pliny the Younger, *Letters*: X.74.16). Tiberius Gracchus embedded his personal signet ring on the doors of Kronos Temple, to be sure that money does not come out without permission (Plutarch, *Lives*, vol. x, *Tiberius Gracchus*: 8). Pompey decided to imprint his seal on the swords of his soldiers to prevent them from fighting each other (Plutarch, *Lives*, vol. v, *Pompey*: 10. 7). The seal corresponds to modern security codes, biometric authentication devices, and signatures. At a time when many people were illiterate, imprinting a personal seal was the only reliable sign of identification (Platt 2006: 234; Richter 1971: i). And also, before the era of postal services, it was necessary to deposit letters by couriers, hence the seal constituted a sign of identification and protection from reading the contents of the letter by an unauthorised person. Thus, for example, the letter Phaedra left for her husband Theseus, the king of Athens, was sealed with her personal signet ring, and Theseus had to untie it in order to read it (Euripides, *Hippolytus*, vol. II: 862–865).

Apart from the papyrus, wooden boards (*tabulae ceratae*) were also used for letters, and especially contracts. These plates were covered with wax on which the writing was done with a *stylus*. In this case, too, a thread or string would have been transferred through the outer edges of the boards and the edges would have been sealed with wax. When the document was particularly important, the wax imprint would have been kept from harm in a little box of bronze. The boxes were sometimes coated with coloured enamel, similar to the clasp pins known in western and central Europe, and might have been made in the same workshops (Henig 1978: 31).

When the imprint was made of wax, it could be warmed slightly, until the bottom melted, and then the letter could be opened without damaging the design on the imprint (Henig 1978: 26). In this way it was possible to open sealed letters, or to transfer seal impressions to documents that were not written by the signet ring owner itself. These sophisticated fraud operations were very difficult to handle. For example, Thucydides documents a case in which a person broke a letter's seal, read it, and re-signed it (*History of the Peloponnesian War*, 1: 132. 5). Lucian also describes how the false prophet Alexander convinced the public of his divine powers, when giving answers to the requests of his believers, supposedly from the god Asclepius, while actually opening the scrolls himself by dissolving the wax of the seal and then closing it again (Lucian of Samosata, *Alexander of Abonuteichos – the False Prophet*: 20–21).

The seal was used to sign legal contracts during the procedures of legal proceedings in Classical Athens. Government officials also used the emperor's seal to sign official documents. The seal also served as a kind of identity card of its wearer, and sometimes represented its owner in his absence. For example, Orestes shows Electra the signet ring of their father, Agamemnon, which he wears, in order to convince her of his identity (Sophocles, *Electra*: 1222). It was also used to confirm a verbal message: when Deianeira sends Lichas to Heracles with her poisoned robe, she also adds the imprint of her seal ring as a sign 'that he will surely recognise' (Sophocles, *The Trachiniae*: 614 ff).

Herodotus describes how Egyptian priests imprinted their seal on the horns of a sacrifice bull (*Historiae*: 2. 38). Plutarch refers to the writer Castor, who mentioned the priests whose job was to imprint the bull sacrificed for Isis and Osiris with a signet ring bearing a representation of a kneeling man, his hands tied behind his back, and a sword resting on his neck (Plutarch, *Moralia*, vol. V, 'Isis and Osiris': 363 B). Statues from Cyprus depicting priests and 'temple boys' document the bearing of seals by priests, wearing a variety of seal necklaces on their chests (Beer 1994: pt. ii, 25–27, n. 133; pt. I, no. 168 and pl. 49, cf. Plantzos 1999: 19–20). Pausanias denotes that in Elis the priests of Dionysus brought three pottery vessels into the temple in order to stamp their seals on them (Pausanias, *Description of Greece*: 6.26.1–2). When in the morning everyone was allowed to inspect the vases, they discovered that they were untouched, full of wine.

The widespread use of engraved gems as seals can be also learned from papyri which were preserved and found sealed (in addition to the literary sources and the general finding that indicates their prevalence). For example, a Hellenistic papyri archive was found in Elephantine, Egypt, which included wills, a marriage contract relating to the maintenance of the dowry, and even documents of a concubine documenting deposits from her patrons (Porten 1996); and large collections of *bullae* (seal impressions on clay), such as that discovered in a building at Cyrene, Libya, where the *bullae* were hardened by the fire occurring during the Jewish revolt that broke out in 115–116 AD (Maddoli 1965: 39–145).

The possibility that a ruler's seal ring might fall into the wrong hands might cause serious consequences, from simple fraud to signifying its owner's defeat in battle. One famous example is the story of the falling of the signet ring of the Roman general Marcellus into the hands of Hannibal. This nearly resulted in the Carthaginians taking various Roman cities (Livy, *Ab urbe condita* XXVII: 28). In order to prevent such acts of deceit, people used to transfer their seal ring to loyal hands, or destroy it before they died. According to Suetonius, Tiberius, on his deathbed, pulled off his ring to give it to a bystander and after some hesitation replaced it on his finger (Suetonius, *De vita Caesarum - Tiberius*: II.73). Petronius, one of Nero's courtiers, was said to have broken his seal ring before committing suicide, so as to prevent its illegal use endangering others (Tacitus, *The Annals of Tacitus* 16: 18–19). Wearing the signet ring of a deceased emperor signalled his successor. The use made by the later emperors of Augustus's portrait, appearing on a seal ring which was made for him by Dioskourides, may indicate this. In addition, according to Plutarch, when Julius Caesar arrived in Egypt after the death of Pompey, his rival's signet ring was handed to him (Plutarch, *Lives*, vol. v, *Pompey*: 80.5). Hellenistic and Roman gems from later sites, may sometimes have been passed down in this way, or they may have been purchased by the last owner on the market as antiques. For the archaeologist, the long life and continued appreciation of old gemstones limit their value as dating evidence (Henig 1994: X). Some of the Greek and Roman gems reached the Middle Ages and continued to be used as seals (Babelon, s.v. 'Gemmae', Daremberg and Saglio (eds), *DAGR*, t. 2.2: 1488; Soeda 1987: 185–192). The use of gems as seals was their main use until the mid 1st century AD. During this period, large quantities are being produced, their quality is reduced and the imprint becomes difficult to understand. The mass production of the gems makes the models become similar to each other (Guiraud 1996: 51). It seems that most of the Hellenistic intaglios were engraved to serve as jewels, or amulets, and not as seals. Discovered clay impressions were sealed by metal rings, and not by engraved gemstones (Plantzos 1999: 23).

B. Engraved Gems as Amulets

Another important role of engraved gems was to serve as amulets. Engraved gems were thought by the Romans to have extraordinary properties, such as protecting against disease, encouraging love or ensuring victory. According to Pliny (*Natural History*: XXXVII.139–143), it was believed that through their wearing it was possible to ward off evil forces or specific demons, to counter poison, as well as promoting any good cause. Amulets were usually worn, perhaps sewn into clothing, worn on a string around the neck, or somewhere else. According to Plutarch, some amuletic devices that could be gems served to neutralise the 'evil-eye' through the use of alien images that supposedly trapped the harmful gaze and thus distanced the negative forces from the gem wearer (Plutarch, *Moralia*, vol. VIII, 'Quaestiones convivales': V.7.681). Such gems were therefore considered apotropaic.

It was believed that an invisible demon dwelt within each gem, and that a secret relationship existed between the gems and the stars because of their similar sparkle. Thus was born the ancient relationship between the gems and the belief that attributed a magical, protective and astrological character to them (Babelon, s.v. 'Gemmae', Daremberg and Saglio (eds), *DAGR*, t. 2.2: 1460). Over time, carved images of gods, priests, etc. began to appear on the gems in order to enhance the magic power. Whenever an individual needed the help of a god he would turn to the aid of his gem, which he always kept close to him and which became an emblem of his personality. A gem could constitute an image or an icon, allowing one direct access to the Divine or it could be amuletic, whose power is innate or implicit. Certain gemstones, including jasper and agate, were ascribed the power to cure disease, as well as being talismanic and possessing protective qualities. Pliny provides a long list of precious and semi-precious stones that were believed to possess such qualities, such as the amethyst, said to prevent intoxication (probably due to its purple-red colour resembling wine); the emerald, detoxifying when carved with the image of an eagle; and the diamond, curing insanity and false fears and protecting against the harmful effects of toxins (Damigeron, *De virtutibus lapidum*: 18; Dioscorides, *De materia medica*: no. 20, 5.126.I; Les lapidaire grecs 1985: *lapidaire orphique* 21; Pliny, *Natural History*: XXXVI, XXXVII.169).

Pliny refers to such beliefs with scepticism and ridicule, but nonetheless attributes to some of the stones healing properties (Thorndike 1964, vol. 1: 80–81) when they are crushed to powder and drunk or when worn as amulets (Pliny, *Natural History*: XXXVII.12, 37, 39, 55). Pliny also repeats the belief specified in Theophrastus and Mucianus, according to which certain stones assist fertility (Pliny, *Natural History*: XXXVI.25, 39).

Although there is no evidence of a belief in the existence of magical gems in Ancient Greece, Homer already mentions some evidence of the Greek belief in magic. In the 5th and 4th centuries BC, magical activities and artefacts are mentioned in the literature, and the existence of amulets is even implied on vase paintings (Bonner 1950: 3–6). At the end of the Classical period and during Hellenistic times magical rings are mentioned in the written sources (Aristophanes, *Wealth (The Plutus)*: 883–885); and during the Roman period the use of gems as amulets started to become widespread, and inscriptions started to appear as well (Bonner 1950: 6–7).

Medical references in the essay 'On stones' confirm an early interest of Classical medicine in stones (Theophrastus, *De Lapidibus*). By the end of the 1st century AD this had become fully developed, as can be seen in the 'Materia Medica', a pharmacology essay by Dioscorides of Anazarbus from Cilicia in southern Asia Minor. The fifth book of Materia Medica deals mainly with the medicinal properties of gems (Dioscorides, *De materia medica*: 5.126). The stones, even when not decorated, were believed to have some innate curative or other power. For example, hematite was recommended for healing eye diseases, sapphire against scorpion stings, and all types of jasper were recommended as amulets that allowed a swift labour for women.

Dioscorides specifies about two hundred types of stones, and suggests that some, softer ones, will be ground to powder in order to be taken orally as a medicine, and the harder ones will be worn as amulets. For many Greeks the dangers that lurked at sea, such as storms and sinking ships, were common sources of concern. A book on gemology related to shipping and seafaring recommended a variety of gemstones that could ward off such dangers (Clark 1986: 83). For example, amulets made of chalcedony were worn by children at sea. Such beliefs, which we would now dismiss as non-scientific, have been taken seriously in the past (Clark 1986: 84). Another genre of gemstone-related research was the *Lithika*, the precursor of the medieval *Lapidaria*. These, unlike the scientific doctrines of Theophrastus and Pliny, deal mainly with the magical properties of the stones. Pliny refers to such works critically. A later one which has survived, from the 3rd or 4th century AD, is the *Lithika*. There is no doubt that this composition is not the 'Book of Eighty Stones' mentioned in 'Suidae Lexicon' (Suidas, s.v. 'Orpheus', in Adler (ed.),*Suidae Lexicon*, vol. III: 564). This book dealt with eighty gemstones and the depictions engraved on them. The book apparently suggested an interpretation of the magical symbols, which according to the Orphian doctrine, should be engraved on certain gemstones. Diodorus Siculus knew of the existence of such a treatise, which he related to the Orphic doctrines, and which was called the *Lithika* (Diodorus Siculus, *Bibliotheca historica*: 7. 1. 1). It is not possible to determine whether this was the book which Suidas noted. The *Lithika* that survived, an essay contained in the Orphic poems, concenrs 29 stones only and their magical properties, but does not discuss the devices engraved on them (Lithika in *Orphica*: 363; 'The Orphic Poems', 36). The poem probably influenced the entire genre of medieval lapidaria. These were long poems, following the tradition of the *Lithika*, and similar poems on gemstones, which discussed the properties of gems regarding religious, magical, or apocalyptic criteria (Plantzos 1999: 10). St. Isidore, the Bishop of Seville (7th century AD), included in his *Etymologiae* a passage on gemstones, in which Pliny's influence on him can be discerned (Isidore of Seville, *Etymologies - Book 16: De Lapidibus et Metallis; Stones and Metals*: XVI). Marbode, the Bishop of Rennes (1101–1067), wrote a Latin poem called *De Lapidibus* based on St. Isidore and Pliny, but also with the influences of *De Virtutibus Lapidum* of the 2nd century BC Damigeron (Damigeron, *The Virtues of Stones: De virtutibus lapidum*; Marbode of Rennes, *De Lapidibus*). These descriptions were influenced by the Christian faith (Plantzos 1999: 10). In 2001, 'The Papyrus of Milan' was published, which includes Posidippus of Pella epigrams from the second half of the 3rd century BC and whose first part, entitled 'Lithika', deals with gemstones (Posidippus of Pella, *Posidippi Pellaei quae supersunt omnia*: Poems 1–20).

In the 1st century AD, there was a significant change in the use of gems, and from this period onwards we find inscribed gems that can be categorised with certainty as amulets. In the majority of cases the inscriptions are in Greek. These gems no longer serve as seals, since their rough style and the engraving in the 'positive' do not create clear impressions. The Egyptian influence on the magical gems is evident, and also the largest amount of magical gems was discovered in Egypt itself (Bonner 1950: 7–44).

A number of scholars have suggested that the definition of magical gems is problematic due to its reductive nature (Nagy 2012: 106; 2002: 153–179), and owing to its assumption that only inscribed ones can be regarded as such (Hamburger 1968: 3–4). Nagy has suggested that it would be more appropriate to regard magical gems as 'Hellenised' versions of amulets (Nagy 2012: 84–87, 106; 2002: 153–156, 169–170). We know from ancient sources like the *Lithika*, and the magical papyri, that there existed a much larger range of gems with magical properties, for example with regard to healing diseases (Nagy 2002: 153–179; 2011; 2012: 85–87; Dasen 2014: 178, note 1). Bonner cites several specimens of uninscribed gems along with their inscribed counterparts, and points out that the lack of an inscription may not always invalidate their magical use. Further, he points out that certain gems, which bear no inscription of a magical character, may, nevertheless, have been worn as amulets (Bonner 1950: 14, cf. Hamburger 1968: 3).

Many different devices appear on the magical gems. In addition to the detailed description of the magical properties of gemstones, Pliny also notes that many of his contemporaries wore as amulets gems which were engraved with symbols, mysterious images and astronomical depictions whose healing abilities were known as wondrous (Babelon, s.v. 'Gemmae', Daremberg and Saglio (eds),

DAGR, t. 2.2: 1481; Pliny, *Natural History*: XXXVI.25, 31, 39; XXXVII.15, 58, 67, 169). In most cases it is difficult to decipher what was the magical purpose of the gem, but sometimes the inscription helps to associate the device with a particular type of magical action. Thus, for example, gems on which appear Heracles battling the Nemean lion were related to the healing of an intestinal disease; Representations of lizards were associated with curing eye diseases (Pliny, *Natural History*: XXIX.129–130); and a depiction of a womb, portrayed as a cupping vessel, often with a key beneath it, had a symbolic value in connection with pregnancy and childbirth (Dasen 2014: 181).

Gems are also known as expressing love, and as a guarantee of personal value and well-being. According to Pliny, seal rings and gems were often emotionally charged: they were often gifts of love for a beloved one (Pliny, *Natural History*: XXXIII.147; XXXVII.18–20, 29). It is also accepted that they defined the place of the individual in society, both within the family and in the wider circle of governments, because they supported and denoted those who performed public functions, ensured the effectiveness of specific functionaries such judges or rulers, and their empowerment, due to the widespread public appreciation of the precious gemstones and precious materials embodied in the symbols of their officiation. Their wearing, then, was actually a status symbol (Clark 1986: 82; Platt 2006: 234–240).

In an Orphic 4th-century AD poem, it is said that Hermes gave these gemstones to mortals in order to prevent suffering, and ordered Orpheus to inform people of their qualities. They were often buried with the deceased to serve as a conveyor to the underworld (Henig 1994: 219). Thus, gems were sometimes found in tombs, placed on sarcophagi along with other valuables such as jewellery, as offerings to the deceased. Gems were also given as precious gifts to the gods, as can be concluded, for example, from inventories of temples that mention rings inlaid with engraved gemstones (Plantzos 1999: V, 12–17). The belief in the magical powers of the pagan images engraved on gems, and also in their precious materials, lasted until the Middle Ages (Soeda 1987: 185–192; Suger, Abbot of Saint Denis, *Abbot Suger On the Abbey Church of St. Denis and its Art Treasures*: 63–65).

C. Engraved Gems as Jewellery

Engraved gems were also used by the Greeks and Romans merely as ornaments, although at first unengraved stones were more often employed, since their varied colours and brilliance had great appeal. Precious gemstones decorated objects such as furniture, statues, vases, and even clothes and hairstyles (Babelon, s.v. 'Gemmae', Daremberg and Saglio (eds), *DAGR*, t. 2.2: 1484–1485; Richter 1971: vol.1, iii). The practice was common in the East long before the Greeks and Romans, but became more prevalent during the Hellenistic period, when the conquests of Alexander the Great in the East made precious stones more accessible to the Greeks. In early Greek times the ornamental use of gems was reserved mostly for public and religious purposes (Richter 1956: XVIII). The throne of the statue of Zeus at Olympia was 'adorned with gold and precious stones, as well as with ebony and ivory' (Pausanias, V, ii). The eyes of statues were inlaid with ivory and precious stones, especially banded agate due to its resemblance to the human eye, such as the eyes set in the Athena Parthenos of Phidias (Babelon, s.v. 'Gemmae', Daremberg and Saglio (eds), *DAGR*, t. 2.2: 1485; Plato, *Hippias Major*, vol. 1, 745; see also Richter 1956: XVIII). The gems were also used to decorate jewellery, the garnet stone being particularly common for this purpose (Clark 1986: 73). In addition, in the Hellenistic period, they decorated vessels for banquets such as *rhyta* and *phialae*, as well as furniture such as *klinai* and tables (Posidippus of Pella, *Posidippi Pellaei quae supersunt omnia*: Poems 1–20. See also Bing 2005: 135–139; Kuttner 2005: 147–149). These were usually not engraved, since the use of engraved gems was reserved for seals. The cameos, where the design was made in relief, were usually used only as decorations, and not as seals (Richter 1971: vol.1, IV). It is known, for example, that Cleopatra's palace walls were decorated with precious stones (Lucan, *Pharsalia* X: 119–122). Gold and silver vases studded with gems were particularly popular in Hellenistic and Roman times, and became almost a craze in the Roman Imperial period. In addition to vases, many articles of apparel were set with precious stones (Richter 1956: XVIII). Claudius, for example, wore emeralds and sard stones; Caligula appeared in public with bejewelled cloaks and bracelets. Both he and Elagabalus were fond of wearing gems on their shoes, and the stones were sometimes engraved (Pliny, *Natural History*: IX.114). Lollia Paulina, the wife of Caligula, is described as wearing emeralds and pearls on her head, hair, ears, neck, arms, and fingers (Pliny, *Natural History*: IX.58). The ring was very important to the external image, and was an inseparable part of everyday garments (Henig 1997: 97).

The use of gems for sealing was altered throughout the Roman era. In the period of the Republic, the use of signet rings, inlaid with engraved gems, was reserved for the holders of various administrative positions. The ring itself was simple and usually made of iron. Wearing a seal ring was evidence of power and high social status, and the right to wear a gold ring was not given to everyone. But later, in Imperial times this privilege gradually extended to the lower classes, until finally, according to Macrobius, only slaves were not allowed to wear gold rings (*Saturnalia* VII: 13.12).

Over time, increasing numbers of rings were worn until some people even put them on all fingers of the hand and sometimes several on one finger, using all three joints (Pliny, *Natural History*: XXXIII.6). It can be concluded that in the Late

Roman period, rings inlaid with engraved gems were no longer used for sealing as their primary purpose (Richter 1956: XIX). In Martin Henig's opinion, these were mostly gifts of love or marriage, and were used as jewellery rather than seals (2006: 57–66). In his opinion, the meaning behind these miniature objects is personal to the wearer, and involves human emotions and desires (Henig 2006: 57, 59, 65). The epigrams written by Posidippus in the 3rd century BC reinforce Henig's argument, since they deal with gemstones and their personal significance for humans. For example, it is said that Timanthes carved a starry lapis lazuli for Demylus, and in return for a gentle kiss, gave it as a gift to dark-haired Nicaea of Cos (Posidippus of Pella, *Posidippi Pellaei quae supersunt omnia*: poem 5).

Ancient engraved gems were often incorporated into medieval artefacts such as prayer book covers, crosses, reliquaries, boxes, and religious furniture, which were then given an *Interpretatio Christiana* (Clark 1986: 88–91, figs 31, 32; Kinney 2011: 97–119; Richter 1971: vol. 2, III).

2. The materials used for ancient gems

Ancient writers mention the materials used for ancient gems: the two main sources are those of Theophrastus (*De Lapidibus*), a 4th-century BC philosopher and Pliny the Elder (*Natural History*: XXXVII), from the 1st century AD. The ancient names do not always match those used today by gemologists, because in ancient times the names were given according to the colour of the stones, and the modern names are determined according to the crystalline composition of the gems.

A. *Chalcedonies or non-crystallising quartzes*

Most of the gems are made of various types of semi-transparent or opaque quartz (Richter 1968: 9–12).

Carnelian – Reddish in colour, shading from dark-red to golden-yellow; sometimes clear and translucent, at other times dull (Marbode of Rennes, *De Lapidibus* 22 (De Cornelio): lines 330–340; Richter 1956: XXV). Carnelian was used for the production of gems from the Minoan era to the Late Roman period, and was in fact the most common gemstone (about half of the ancient gems known today are made of it).

Sard – Light yellowish-brown or dark in colour. It is often difficult to distinguish from carnelian. The ancient writers refer both to carnelian and sard by the term *sardion* (Richter 1956: XXV).

Chalcedony – Of pale, smoky, milky-white, yellowish, or bluish-grey colour; generally only semi-translucent. This stone was used during the Minoan period and became the main material for Ionic Greek and Greco-Persian gems of the 5th and 4th centuries BC. The ancient name of this stone was *iaspis* (Damigeron, *The Virtues of Stones: De virtutibus lapidum*: 48; Richter 1956: XXV).

Plasma – Green and semi-translucent plasma was common in the Hellenistic and Roman periods. The ancient name of this stone was green *iaspis*. In fact, the term plasma included several types of stones: Prase: of greyish-green colour; and Chrysoprase: of bright-green colour (Pliny, *Natural History*: XXXVII.118-119; Spier 1992: 5).

Jasper –These stones are opaque and their colours are varied: red, yellow, green, brown or black. Red jasper is common in the Augustan period, and even more so in the Late Roman times. It is perhaps a variety of the ancient *haematitis*. Yellow jasper occurs only in the Late Roman period. Green jasper was commonly used for 'Greco-Phoenician gems' and in the Late Roman era. The heliotrope is a variety of green jasper, of dark-green colour with red spots (commonly referred to as 'bloodstone'). Its use is confined to Late Roman times (Richter 1956: XXV–XXVI).

Agate – A variegated quartz which is formed by being deposited in various layers. Its ancient name is achate. It consists of layers of varying degrees of transparency and different shades of black, brown, grey and white. Depending on the colour and nature of the layers, different names are given to the agate types: for example, when the stone is cut transversely and the layers are more or less level so that they appear in bands, it is commonly referred to as banded agate. Banded agate was popular in the Minoan period, and during the 6th–4th centuries BC both in Greece and Etruria. After that it disappears. When the stone is cut horizontally so that the layers are superimposed, it is called either onyx or sardonyx; when one of the layers is of sard, the stone is termed sardonyx, otherwise the term onyx is generally used. Onyx and sardonyx were used by the Greeks from early times, and were also popular with the Etruscans, especially in the later periods. Sardonyx is the main material used for cameos in the Hellenistic and Roman eras. Nicolo is the name given to a special variety of two-layered onyx in which the lower layer is usually of black jasper, sometimes of a dark sard, and the upper layer thin and of bluish-white colour. Nicolo began to be used in the 1st century BC and lasted throughout the Roman period (Richter 1956: XXVI).

B. Crystallising quartzes

Rock Crystal – Transparent and colourless. It was used in Minoan and classical Greek times. In Italy it does not appear until the 1st century BC. The ancient name of the stone was *crystallum* (Richter 1956: XXVI).

Amethyst – Transparent and of a purple colour. It was used from the Minoan period onwards. It is common in the Hellenistic and Roman times. The lighter variety is probably identical with the ancient *hyacinthus* (Richter 1956: XXVII).

C. Harder, more precious stones

Garnet – Transparent and of various deep-red, orange or violet colours. It was used during the Hellenistic and Late Roman periods, and in Byzantine times in workshops of the Eastern Empire. Its ancient names change according to the various colours: the pure red stones are called *pyrope* or Syrian garnet, the garnets with orange and brown tints are called *hyacinthine* garnets, and the garnets with a violet hue are called almandine garnets. The garnet stone is usually cut with a very convex surface (en cabochon), which increases its beauty. When the stones are cut in this way they are referred to as carbuncles. The ancient name for the garnet is *carbunculus* (Richter 1956: XXVII).

Beryl – There are two chief types:

Emerald, of a deep-green, transparent colour is known from the Archaic Greek period onwards, but it is never common. Its ancient name was *smargdus.*

Aquamarine, of bluish or greenish colour and highly transparent. It is known from the Hellenistic period onwards, and later became popular during the Augustan period. The ancient name was *beryllus* (Richter 1956: XXVII).

Other hard stones used in Greek and Roman times include:

Topaz – Transparent and of yellow colour, occurs occasionally in Hellenistic and Roman periods. The ancient name was *topazon* or perhaps *chrysolithus* (Richter 1956: XXVII).

Peridot *or* Chrysolite – A yellowish-green colour, sometimes translucent, sometimes semi-transparent, occurs only rarely. Variously identified as the ancient *topazon* and *chrysolithus* (Richter 1956: XXVII).

Sapphire – A rare gemstone, transparent and of blue colour, occurs only in the Roman period. The hardest stone used in ancient glyptic art. The ancient name is not known: it is not sapphire (Richter 1956: XXVIII).

Lapis lazuli – Deep blue in colour, opaque, often with gold-coloured particles of pyrite. It occurs rarely; occasionally as early as the 5th and 4th centuries BC; but is more prevalent in the Roman period (Richter 1956: XXVIII).

Turquoise– Opaque greenish or sky-blue in colour. The stone does not occur in ancient intaglios, but sometimes used for cameos, and for Augustan period creations (Richter 1956: XXVIII).

Malachite– Green and opaque, rarely used.

D. Inferior varieties

Other materials from which gemstones are carved are:

Hematite, steatite, serpentine, porphyry, obsidian, amber and glass. Glass was used throughout antiquity as a substitute for precious stones. Glass gems were mostly cast in moulds taken from engraved stones (Richter 1956: XXVIII).

3. The themes depicted on gems

The variety of designs that appears on the engraved gems is very wide.

In Mesopotamia, the favoured themes were mainly ritual scenes, while the Egyptians carved mostly inscriptions. The Greeks, on the other hand, drew their inspiration from the life around them and from their many legends. The principal design was pictorial and included a favourite deity, or mythological hero, or animal, or portrait, or symbol. Often the meaning of a scene and of the engraved symbols, now escapes us, because we lack the historical context (as opposed to coins) to help in the interpretation (Richter 1956: XX). But mostly, the devices depicted on the gems are borrowed (or supplementary to) from prevalent Greek and Roman artistic stock. These seals feature the same gods, myths and scenes from everyday life, but in a concise manner.

The fauna provided a wide range of motifs for seals from all periods, and animal representations are very common on gemstones (Henig 1997: 45–53). In the Late Hellenistic period and during the Augustan period, a new interest in animals and plants arose among the artists (Plantzos 1999: 99). Many subjects drawn from Greek mythology have served as endless sources of inspiration for animal depictions, such as Heracles' labours, the Calydonian Hunt, horseback riding, or chariot races (Klingender 1971: 64). In the Augustan period these representations should be seen as part of the overall programme of Imperial propaganda (Zanker 1988: 177–188). The repertoire of themes in use during the Imperial Roman period often drew inspiration from works of art in various media: sculpture, wall-paintings and vase paintings; as well as from different periods: from the Archaic period to the end of the Hellenistic period. Sometimes gems have remained the only evidence of Imperial portraits as well as of Greek and Roman sculptures and wall-paintings that have long since been lost (Henig 1999: 390, fig. Ic; Henig 2000: 131, no. 3). However, when interpreting the visual depictions of animals it is likely to encounter a number of obstacles. The difficulty in understanding lies in the perspective of time, the incomplete information, ambiguous information and the multiple versions which are often contradictory. Each visual representation usually had more than one meaning and more than one role, and the visual and literary sources do not provide all the answers, leaving much room for speculation. The more complex the depiction, the more proposals there are for its interpretation (Gersht 2007: 80).

4. References to gemstones in ancient literary sources

The types of stones used for gems are mentioned by Theophrastus in his essay (*De Lapidibus*), which gives a great deal of information about gemstones and glyptic art, and also by Pliny (*Natural History*: XXXVII), who dedicates a wide discussion regarding gems, while mentioning names and types of the wide range of gemstones, indicating their characteristics, their places of origin, their classification by colour and prevalence and their carving technique. At the beginning of the 7th century AD, Isidore of Seville wrote his book (*Etymologiae: Book 16: De Lapidibus et Metallis; Stones and Metals*: IV–XIV), which contained descriptions of the miraculous powers of gemstones.

The importance attributed to gems can be deduced from many ancient sources, such as Suetonius, denoting that Caesar was an enthusiastic collector of them and is said to have deposited as many as six cabinets (*dactyliothecae*) in the temple of Venus Genetrix (Suetonius, *De vita caesarum - Julius Caesar*: 47). Many other sources mention myths associated with gems, for example Herodotus mentions the signet ring of the tyrant Polykrates, which was encased in gold and featuring an emerald stone. He threw it into the sea because he had to choose his most valued possession in order to forestall the gods' envy at his good fortune (Herodotus, *Historiae*: 3.41). According to Posidippus, the stone was engraved with an image of the lyre of a favourite poet who used to sing and play for the tyrant (Posidippus of Pella, *Posidippi Pellaei quae supersunt omnia*: 31, poem 9, 1–2; *The New Posidippus: a Hellenistic Poetry Book*: 19, poem 9. 1–2). Pliny mentions an unengraved sardonyx that was centuries later displayed in Rome as Polykrates' stone (Pliny, *Natural History*: XXXVII, II.3–5, IV.8). An Archaic Greek scarab from Aegina made of agate reads: 'I am the sign (sama/sêma) of Thersis: do not open me' (Boardman 1968: 73–74, no. 176). The use of the term sama/sêma is significant because it demonstrates that there was a parallel between the seal and its owner, with the image carved on the gem perceived as a specific identity marker and proclaiming an individual's continued presence even during their physical absence. The seals are also known in Greek as *symbola, sêmanteria, sêmantra, sêmeia*, and in Latin as *signa* -

whereby all the terms express the semiotic function of the seals (Platt 2006: 240–241). A seal was considered as a powerful metaphor of an individual and as that individual's relationship with the surrounding world. Indeed, the seal imprint became such a powerful image that the term *tupôsis* (the action of imprinting the seal on wax) was used as a philosophical metaphor by Plato, and later on in the Stoic writings, in order to explain the nature of knowledge and the relationship between sensory perception and the soul (Plato, *Theaetetus*: 191D–E, 193C, 194C, D; Diogenes Laertius, *Lives of Eminent Philosophers* (*Life of Zeno*): 7.177, 7.45–46, 7.50). Socrates proposes a model whereby the mind is like a block of wax. The perceptions or thoughts are interpreted by it 'like the imprints of seals or the images on rings'. But the knowledge is not identical to the 'thing' itself (any image we experienced in our senses, for example through sight, hearing and touch), just as the imprint is not identical to the seal. Nevertheless, it would seem that the owners of these gems had expected to make their impression and mark in the world by the very act of imprinting their signet-ring in wax. They thereby created a chain of signs, a series of replications that related to the 'self', in the most personal sense, as well as to the public and social roles; identifying the 'self' as a rational, moral and, finally, as a genuine being (Platt 2006: 251).

5. Dating methods

The origin of most of the engraved gems found in museums and private collections is unknown: they were not discovered in excavations, and thus cannot be dated on the basis of archaeological context. Thus dating methods which rely on other aspects, such as the style and technique of carving, the choice of designs on the gems, and material and shape were evolved.

The dating of these eclectic gems from the Israel Museum is extremely difficult, since their archaeological context is unknown. The sorting method developed by Marianne Maaskant-Kleibrink (1978), who dealt with a similar collection, has therefore been very useful in dating the gems for the present study. Maaskant-Kleibrink sorted the gems according to style and engraving technique rather than workshop, since it was clear that they had been executed in different provinces. In addition, the material and the shape of the stones themselves have helped in establishing the correct date, or at least an approximate one, since different materials were typical for different periods. These features were highly dependent on changes in 'fashion' and related to the different shapes for finger-rings (Maaskant-Kleibrink 1978: 59–61).

In this study I will refer mainly to Greek and Roman gems, although there are also some Etruscan scarabs, Classical Phoenician scarabs and neo-Classical ones.

A. *Archaeological context*

Gems discovered in archaeological excavations can be dated to the time they went out of use, based on pottery and coins found there. Large assemblages of gems discovered in archaeological excavations made it possible to study the development of the art of engraved gems in terms of style, subjects and types of stones. One of the important assemblages included 88 gems discovered in the baths of the Legionary fortress in Caerleon, Britain, which are divided into two groups. The earliest is dated to AD 75–110 and the later to AD 160–230. When comparing the two groups there were differences in the choice of subjects and types of stones. The early group included more depictions of 'fertility symbols' and pastoral scenes, while the later group included various figures of gods, animals and 'combination gems', many of them with a military connection. The early group showed a preference for transparent stones (yellow sard and amethyst), in contrast to the preference for opaque ones in the later group (the most common being red jasper). A similar trend was repeated in other dated assemblages as well (Henig 1978: 31).

However, it should be remembered that dating according to archaeological context is not without limitations, because this method can determine only the latest date (*terminus ante quem*), which is not necessarily the date of the manufacture of the gems. Engraved gems are valuable objects and were inherited from generation to generation. There are several examples of Hellenistic gems that have apparently remained in use for a long time, as they were discovered in later assemblages (Henig 1978: 31).

B. *The type and shape of the gemstone*

1. Materials: The type of material of a particular gemstone can also provide clues for dating. Pliny implies that transparent stones were preferred over others (*Natural History*: XXXVII.28, 120). Although carnelian was popular during the Roman period, in archaeological assemblages from Pliny's era plasma, sard, yellow, amethyst and garnet gemstones are more common. The reason for this is not clear, although it should be noted that the trade between the Roman Empire and India was more important in the 1st century than later, and many of the better quality gems were imported from the East (Pliny, *Natural History*: VI.101). Red jasper, which is perhaps the most common opaque stone, became widespread, starting from the 2nd century AD (Richter 1956: 61). The advantage of jasper is that the carved images stand out from the background, which was particularly valuable when the ornamental value of the intaglios increased in the 2nd and 3rd centuries, and they were no longer used solely for sealing purposes. Glass gems from the beginning of the Empire, which were of different colours and usually transparent, were replaced in the 2nd and 3rd centuries AD almost entirely by gems of crushed glass (pastes) imitating blue nicolo (Henig 1978: 31).

Gem transparency can then be an indication of date. For example, in the bathhouse of the Legionary fortress in Caerleon, mentioned above, of the 88 gems found in the drainage channel, 32 were discovered in the lower strata, dating to the Flavian and Trajan periods, while the rest came from the later strata of the canal, dating back to c. 160 AD. In the later assemblages of AD 230, no gems were discovered. The earliest groups of gems included more transparent stones, such as sard, amethyst and others, while later groups included very few transparent stones. In other words, sometime between AD 110–100 and 160–150 there was a change in the fashion of seal rings and the preference changed from transparent to opaque stones. The reasons for this change are unclear, and it is possible that when the gems were increasingly used as amulets, and their use as seals decreased, the importance of presenting the design clearly on the gem was increased, while that of the imprint diminished. As mentioned above, the images stand out from the background better on opaque stones. In addition, it is possible that certain sources of semi-precious stones were lost, although there is no evidence for that in ancient literature.

It is also possible to discern a connection between the carved subject and the type of gemstone. In the later group from Caerleon it can be seen that gods are usually depicted on carnelian, while cupids, heroes, animals and combinations appear on red jasper. These differences may be related to the magical properties of the various stones (Henig 1978: 41).

2. Shape: Small gems with convex surfaces are usually earlier. This is especially true for plasma gems. Sena-Chiesa noticed a workshop for these stones in Aquileia, which operated in the 1st century AD. Large convex gemstones with straight sides usually belong to the 2nd or 3rd centuries AD. When the gem is elongated it was most likely intended to fit into rings of the 3rd century AD (Henig 1978: 32). This topic will be discussed later in more detail.

C. The technique and style of the gemstone

1. Greek gems

Archaic

Archaic period gems can be dated according to their prevalent scarab shape. The most common material during this period was carnelian and other types of quartz stones (Boardman 1968: 9, 13–17; Boardman and Vollenweider 1978, vol. 1: 11–18).

Late Archaic and Classical

In the Classical period the scarab shape disappears and is replaced by the scaraboid, which is an aesthetic refinement of the former scarab, i.e. having undecorated convex reverses, and considerably larger in format and also thicker. The lineal frame surrounding the design carved on the scarab disappears, and sometimes a simple line appears in its place. Carnelian continues to be widespread, but semi-translucent chalcedony, especially bluish, is the preferred material for contemporary gems (Boardman 1968: 89; Boardman 1970: 189–194; Boardman and Vollenweider 1978, vol. 1: 23, 72; Maaskant-Kleibrink 1978: 76).

Hellenistic

During the Hellenistic period, new and colourful stones were introduced in the wake of the conquests of Alexander the Great, such as the garnet, amethyst and aquamarine. The shape was usually an elongated oval for single figure compositions and a broad oval, or round, when several figures or busts were shown. In addition, the convex shape occurred, such as in the case of garnet, which is usually cut with a very convex surface (*en cabochon*), which increases its beauty. An important subject was the portrait, which is evident from the many Ptolemy and Seleucid portraits on clay sealings from Hellenistic archives. There was also a preference for particularly elongated shapes that were not rendered in much detail during the Hellenistic period (Boardman and Vollenweider 1978, vol. 1: 66; Maaskant-Kleibrink 1978: 82; Plantzos 1999: 90–91).

In addition, the dating method in the Greek world is based on the tradition of stylistic dating that is identical to that used in other media. Greek gems can be dated according to their style because Greek art is characterised by a uniform style in the various media during the Archaic, Classical and Hellenistic periods, although each medium is marked by its own iconography. The Archaic period is represented by rigid and static expression, the filling of the space sometimes in a forced manner, and the muscular design of the body; but the anatomy is still not precise, with the figures having a large head, wide thighs, narrow waist and a fleshy chest (Boardman 1968: 10, 28–30, 45, 51–52, 59). The Classical period is marked by a more accurate anatomical depiction, more naturalistic, thinner and refined characters than in the Archaic period, and also the necessity to fill the void disappeared with the figures freely placed within it (Boardman 1968: 103; Boardman 1970: 17–18; Boardman and Vollenweider 1978, vol. 1: 69). During the Hellenistic period, various dynamic designs appear in which there are multiple influences, in contrast to the limited range of images in the Classical period, which was characterised by *sophrosyne*.

2. Etruscan scarabs

Hard-stone gem engraving on scarabs began in Etruria in the second half of the 6th century BC, under the immediate influence of Greek Archaic engraving and probably in the hands of Greek artists. Nuances of style point to Ionian engravers, who were also the earliest in the Greek world. From the very beginning the subjects adopted were taken from Greek mythology, but not always completely understood, or it is given a somewhat different narrative. Winged demons had a special place in Etruscan art, and so did Heracles. In the 5th and 4th centuries, motifs from Greek red-figure vase painting were very popular. By far the largest proportion of Etruscan scarabs are of the A 'globolo' type. Developing in the 4th century, they were the predominant type in the 3rd century BC. The figures in the designs were composed of large rounded areas, with no detailing whatsoever. The tool was the large round *bouterolle* (*globolo tondo* in Italian). The figures and animals shown on A 'globolo' intaglios are thus largely abstract in character and draw their charm from their panache and variety. It would seem out of the question that these designs were used for sealing purpose. Besides, the A 'globolo' scarabs are not found only in finger-rings but also in other jewellery such as necklace (Henig 1994: 58; Maaskant-Kleibrink 1978: 86, no. 54).

The material is exclusively dark-red carnelian, although in the latter part of the period there are also banded agate scarabs. The shape is invariably the scarab, with a more elaborately cut beetle-back than the Greek type and it often has a decorated base. The scarab backs are far more carefully worked than most Greek examples, a speciality being a patterned upright border or plinth to each stone; some have relief figures on their backs, like cameos.

In his book *Etruskische Skarabäen*, P. Zazoff classified Etruscan scarabs according to the following styles:

    a.   Archaic Style (second half of the 6th century BC – *c*. 500 BC).
    b.   Severe Style (strongly influenced by red-figure vases; strong schematisation of the figures at the end of the period; first half of 5th century BC – first half of 4th century BC).
    c.   Free Style (influenced by imported Greek vases and by Greek painting and reliefs. In the 4th century a transitional period leading to the A 'globolo' style can be distinguished; from *c*. 480 – *c*. 300 BC).
    d.   A 'globolo' type (P. Zazoff makes a plausible case for saying that most of the A 'globolo' scarabs originate in the 3rd century).

The styles to the end of the 5th century BC are close to Greek examples but Archaic styles tend to linger. At their best they are as good as any Greek scarabs, especially the anatomical studies of heroes. In the 4th century BC the A 'globolo' style begins – rendering figures mainly with the drill, in groups of 'blobs'. This stylesoon becomes dominant and even more simplified with animal studies (Henig 1994: 58; Maaskant-Kleibrink 1978: 86, 93, no. 54).

3. Classical Phoenician scarabs

'Classical Phoenician scarabs' were made in Phoenician workshops in the period of the Achaemenid Persian Empire. They are made of green jasper, the colour probably being of as much importance as their intaglios since it enhances their amuletic value. The earliest ones are dated to the end of the 6th century BC, and the later ones were found in tombs from the mid 4th century BC (Boardman 2003: 3–8). These scarabs were worn as pendants and not on rings. The perforated ones were clearly designed to be suspended on strings, others were given precious metal mounts. They served as jewellery, as offerings in tombs and sanctuaries, and for their primary function of sealing. These scarabs feature Egyptianising, Levantine and Hellenising subjects as their devices. But there are also many miscellaneous forms, and much overlapping of categories. Most of them were found in the western Phoenician (Punic) cemeteries of Carthage, Sardinia and Ibiza (Spain), but there are also many from the East Mediterranean. Many have been called Greco-Phoenician because their subjects and styles are Late Archaic (Boardman 1968: 169–171; Boardman 2003: 17). The colour green was perceived as lucky in the East and in Egypt, being the colour of new vegetation, growing crops and fertility, and hence of new life, youth and well-being, and even resurrection (Boardman 1991: 31). It was, in particular, the colour of the papyrus plant, which when represented in hieroglyphs produced the word 'wadj', meaning 'to flourish' or 'be healthy' (Andrews 1990: 37). In Sardinia, for example, the stone called 'verde di Sardegna' is known, made of serpentine, a softer mineral than green jasper. In the East, green jasper was available in Egypt and around the Dead Sea coast. It was used for making seals in the late Bronze Age of Phoenicia, and sometimes for amulets in Egypt (Boardman 2003: 6; Moorey 1994: 98–99). In the mid 6th century BC Greek artists adopted the scarab form, originated from the Phoenician workshops of Cyprus (Boardman and Vollenweider 1978, vol. 1: 12).

4. Roman gems

In the Roman Imperial era the production of gems became a mass industry, and consequently the motifs and styles became standard. Therefore, dating Roman gems according to their style is very difficult. In addition, the chronological boundaries of the styles actually overlap. One style does not succeed the other, but two or three styles are popular during the same period, depending on the type of customers and their taste (Guiraud 1996: 59). In the absence of a consistent dating method, the early catalogues dealt only with iconography. Furtwängler was the first to attempt to classify Imperial Roman gems in chronological order at the beginning of the 20th century (Furtwängler 1900). He speculated that during the Julio-Claudian period the classicist style prevailed. In the second half of the 1st century AD, schematic models start to appear, and many of the gems that were produced in the second half of the 2nd century AD are typified by careless and concise engraving, produced hastily and coarsely, with no detailing. At the same time, however, naturalistic styled gems with great attention to detail continue to be produced as well. Therefore, the attempt to associate gems with various workshops, even those found in a well-dated archaeological context, is almost impossible. The initial attempt of Sena-Chiesa in the 1960s to assign the Aquileia gems into workshops and to date them is a landmark (1966). While some of her work remains speculative, it is possible to learn from the large number of gems in the collection and from the multiple stylistic connections about the importance of Aquileia as a centre for engraving gems. Sena-Chiesa used for the first time gems from dated complexes, and paralleled them in her study to the Aquileia ones in order to establish their dating. In the 1970s Zwierlein-Diehl and Maaskant-Kleibrink categorised the large collections in Germany and the Netherlands according to style rather than workshops, since it was clear that the gems came from various provinces. It was reasonable to assume that the use of the drill had changed over time, and that the materials and shapes of the gems also had chronological implications. Maaskant-Kleibrink, who published the catalogue of gems from the Royal Coin Cabinet, The Hague (Maaskant-Kleibrink 1978), divided the main styles into subgroups according to the following chronological order:

I. Italic and Roman Republican ringstone groups (3rd century BC–AD 30):

   a. **'Italic Elongated Figure Style' (2nd century BC – 100 BC)** – This style is found mainly on banded agate ringstones, which were adapted to the elongated figures depicted on them. These are very thin and flat on both sides (Maaskant-Kleibrink 1978: 101).
   b. **'Italic A Globolo-like Style' (2nd century BC)** – This style can be seen in very convex carnelian and chalcedony stones. The basic design is done with a large round bouterolle or round-wheel-drill, and the small details are done by small bouterolles or wheel grooves. They are influenced by the technique of Etruscan scarabs (Maaskant-Kleibrink 1978: 105).

c. **'Campanian- and Hellenistic-Roman Styles' (3rd – beginning of 1st century BC)** – The gemstones cut in this style are mainly convex carnelian, amethyst, and chalcedony, which have a broad oval or almost round shape. The motifs on the Campanian-Roman gems are Hellenistic in origin and reworked in characteristic Campanian style. The figures are round and heavy, cut with thick, rounded drills and the details of the eyes, knees, hair, etc., are given with a small round bouterolle. The execution is plastic, and three-quarter frontal figures and heads are most common. There are stylistic parallels between these gems and Campanian coins and terracottas. They are datable based on these comparisons, as well as the ring types in which they are set (Maaskant-Kleibrink 1978: 108–109).

d. **'Italic-Republican Blob Style' (c. 200 – first half of 1st century BC)** – This style is characterised by convex ringstones, engraved by a large round bouterolle, and detailed by a smaller round bouterolle or a few wheel grooves. The term 'Blob Style' refers to its summary style of engraving. While it is mostly found on banded agate ringstones, it is also used in carnelian and chalcedony ringstones (Maaskant-Kleibrink 1978: 124-125).

e. **'Italic-Republican Pellet Style' (2nd – 1st century BC)** – This style has the common stylistic feature of numerous small pellets in the design, rendered with a tiny round bouterolle, which produces little holes in details such as hair, eyes, beards, elbows, etc. Pelleting is also found on Roman-Republican coins. Carnelian, amethyst, and chalcedony are used, as well as banded agate. They are no longer elongated, but have a broad shape (Maaskant-Kleibrink 1978: 131–132).

f. **'Republican Extinguishing Pellet Style' (second half of 1st century BC – first half of 1st century AD)** – These workshops employed tiny blobs only for hair, beards, knees and feet. This milder form of pelleting is also encountered on coins. The ringstones cut in this style are smaller and more oval shaped than those of the earlier Pellet Style. Usually they are cut from carnelian or amethyst and chalcedony, nicolos also become more frequent (Maaskant-Kleibrink 1978: 145).

g. **'Republican Wheel Style'** – A group of gems in which parallel and short grooves are used for detailing, e.g. for the hair and for the folds of garments. The grooves range from fairly thin to rather thick and their sides are fairly straight or curved. This indicates that they were formed by wheel- or disk-shaped drill ends of varying thicknesses and whose sides had varying degrees of roundness. The large shapes in these gems, such as the body, were probably carved with a blunted drill or a very thick round-sided disk. It is possible to estimate according to the degree of curvature of the sides of the large areas what the approximate thickness of the instruments must have been (Maaskant-Kleibrink 1978: 154).

Additional features of the Republican Wheel Style workshops are:

1. The hair in a roll around the head, stylised and looking like a hat with a rim.
2. Short grooves for the ribs, especially in male torsos.
3. Short protruding grooves for the chin, lips and nose.

The workshops that produced gems in the Wheel Style mainly chose Dionysian themes: sacrificial scenes (chiefly offerings for Priapus) and rural scenes, especially those of the shepherds milking goats. In addition, there are a considerable number of Wheel Style intaglios with masks, heads and portraits. In Aquileia there are an unusually large number of Wheel Style gems. Sena-Chiesa sorted them according to stylistic characteristics into a number of workshops. It is quite possible that some of The Hague collection gems (now in the Rijksmuseum van Oudheden, Leiden) originated in Aquileia. It can be assumed that the Wheel Style gems had northern origins, partly because they occur less frequently in southern Italian collections. This style can also be found in collections from the Middle East, but may have been imported there. Many archaeologists have pointed out the Hellenistic origin of the rural scenes and the attributes shown on these gems. The Late Republic dating of the gems is supported by the ring types containing Wheel Style intaglios depicting rustic scenes. Over time, the characters become smaller and rigid and the carving of the head and body becomes coarse, careless and concise, with no detailing. The usual forms for gemstones are broad oval or round (Maaskant-Kleibrink 1978: 154–155).

h. **'Flat Bouterolle Style'** – A group of gems that display exaggeration in the use of the large blunted drill for engraving the larger shapes such as bodies and heads. The detailing is done with rounded wheel grooves but, compared with the detailing in the Wheel Style gems, it is limited. Zwierlein-Diehl points out that a similar style is depicted on coins. In this class of gems there is also a preference for the round shape, although broad oval ringstones do occur also (Maaskant-Kleibrink 1978: 179–180).

II. Roman Imperial Ringstone Groups (Augustan period – 3rd century AD)

a. Imperial classicising styles (Augustan – early 2nd century AD)

From the last decades of the 1st century BC onward, ringstone styles were increasingly influenced by earlier and contemporary 'Greek' workshops.

These workshops, apparently situated in Rome, Pompeii, etc., were manned by Greek immigrant engravers who created masterpieces which were frequently inscribed with their own names. The gems they produced were in most cases larger than the Roman ones and were intended for display in the *dactyliothecae* kept by the Roman aristocracy and for personal ornament. The motifs of theses larger gems were inspired by Classical Greek art of the 5th and 4th centuries BC, especially famous sculptures and reliefs.

However, this revival of well-known Classical motifs is mixed with a considerable Hellenistic influence. The figures are often very small, and the modeling is deep and rounded. They were probably produced with small, very rounded drills. Faces and hands are rendered with very short grooves often resembling pellets. The detailing is done with disks or wheels producing slightly rounded grooves. The hairstyle is often that of the hair-roll around the head, rendered by means of small parallel grooves, as popularised by the earlier Wheel Style workshops. With female figures the drapery is rendered in a striped style: parallel rounded wheel grooves indicate folds of the *chiton* and *himation*. The motifs are strongly Classicising or Hellenising ones, and adaptions from famous Greek sculpture-types, mythological motifs and a preference of subjects such as Cupid, Bacchic motifs and rural animal scenes are clearly seen (Maaskant-Kleibrink 1978: 195–197).

b. Imperial transitional styles (1st–early 3rd century AD)

These styles stem from the Classicising Style, but their engraving technique becomes simplified. However, they are not identical to the later Imperial Styles in their coarse incoherent grooves. Two types of simplification are found: rounded grooves of varying thickness ('Small Grooves', 'Chin-Mouth-Nose' and 'Plain Grooves Styles') and large rounded and undetailed forms ('Round Head', 'Cap-With-Rim Styles'). In addition, after the Flavian period the Roman ring becomes broader and somewhat larger when most of them are nicolos and carnelians, but chalcedonies and jaspers were also popular at that time. The motifs depicted are similar to those on 1st- and 2nd-century Roman coins: Jupiter enthroned, Mercury standing or seated, Fortune, etc. (Maaskant-Kleibrink 1978: 251).

Transitional Styles include the following subgroups:

b1. 'Imperial Small Grooves Style' (1st–2nd century AD) – The figures on these gems are coarsely engraved with thick rounded grooves, probably produced by means of a thick rounded wheel or disk drills. The bodies of the figures have a rubbery quality, they lack a display of movement and the limbs are lumpy and undetailed. The male chest is indicated by two, four, or six small grooves. Draperies are indicated by a few parallel straight grooves and the hair, depicted in a roll, is similarly engraved. Sometimes facial features are also engraved by means of three or four parallel small horizontal grooves to indicate the chin, mouth and nose (Maaskant-Kleibrink 1978: 251–252).

b2. 'Round Head Style' (1st–2nd century AD) – Following the simpler carving style many gem artists engraved the heads of the figures as round globules. Only rarely is there any detailing in the form of a spiky diadem or helmet rim. The engravers usually added short wheel grooves for the nose, mouth, and chin. The head and other basic shapes are concisely carved with a large rounded drill. The details, and especially the draperies, are distinguished, being indicated only by a small number of thin, sharp wheel-drill grooves (Maaskant-Kleibrink 1978: 285).

b3. 'Chin-Mouth-Nose Style' (1st–2nd century AD) – Many gems combine the properties of several subgroups and have the additional characteristic of a striking stylization of the nose, mouth and chin, with four or three horizontal short horizontal grooves used to denote these features. Such simplification of the face can also be found in Republican Wheel Style gems, although the technique was employed differently. The outlines of the figures are indicated by a few thick rounded grooves. The hair is done in a stylised roll around the head and is detailed with short grooves. The folds of the garments are carved with numerous thin or thick lines. In addition, this style has a special striped pattern (Maaskant-Kleibrink 1978: 294).

b4. 'Cap-With-Rim Style' (end of 1st–2nd century AD) – The figures depicted on the gems in this style are smaller and summary in detail. They are carved with large rounded drills, or a broad rounded wheel. The hair of the characters appears not only as a roll around the head, as in the previous styles, but as a close-fitting hat. The nose, mouth and chin are rarely stylised into horizontal grooves. The feet are pointed and unwieldy (Maaskant-Kleibrink 1978: 302).

b5. 'Plain Grooves Style' (1st–3rdcentury AD) – This group of gems differs from the others through being engraved with thick rounded wheel grooves. In general there is no detailing for hands, hair and faces. It was one of the most common styles during the 2nd century AD, especially for nicolos and three-layered agates (Maaskant-Kleibrink 1978: 311).

c. Imperial coarse styles (late 2nd–3rd century AD)

A large number of Roman gems were carved in a hasty style, with the characters shaped only by a few lines that are generally incoherently joined together. The attributes are represented only by a line or a scratch. As a result, many of the models on these ringstones cannot be deciphered unless they are compared to similar models of better quality. Many magical amulets are carved in this style (Maaskant-Kleibrink 1978: 320).

In these intaglios, two main styles can be discerned:

c1. 'Rigid Chin-Mouth-Nose Style' (end of 2nd–3rd century AD) – This style is similar to the 'Chin-Mouth-Nose Style', but it is noted for its even stiffer forms. The contours of the figures are engraved with a large rounded drill and the detailing is composed of many sharp wheel grooves which often criss-cross the representation. Sometimes there are no outlines at all, with the characters depicted by short lines (Maaskant-Kleibrink 1978: 321).

c2. 'Incoherent Grooves Style' (3rd century AD) – Animals and symbols were depicted in this careless style, gods and human beings. The representations are very concise, the figures are made of several scratches or blobs, which are loosely and inaccurately connected. The detailing, in cases where it exists, consists of a few wheel grooves. It is very difficult to decipher the images, and therefore it can be assumed that these were not used to sign documents. The engraving technique of these gems is very reminiscent of magical amulets (Maaskant-Kleibrink 1978: 326).

The classification method of Maaskant-Kleibrink was widely accepted, with most studies on Roman gems published afterwards following her classifications.

In addition, Henig, based on findings from excavations in Britain, suggests a simpler division:

1. **The Augustan Style ('Wheel Style') 50 BC–AD 20** – Henig compares the Augustan style of engraving gems to the typical contemporary sculptural styles, such as the Ara Pacis mythological panels and the neo-Attic reliefs (Henig 1988: 145, 151).

2. **The Classicising Style (AD 20–70)** – This style continues the tradition of late Hellenistic art, until in Nero's time the preoccupation with the textures themselves became more central than the naturalistic depiction of the body.

3. **The Flavian Style ('Small Grooves Style') AD 70–120** – For the gems produced during this period it seems that the interest in texture became more important than shape. There is a tendency to use shorter and less flowing grooves.

4. **The Patterned Style (AD 120–180)** – Characterised by a linear depiction of the body and objects on the gems, as well as a tendency to break the naturalistic forms into repetitive patterns.

5. **The Late Patterned Style (AD 180–220)** – During this period the gemstones used by the artists become larger.
6. **'The Incoherent Grooves Style' (AD140–220)** – Characterised by a slapdash, careless carving of broad coarse diagonal lines.

D. Choice of themes

During the Hellenistic period syncretistic depictions of deities, such as Isis and Serapis, appeared on Ptolemaic gems, as well as portraits of rulers, along with the usual repertoire of deities, Erotes, nymphs, masks and marine subjects (Plantzos 1999: 83–84, 90–91, 96).

Gems implying historical events or featuring portraits with characteristic hair styles are easy to date.

The goddess Ceres appears on Imperial coins from the end of the 1st century until the beginning of the 3rd century AD, and on gems only in the 2nd century AD.

Pastoral scenes and representations evoking a sense of abundance and prosperity on gems, such as shepherds watching over their flocks, were common in the Flavian period, as is also seen on Imperial coins, and were intended to publicise post-Civil War Italy's economic recovery (Henig 1978: 32–33; Henig 1997: 100).

Famous sculptures are often carved on small, green plasma gems dating back to the early days of the Empire (Henig 1978: 33).

From the time of Augustus to the beginning of the 2nd century AD, the motifs are very classicising or Hellenistic: mythological scenes, depictions of famous Greek statues, Cupids, Dionysian themes and rural scenes. The common themes of Roman coins, such as Jupiter seated, Mars, Bacchus, Minerva and other Olympic gods, were also added to the repertoire of gems from the 1st century AD, and their popularity even increased in the second half of the century (Henig 1978: 32–34).

E. Comparison to works in other media

Greek art is typified by uniform styles in various media during the Archaic and Classical periods, although each medium is characterised by its own iconography. Therefore, it is possible to date gems of these periods according to style, such as a vase, a statue or a coin.

In the 5th century BC, sculptures start to be copied on gems, and in the beginning of the Roman period, in the 1st century BC, this tendency becomes more prevalent. However, the style of the copied sculpture does not indicate the dating of the gem itself, since it was usually created earlier (Boardman 1997: 13–17).

The coins appear to be closest to the carved gemstones, both due to the similar dimensions and to the preparation in negative. In both cases, there is a tendency to use a clear summarised language, thus enabling the artist to omit excessive detail (Guiraud 1996: 97).

In addition, taking for example the subject of gods, both coins and gems were then influenced by models of Greek or Roman statues, but the absence of a base under the feet of the depicted figures, and the presentation of the face in profile, as evidenced in many representations of deities on gems, are more reminiscent of common coins motifs than of sculptures (Guiraud 1996: 97–98; Richter 1956: XXI).

Some scholars argue that, in fact, the two arts were not separate, and engraved gem workshops also prepared moulds for casting coins (Hamburger 1968: 1; Maaskant-Kleibrink 1978: 196; Vermeule 1957: nos 242–255). Indeed, sometimes the same designs can be seen appearing both on gems and coins (Meshorer 1984: 83). At the same time, however, in Aquileia, where a workshop for producing gems was discovered, no connection to preparing coin moulds was found (Henig 1978: 34).

In any case, it is problematic to date gems only on the basis of their motifs bearing similarities to those appearing on coins, since the same motifs reappear on coins of different periods. In addition, there is a fundamental difference between gems and coins. The gems reflect personal taste and identity, while the coins represent public taste. Certain themes, for example erotic ones, appear regularly on gems, but are not suitable for depiction on coins (Richter 1956: 62).

Other media such as wall-paintings, mosaics and ceramics decorated with paintings and reliefs, especially clay oil-lamps, bronze and pottery figurines and marble statuettes can be used as a source of comparison: sometimes stylistic but mainly iconographic. However, it should be remembered that the art of engraved gems is of a very varied nature and few areas have so many types and models (Henig 1978: 141–151).

6. Carving technique

Our knowledge of the methods used by Greek and Roman gem engravers is based on: written sources such as Pliny; visual depictions of tools on ancient monuments; archaeological excavations at workshops of gem engravers;

comparison to carving techniques of gems in modern times; and examination of the stones themselves, often magnified under a microscope lens.

The ancient gems, which were mostly made of hard stones, were carved using drills dipped in a mixture of oil and a grinding powder. The stones were worked with variously shaped drills that are made to rotate with the help of the wheel, or some other device such as a bow. The actual cutting was not done by the drills, but by the powder that was rubbed into the stone with the drill. This is nowadays a diamond-powder, mixed with oil. The Greeks probably used the so-called Naxian stone (naxium), a form of corundum found on the island of Naxos. Diamond-powder must have been accessible in Roman times, as it is mentioned both by Pliny (*Natural History*: XXXVII.15) and M. Manilius (*Astronomicon*: IV, 926).

On the gravestone of a gem cutter of the Roman Empire (2nd century AD), found at Philadelphia in Asia Minor, a tool is represented which looks like the bow used by modern jewellers. By being drawn quickly back and forth, the bow could impart a rotating movement similar to that of the wheel. As, however, the wheel was well known to the ancients in the making of pottery, it is probable that they also made use of it for gem engraving (Maaskant-Kleibrink 1989: 189–190; Richter 1956: XXII–XXIII).

Lorenz Natter, the 18th-century gem artist, in his work (1754) on ancient gemstone carving techniques compared to modern methods, described the main types of drills used for carving gemstones (*Traité de la méthode antique de graver en pierres fines comparés avec la méthode moderne*). In his opinion, they have not changed much since ancient times, and included two types – a vertical drill and a horizontal drill. The vertical form is a short metal rod, to which a hollow cylindrical copper drill is connected. Rounded heads of different thicknesses can be attached, so as to drill out convex and rounded shapes. The horizontal drill is a rod with a small bronze wheel connected to it, capable of creating different grooves (Maaskant-Kleibrink 1989: 189–190).

In most cases, the gemstones arrived semi-processed, in a shape suitable for inlaying in a ring or pendant, although sometimes the artists themselves prepared the initial shape of the gem from the raw material blocks. When preparing the general shape of the gem, the artist selected its dimensions. In gems of several layers, used for making cameos, their thickness had a special importance. After the gem engraver had finished preparing the general shape and polished it, he would cover the surface of the gem with wax, on which he outlined the general shape of his design. In gems that were used as intaglios, in order to obtain the correct outline for the imprint, the artist had to engrave it slightly behind the line he drew on the wax. In the next stage, the artist removed the large areas of the motif with the help of a round-headed drill, and added the small details with the help of variously shaped drills. Finally he had to polish the surface. According to Pliny, the ancients used Naxian stone (naxium) for polishing (*Natural History*: XXVI.10). Work on each gem was prolonged, depending on the size of the stone and the complexity of the subject. There are estimates that the work on the Gemma Augustea, for example, lasted five years (Guiraud 1996: 54–56).

During the Roman period large amounts of glass gems were also produced. These were cast from terracotta moulds made from existing stone gems, both intaglios and cameos. The colour was obtained by various metallic oxides added to the glass, such as cobalt for blue and magnesium for the yellow colour. The moulds were heated to a temperature of about 1000 degrees Celsius to melt the glass. Usually the glass gems are of lower quality, since the same pattern was used repeatedly and the model became worn and unclear (Guiraud 1996: 57–58).

It is not definitely known whether the Greek or Roman gem artists made use of the magnifying glass, although some crystal-convex lenses were discovered in ancient assemblages, mainly in tombs. The general principle of magnification by concentrating rays was indeed known to Aristophanes (*Clouds*: 766). Pliny mentions balls of glass or crystal brought into contact with the rays of the sun to generate heat (*Natural History*: XXXVI.67; XXXVII.10). Although we find it difficult to believe that gem artists were able to perform such delicate and precise work without using magnifying lenses. However, even today, when strong lenses are easily available, they do not always use them, but only in their later years (Guiraud 1996: 56; Richter 1956: XXIV).

7. Artists and workshops

To date, only a few workshops have been discovered, despite the fact that the enormous number of engraved gems created in ancient times, and their great variety, attest to the existence of many workshops. In Herculaneum, a shop of a gem engraver was found with the final products displayed on a table, and gems in the process of being making discovered in the back of the store (Deiss 1989: 108). Also in a Pompeian house, perhaps that of a gem artist, a box with partly processed gems was found (Henig 1978: 29). In Aquileia there were apparently several workshops, although no archaeological evidence has yet been found (Henig 1999: 52). The reason researchers assume with a high degree of probability that such workshops existed is the large amount of gems discovered there, and the stylistic similarity between many of the gems. The site was apparently an important production centre starting from the 1st century BC to the 3rd century AD. Similar assumptions exist for other sites, where workshops have not yet been discovered (Henig 1999: 52).

From the middle of the 2nd century AD, it is assumed that it was relatively simple for travelling artists to set up a workshop wherever there was a demand for gems. In this period the mass production of gems began, and a gem engraver needed only a small number of drills of different sizes, a small wooden drill, some stones and grinding powder, all of which were small and easy to carry (Maaskant-Kleibrink 1997: 25).

Of the gem artists themselves, we can learn a little from the number of gems inscribed with their signature and based on a few comments in ancient literature. It is impossible to identify and trace the stylistic development of a particular artist, because only very rarely has more than one gem been discovered signed by the same artist. In the Roman period, the difficulty increases, because the artists collected and assembled their models from different sources of different styles.

The artist's signature, in cases where it occurs, is small compared to the name of the owner appearing in larger letters. All the surviving names of artists are Greek, even in the Roman period (although there were Roman engravers as well). The most famous gem artists were Epimenes, from the end of the Archaic period; Dexamenos, from the second half of the 5th century BC; Pyrgoteles from the period of Alexander the Great; and Dioskourides, from the Augustan period (Richter 1956: XXXII–XXXIII). The sons of Dioskourides (Herphilos, Hylos and Eutiches) were also gem artists and their signatures are found on a number of gems (Henig 1997: 89–90).

Animal images and their meaning

The ancient Greeks adored animals and regarded them as the embodiment of the forces of nature (Prieur 1988: 54). Often they were painstakingly depicted in art, depictions which were also full of meaning. Animals played an important role in ancient Greece, both in everyday life and myth. Myths dealing with heroes and animals constituted an endless source of inspiration for depictions on gemstones as well as other media: Heracles battling the Nemean Lion, Leda and the Swan, Bellerophon and Pegasus, and many more. The artists in ancient Greece watched animal behaviour and used their representations to decorate their environment and also to comment metaphorically on many aspects of human life. Using animals, they transferred visual messages related to social status, rituals, social ceremonies, age and gender (Klinger 1999: 26).

Animals were ambivalently described in ancient literature: on the one hand as resembling human beings and expressing the same feelings, such as joy and sadness, anger, courage and fear, and on the other hand as expressing the impulsive instincts and the irrational aspect in the human soul (Dierauer 1997: 3–4). Animals have been associated with deities, often accompanying them, and sometimes the gods used animals as their envoys, to intervene in life on earth and to communicate with humans (Prieur 1988: 135–139). Various animals served as attributes of different gods, sharing with them similar qualities, mythology and cult. Some believe that an animal that was venerated as a deity in the past became later an attribute of this god. The presence of the animal can indicate that it comes before the anthropomorphic images that replaced it (Prieur 1988: 27, 33, 57). For example it is possible that Hera, called ox-eyed by Homer (Homer, *Iliad*: 1.553), was venerated in the past as a sacred cow (Ovid, *Metamorphoses*: 5.330).

In the Roman world animals also took part in all areas of life, and were often portrayed on sculptures and reliefs when accompanying gods, goddesses and heroes. Animals appear in religious ceremonies, hunting and battle scenes

– mythological, and of their time, as well as everyday life and burial scenes (Gersht 1999: 35).

Of animals, their importance and significance, one can learn from a variety of ancient sources, such as Aelian's *De Natura Animalium*, which includes facts about the history of nature alongside allegorical shortstories about animals, usually with a moral; Aristotle in his *Historia Animalium* discusses at length animal features; Varro in his work *De Re Rustica* specifies instructions for agricultural farm management as well as the handling of its animals; and Xenophon discusses the art of horse-breeding in his essay *De Re Equestri*.

Plato in Phaedrus, and Laches describes the soul as consisting metaphorically of two wild beasts: the lion and the wild boar, and of two more domesticated ones: the horse and the dog (*Laches*: 196 E; Plato, *Phaedrus*: 249 D; see also Frère 1997: 433).

According to Pythagoras, the concept of reincarnation means that the soul of humans can pass to animals and vice versa, whereas human existence is considered supreme (Dierauer 1997: 4–5). According to Plato, as noted by Empedocles, living as a human being is the acme and the last link in the chain of life, and then re-births are concluded (*Empedocles*: 31 B 146; see Diels and Kranz 1952). Anaxagoras, like Aristotle and Empedocles, attributes to animals a certain degree of wisdom, while Plato believes that animals lack logic and behave in irrational ways. In his opinion, while animals do exhibit traits such as courage and passion, they do not possess logic and intelligence (*Anaxagore: 59 B 12, 59 A 102; see* Diels and Kranz 1952; Plato, *Republic*: 589 D, 591 B, 441 A–B).

In the following chapters will be discussed the possible interpretations of animals depictions on gems: as attributes of gods; as participants in the myths of gods and heroes; as symbols of victory, wealth and fertility; as bearers of apotropaic, magical and healing meanings; as astrological signs; as participating in pastoral scenes; and as the bearers of political propaganda. The animal gems are divided into groups, since it should be noted that there are gems that can be read in different ways. For example the lion in 'Heracles and the Lion' motif on gems is a participant in the myth of the hero, but has a relevance to healing intestinal disease as well.

Mammals

Cattle

A green jasper Classical-Phoenician scarab from the Israel Museum, which dates to the first half of the 5th century BC, depicts a cow suckling a kneeling calf, and its large head is frontal while the flanks are directed toward the observer (Figures 1a and b) (Boardman 2003: 122, pl. 40/55). The calf seems newly born and still having difficulty standing up, opening his mouth to suckle, his front legs are bent while the hind legs are quite straight. The cow has a unique styling of the hair above its eyes and between its two horns. Above them features a grasshopper that occupies a significant part of the background.[2] Both the cow and calf are standing on the *neb*-basket.[3] As previously noted, the scarab is made of green jasper, the colour being probably of as much importance as its intaglio since it enhances its amuletic value.

Figure 1a. A Cow Suckling her Calf and a grasshopper, green jasper, 12x16x8.5 mm, a Classical-Phoenician scarab, first half of the 5th century BC.
The Israel Museum Jerusalem, The Harry Stern Collection, bequeathed by Dr Kurt Stern, London . In memory of his parents and his brother who perished at Sobibor. IMJ76.42.2420. ©Photo: The Israel Museum, Jerusalem, by Vladimir Naikhin.

---

[2] I am grateful to Dr Ariel-Leib-Leonid Friedman, Entomologist, the Steinhardt Museum of Natural History, Tel Aviv University for identifying the insect.
[3] The *neb*-basket signified 'goddess' in Egyptian hieroglyphics (Boardman 1968: 20).

Figure 1b. Impression of the green jasper scarab.
©Photo: The Israel Museum, Jerusalem.

Boardman notes that the origin of this scarab is the Eastern Mediterranean: Syria-Palestine, Cyprus or Egypt. The theme might be Egyptian, from the Eastern Mediterranean, Greek, or combined. Boardman also notes that the perspective of the depiction is rare (Boardman 2003: 6, 17, 121). The cow suckling a calf motif has been known already from reliefs of the Old Kingdom of Egypt. It is common on Minoan and Mycenaean seal stones (Boardman 1970: pl. 174), decorating ivory plates of palaces from the East, Mesopotamian cylinder seals and Phoenician metal bowls (Ward 1992: 70). It is found on objects as varied as a Minoan sarcophagus, a silver ring of Syracuse, and fragments of pottery from Cana'an. The theme can be linked in some cases with specific gods, and was offered different interpretations. Possessing many calves has been related to abundance and wealth since Biblical times. It was also a depiction that artists copied from nature. However, the most acceptable explanation among scholars is that the source of the motif is Egyptian, symbolising Isis suckling her son Horus (Ward 1992: 70–77). Isis is often represented in the act of protecting her dead husband. This image made her one of the goddesses famous for warding off evil and, as such, her figure was often represented on amulets (Tiradritti 1998: 3). Isis was regarded as the feminine aspect of nature, the fertile agency, associated with procreation, with an innate love for all creatures, and identical with the good that she longs for and rejecting evil (Plutarch, *Moralia, vol. V, Isis and Osiris*: 372.53). Some researchers believe that the theme was originally Mesopotamian, hence symbolising Ishtar or similar goddesses of fertility, or originating from the Mediterranean region and then representing Astarte or Anat (Ward 1992: 70–73). According to Plutarch, the Egyptians saw the cow as the image of Isis, the great goddess of Egypt (*Moralia*, vol. V, 'Isis and Osiris': 366.3919). Isis is depicted as wearing a crown of cow horns surrounding the solar disk. Aelian notes that in Egypt sculptors and painters depicted Isis with cow horns – an animal that has strong associations with passion and love (*De natura animalium*, X. 27). Isis had an important role in carrying out rituals in honour of the deceased, and these roles were also attributed to her during the Greco-Roman period. Isis was the Great Goddess, the benevolent mother, whose influence and love dominated the entire universe – heaven, earth and the Underworld. She was the epitome of femininity, a creative power with the ability to conceive and give life to all. She protected every creature, nourished and cared for them (Budge 2004 (1904): vol. 2, 203). Her cult was associated with mysteries from very ancient times, and in this context she had the ability to bring about the resurrection of the dead, since humans hoped that in the same way she had managed to revive Osiris, and also her son Horus, who was stung by a scorpion, so could she help mortals. All references to Isis in the *Book of the Dead* relate to her as a giver of life and provider of nourishment for the deceased, and as one of the justices of the dead along with Osiris (Budge 2004 (1904): vol. 2, 204–205). In addition, magical powers and skills were attributed to Isis. In the *Book of the Dead* there is a chapter written in order to deliver to the deceased some of the magical powers of this goddess. This section was designed to be quoted on an amulet called *thet*, made of carnelian, and which was believed to protect the deceased if laid on his neck; since then he would be under the protection of Isis he could go wherever he wished in the Afterlife (Budge 2004 (1904): vol. 2, 214–215). Horus, the son of Isis and Osiris, generally represented the sun, and was for the Egyptians what Apollo was for the Greeks. Many temples were built for him throughout Egypt, since he represented life and resurrection – the yearning of all mortals (Budge 2004 (1904): vol. 1, 486–487). The common belief was that Horus helped the dead in his role as a mediator between them and the judge of the Underworld. Horus also took care of the bodies of the deceased and supervised the execution of burial rites (Budge 2004 (1904): vol. 1, 490).

The cow suckling a calf motif is found on scarabs that originated from around the Mediterranean: mostly from North Africa, Sardinia, Ibiza, Italy and Greece, and few from the Eastern Mediterranean: Syria-Palestine, Cyprus and Egypt (Ward 1992: 68, cat. 1–31). In most of the examples there is an empty space in the background, but sometimes a scorpion, star, pomegranate, papyrus plant, or a rosette are depicted, all of which were sacred or associated with Isis (Budge 2004 (1904): vol. 1, 487–488; vol. 2, 215–217, 249). The dating of these scarabs range from the 6th–4th centuries BC, belonging to a group of Phoenician scarabs, sometimes also called 'Greco-Phoenician' because of their relationship to Archaic Greek iconography and style of engraving (Ward 1992: 68). Sometimes a star, rosette, or, more frequently, a crescent moon and a disk appear on Phoenician scarabs, reflecting aspects of a moon-goddess worship that was common in the Eastern Mediterranean (Boardman 2003: 9). According to Plutarch, Isis was considered a moon-goddess. In the eastern regions of the Mediterranean basin Ishtar and Inanna were recognised as goddesses of the moon (*Moralia, vol. V, Isis and Osiris*: 372.53).

The grasshopper bears associations to immortality and resurrection both in Greek and Egyptian mythology. In Greek mythology the myth of Tithonus and Eos is well known, while in Egyptian mythology the grasshopper might serve as a guide to the deceased on their journey to achieve eternal life (Maspero 1901-1904: 263). In addition, according to Horapollo when the Egyptians 'would symbolize a mystic man, and one of the initiated, they delineate a grasshopper; for he does not utter sounds through his mouth, but chirping by means of his spine, sings a sweet melody' (Horapollo, *Hieroglyphica*: II. LV). The grasshopper, then, which uttered a voice that did not come from its mouth, was a living type of superhuman power. Renouf explains that various animal hieroglyphics showing animals which characteristically sprang or flew up into the sky, such as the hare, grouse, grasshopper, were used to express the concept of ascending or leaping into heaven (Renouf 1893, 281-294 cf. Troy 1976: 18). The grasshopper is a symbol of rebirth and immortality because it is an embodiment of 'springing forth': the dead 'arrive in heaven like the grasshopper of Rā' (Budge 2004 (1904), vol. 2, 379), and with the grasshopper ideas of religious enjoyment seem to have been associated, for in the *Book of the Dead* the deceased says 'I have rested in Hemet, to the north of the field of the grasshoppers' (*Book of the Dead*: chap. cxxv.).

It is probable that the choice to depict specifically on green jasper a cow with its suckling calf was not random, especially given this mineral's association with fertility, new life and health, as noted above. In addition, these figures identified as Isis and Horus, an image with implications associated with fertility, birth, rebirth, and resurrection is emphasized by the presence of a grasshopper also bearing associations to immortality and resurrection both in Greek and Egyptian mythology.

A carnelian gem from the Israel Museum (Figures 2a, b and c), dated to the 1st century BC-AD 30, features a bull stamping its feet, above it an octagonal star, and on the other side of the gem a woman's head is depicted, whose hair is bunched at the back of her neck, a ribbon adorns her head and a feather (?) is seen above her forehead. In the Roman period, stars (together with the sun and the moon) symbolised the *aeternitas*, or eternity, of the sky; when they appeared in tombs they represented immortal life, and also everlasting love, when given as gifts of love, for example, in jewellery (Henig 2006: 62). The depiction on this gem can be interpreted as the Taurus astrological sign of the Zodiac, since gems illustrating a Zodiacal sign together with a star are usually considered to have astrological significance (Henig 1994: 175, no. 381; Plantzos 1999: 99).

Figure 2a. Double sided gem: side a – a bull and a star, drawing, carnelian, 10 x 7.5 x 2.5 mm, 1st BC–AD 30.
The Israel Museum Jerusalem, Bequest of Mr Adolphe Doreen, Paris. IMJ70.62.351.
©Drawing: The Israel Museum, Jerusalem, by Pnina Arad.

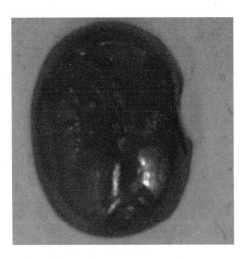

Figure 2b. Side b – head of a woman.
©Photo: The Israel Museum, Jerusalem.

Figure 2c. Side b – head of a woman, drawing.
©Drawing: The Israel Museum, Jerusalem, by Pnina Arad.

Very similar in iconography, and presumably also date, is a gem from the end of the 1st century BC in the Fitzwilliam Museum, Cambridge, although without a portrait of a woman on the reverse (Henig 1994: 120, no. 226). In Henig's opinion, there is no connection between the two sides of the gem. He assumes that the device of Taurus is earlier, and then the owner may have ordered another image on the reverse of the gem, being tired of the previous image. The woman's head engraving might refer to the goddess Artemis (M. Henig, personal communication, September 2011). The intaglio can be compared to a two-sided gem from Bedfordshire, published by Henig – on one side an armed naked man is seen, probably Achilles, and on the other side appears the thunderbolt of Jupiter (Henig 2010: 155–156). Henig believes that there are three reasons for the existence of two-sided Roman gems: first, that the engraver made a mistake in the carving of the device, and decided to use the gem once again, knowing that his failed attempt would be concealed by embedding in the ring; the second is that it may have been a gem used to train young gems artists; and the third, and the most likely explanation in Henig's opinion, that the owner of the gem decided to renew the engraving according to the vogue at the time, and therefore gave the gem in his possession to be re-carved. A similar case is probably demonstrated by an Augustan gem from the Fitzwilliam Museum, which bears a representation of a cow nursing a calf on one side and the reverse features a 3rd-century AD cameo showing Cupid grieving (Henig 2010: 156).

The theme of cattle among trees, grazing or nursing their offspring, belongs to depictions of pastoral and idyllic scenes. An Etruscan 3rd-century BC scarab (Figure 3), from 350 BC, made in the 'globolo' style and kept at the Israel Museum, portrays a grazing bull, similar to the bull on an Etruscan scarab from The Hague Collection, now in the Rijksmuseum van Oudheden, Leiden (Maaskant-Kleibrink 1978: 93, no. 54).

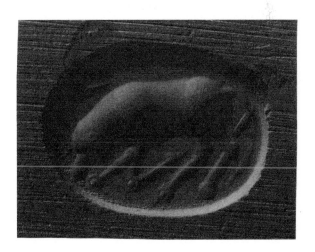

Figure 3. Grazing bull, impression of carnelian stone, 10 x 7.5 x 5.5 mm, an Etruscan 'globolo' style scarab, 350 BC.
The Israel Museum Jerusalem, The Harry Stern Collection, bequeathed by Dr Kurt Stern, London. In memory of his parents and his brother who perished at Sobibor. IMJ76.42.2382.
©Photo: The Israel Museum, Jerusalem.

A carnelian gem from the Israel Museum bears a representation of a bull facing a tree with head bowed (Figure 4). It is made in the 'Imperial Classicising Style', hence dates to the 1st century AD (Maaskant-Kleibrink 1978: 195). Vollenweider mentions a gem depicting the same motif signed by Hyllos, and Henig indicates a similar gem from the Augustan period (Henig 1994: 120, no. 226; Vollenweider 1966: pl. 78, 1, 2, 4).

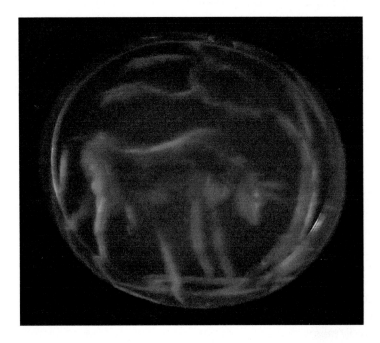

Figure 4. Bull and tree, carnelian, 13.5 x 11 x 2 mm, 1st century AD.
The Israel Museum Jerusalem, Bequest of Mr. Adolphe Doreen, Paris. IMJ70.62.390.
©Photo: The Israel Museum, Jerusalem.

Early examples of the subject are also known, for example, among Greek gems (Boardman 1970: pls. 498, 499), and also among Roman gems kept at The Hague Collection, now in the Rijksmuseum van Oudheden, Leiden (Maaskant-Kleibrink 1978: no. 418), and at the Metropolitan Museum of Art (Richter 1956: no. 508). A black onyx gem from the Israel Museum (Figures 5a and b) features a cow pacing to the right. This gem can be dated to the second half of the 1st century and the early years of the 2nd century AD because the gold ring is Type II (see: Henig 2007, fig. 1, 9-12). A similar cow, though Augustan, is also seen, for example, on a gem kept at the Fitzwilliam Museum (Henig 1994: 126, no. 244). In the *Anthologia Graeca* (IX.747) a small jasper stone is described, on which five grazing cows were engraved so realistically that they might have bolted if not being trapped inside the golden ring in which the gem was embedded.

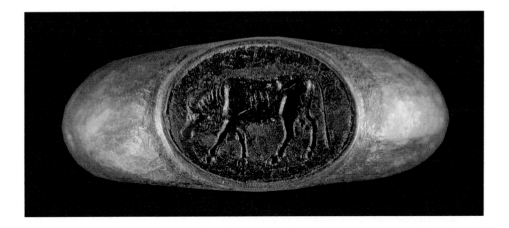

Figure 5a. Cow, onyx, 14 x 9.5 mm, the second half of the 1st century BC–beginning of the 2nd century AD.
The Israel Museum Jerusalem, The Harry Stern Collection, bequeathed by Dr Kurt Stern, London . In memory of his parents and his brother who perished at Sobibor. IMJ76.42.2418. ©Photo: The Israel Museum, Jerusalem, by Vladimir Naikhin.

Figure 5b. Impression of the onyx stone.
©Photo: The Israel Museum, Jerusalem, by Vladimir Naikhin.

Another Augustan gem, made of carnelian (Figure 6), and embedded in a Type III gold ring, depicts a cow which is suckling a calf. A cow and calf as depiction imitating nature was a common motif on Roman intaglios, with the possession of many calves indicating wealth and abundance. Domestic animals on gems often represent the fecundity and plenty of nature, especially when they are depicted with their young in a pastoral setting, grazing, or holding fertility symbols such as ears of corn, horns of plenty, and wine cups (Henig 1997: 48). The motif of a suckling calf on gem-devices could also signify, in addition to a symbol of prosperity and fertility, an expression of affection for a loved one (Henig 1997: 52, note 24). The world of nature was an infinitely adaptable source for the succinct expression of messages, and even if nowadays the nuances of meaning are not always caught, that does not mean that the person who commissioned a particular seal device did not have a very clear idea of what he or she meant to convey to a contemporary loved one (Henig 1997: 52).

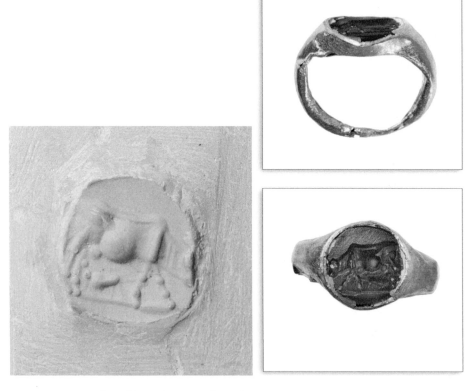

Figure 6. A cow and a calf, carnelian, intaglio and impression, 10 x 7.5 x 2.5 mm, c. 31 BC–AD 14. The Israel Museum Jerusalem, The Harry Stern Collection, bequeathed by Dr Kurt Stern, London. In memory of his parents and his brother who perished at Sobibor. IMJ76.42.2419. ©Photo: The Israel Museum, Jerusalem.

A red jasper gem from the Israel Museum shows a herdsman driving an ox-drawn plough (Figures 7a and b). The rarity of the motif indicates that it was not a common symbol for abundance, in the same way as cornucopias, ears of corn, poppy heads, or calves. The limited time span in which this theme appears (none of which is later than the 1st or beginning of the 2nd century AD) suggests that the subject was popular for a relatively short period of time, the period of the establishment of the colonies, at the end of the Republic and the beginning of the Imperial period (Henig 2001: 309). In addition, this gem can be assigned to the 'small grooves style' typified by rounded wheel grooves employed for detailing, hence can be dated to the beginning of the 2nd century AD (see Maaskant-Kleibrink 1978, 251–252, 268, no. 727).

Figure 7a. Herdsman driving an ox-drawn plough, red jasper, 15 x 11.5 x 2 mm, the beginning of the 2nd century AD.
The Israel Museum Jerusalem, Bequest of Mr. Adolphe Doreen, Paris, through the Israel Embassy, Paris. IMJ70.62.112.
©Photo: The Israel Museum, Jerusalem.

Figure 7b. Herdsman driving an ox-drawn plough, drawing.
©Drawing: The Israel Museum, Jerusalem, by Pnina Arad.

The ox and the cow are often used as guides to the founding of cities. Cadmus, after consultation with the oracle at Delphi, was ordered to follow a cow in order to know where to found the city of Thebes. In the same way, Ilos followed a cow to ascertain where to establish the city of Ilion (Billerbeck, Gaertner, Wyss and Zubler (eds), *Stephani Byzantii Ethnica*: 2006, s.v. 'Ilion'; Cunningham, Hansen, Latte (eds), *Hesychii Alexandrini lexicon*: 2009, s.v. 'Atiolophos'). Later, when the Sabines decided to migrate, their new residence was determined by a leading bull (Strabo, *Geography*: V, 4). The founding of a new city involved a ceremony in which the *sulcus primigenius* was plowed by an ox and a cow together, around the place where it was to be built, to delimit its boundaries. The ceremony is considered to be very ancient and is believed to have begun with Romulus, who founded Rome in this manner. Dionysus of Halicarnassus pointed out that Romulus' act was later used as a model for the Romans, who afterwards established their colonies in a similar way (Dionysius of Halicarnassus, *The Roman Antiquities (Antiquitates Romanae)*: 1.88). This ceremony had fixed rules, involving the augurs' interpretation of allegedly divine omens, such as the flight patterns of birds. According to Plutarch, when Romulus performed the ceremony in Rome, he created the *pomoerium* of the city, namely the limited area that defined the new city, as well as certain aspects of its religious life. The orbit done by the governor of the colony, as he plowed the furrow (while murmuring a fixed prayer), marked its *pomoerium* (Plutarch, *Lives, Romulus*: 11; Varro, *De lingua Latina*: 5.143). Julius Caesar, Mark Antony and Octavian used this ceremony to establish their colonies, and the settlers themselves perpetuated the founding of their colonies by minting coins depicting their *conditor* with the plough (Gargola 1995: 74–75). *Denarii*, apparently minted in 34 BC, show Octavian leading such a team, thus seeking to present himself as the founder of colonies, or a ruler who increased the *pomoerium*. The motif appears on a *sesterius* of Trajan, minted in 106 AD, commemorating the establishment of the Trajanian colony of Sarmizegethusa in Dacia, as well as on provincial coins of Nero from Ptolemais in present-day Libya, and of Septimius Severus from Tyre, currently Lebanon (Henig 2001: 308). Therefore, the owner of the gem in the Israel Museum was apparently a settler of a newly built colony, perhaps the founder himself, and in addition the intaglio could have served as a constant reminder of the connections between their colony and Rome.

Deer

An Archaic late 5th-century BC agate scarab from the Israel Museum bears a representation of a sitting stag in profile, with long and branched antlers (Figures 8a, b and c). Very similar in iconography, but later in date, are some gems and scaraboids mentioned by Boardman (Boardman 1970: 202, pls. 562, 564–567). Although scarabs are rare after the middle of the 5th century, it is interesting to note that the style of those mentioned by Boardman is very similar to the Israel

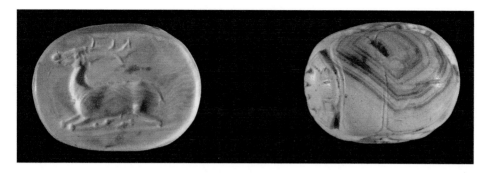

Figure 8a. Sitting stag, banded agate, an Archaic late 5th-century BC scarab
The Israel Museum Jerusalem, Gift of Norbert Schimmel, New York, to American
Friends of the Israel Museum. MJ69.80.250 (2000.121.37).
©Photo: The Israel Museum, Jerusalem, by Vladimir Naikhin.

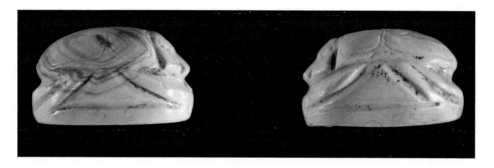

Figure 8b. Archaic agate scarab
©Photo: The Israel Museum, Jerusalem, by Vladimir Naikhin.

Figure 8c. Impression of the agate scarab.
©Photo: The Israel Museum, Jerusalem.

Museum scarab. The studies of stags are the most typical of this group of gems, which Boardman calls 'After Dexamenos' and dates to the end of the 5th century BC. The deer are portrayed with heavy, smooth bodies and slim, brittle legs, much like the Jerusalem one. These stag representations bring us very close to the work of Greeks and for Persians within their territories. In addition, a Greco-Persian scarab in the Ashmolean Museum also bears a similar iconography and style to the Israel Museum example (Boardman and Vollenweider 1978: no. 192). Thus this Jerusalem scarab is probably from an eastern Greek studio in touch with more provincial workshops in the Persian Empire.

A leaping deer is portrayed on an Etruscan 'globolo' style scarab from the Israel Museum, which dates to the third century BC (Figures 9a and b).[4] It is similar to other Etruscan scarabs from the Fitzwilliam Museum (Henig 1994: 70, no. 117), the Royal Coin Cabinet, The Hague, and now in the Rijksmuseum van Oudheden, Leiden (Maaskant-Kleibrink 1978: no. 52), and from the British Museum (Zazoff 1983: Taf. 62, 13).

Figure 9a. Leaping deer, carnelian, 11 x 9 x 7 mm,
an Etruscan 'globolo' style scarab, third century BC.
The Israel Museum Jerusalem, The Harry Stern Collection, bequeathed by Dr Kurt Stern, London. In memory of his parents and his brother who perished at Sobibor. IMJ76.42.2379. ©Photo: The Israel Museum, Jerusalem, by Vladimir Naikhin.

---

[4] Globolo – Etruscan engraving technique, wherein the representation in the stone is carved with a spherical headed drill and the image seems to be composed of round dimples.

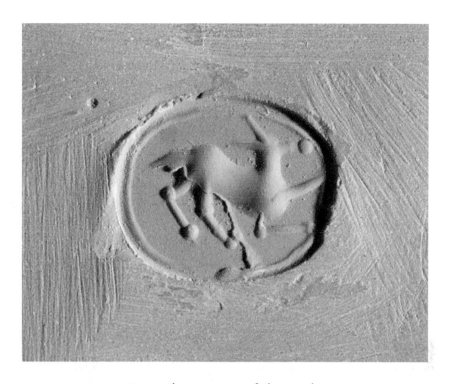

Figure 9b. Impression of the scarab.
©Photo: The Israel Museum, Jerusalem, by Vladimir Naikhin.

The deer was the fastest animal known in the Archaic period, referred to as a noble animal by many contemporary poets, and a symbol of masculinity, virility and good luck. Its impressive shape, with long neck, delicate legs, and flexible and graceful poses, gave the Greek artists great pleasure – as, indeed, we feel today. Both deer and gazelles appear frequently in Greek art, for instance on reliefs, small statuettes, coins, and bronze and terracotta figurines (Richter 1930: 28). A terracotta statuette of 500 BC in the Metropolitan Museum is one of the earliest known examples (Richter 1930: fig. 144). From the second half of the 5th century a bronze statuette in the Louvre, the miniature depictions from the Boston gems, and the Kaulonia coin, now in the British Museum, can be noted (Richter 1930: 29, figs 145, 147–148). The deer hunted depicted on the 'Alexander Sarcophagus' in the Istanbul Archaeological Museum, dating to 330–325 BC, presents a very detailed depiction, typical of the Hellenistic period (Richter 1930: fig. 151).

The deer is mentioned in many myths, such as those of Heracles and the Ceryneian hind, Iphigenia in Aulis, and Artemis and Actaeon (Nonnus, *Dionysiaca*: V, 300–370). Telephus, the legendary founder of Pergamon, was suckled by a doe (Diodorus Siculus, *Bibliotheca historica*: IV, 33). Cyparissus is depicted along with his beloved stag, which he accidentally killed, on wall-paintings at Pompeii (Reinach 1922: 28, no. 2; 182, no. 4), as well as on later mosaics, such as the one from Leicester (Toynbee 1963: 197, 198, no. 183, pl. 219). In Rome, this myth is echoed in that of the favourite stag loved by Silvia (Virgil, *Aeneid*: VII, 483–502). These myths suggest that deer were kept in private homes as pets.

But, primarily, the stag was a sacred animal attributed to Artemis in Greek mythology (called Artumes by the Etruscans). The deer's traits, such as its agility and swiftness, are linked to the attributes of the goddess of hunting. Artemis sometimes turns herself into a doe, for example in the myth of Otus and Ephialtes (Apollodorus, *Bibliotheca*: I.VII.4). The connection between them was a complex one: on the one hand the stag was her victim, and, on the other, her protégée. In the *Odyssey* and the *Homeric Hymns* Artemis is already presented as a hunter who likes to hunt deer (Homer, *Odyssey*: 6.102–104; *Homeric Hymns*: XXVII, 'To Artemis'). This habit also continues to characterise the goddess in later works (Callimachus, *Hymns and Epigrams*, iii, 'Hymn to Artemis', 94–109), as well as in her visual representations, in which the deer are essentially her attribute, like the bow, arrow and quiver. Her epithet, *Elaphia*, also reflects this (Strabo, *Geography*: 343). It was only natural, therefore, that hunters would dedicated some of their quarry to Artemis. One of the inscriptions describes how Likormas hung the skin and antlers of a stag inside the temple of Artemis Agrothera, and in addition it was also customary to sacrifice a deer to Artemis in her sanctuaries (Bevan 1986: 100, 105). Ephesian coins from the 3rd century BC depicting the head of Artemis on one side and a stag on the other, demonstrate the significance of the deer ritual at the Artemision at Ephesus, for example (Head 1892: 57–60, pl. 10.8; pl. 11.1–3). The ambiguity in the character of the goddess is also embodied in her sacred enclosure at Skillous. Although the antelope and stags held there were seen as sacred to her, they were also hunted during her festival (Xenophon, *Anabasis*: V.3.9–10). The stag also accompanies the goddess on marble reliefs, painted terracotta tablets and figurines such, as the 300 terracotta figurines discovered in her temple at Corcyra, and in other places of worship, although to a lesser amount, for example, at Brauron and Calydon (Kahil, s.v. 'Artemis', in *LIMC*, II.1, 743). Terracotta figurines of Artemis accompanied by a deer began to appear at the end of the Archaic period, and the terracotta votive tablets from Brauron, dated to the 6th century BC, are among the earliest representations of the goddess and her favourite companion (although deer depictions on offerings made to the goddess are already evident from the Geometric and Early Archaic periods) (Bevan 1986: 108).[5] Callimachus

---

[5] However it should be noted that the theme itself – a goddess accompanied by a deer – was not a renovation of Late Archaic times, since 'Potnia Theron', the 'mistress of animals' of Minoan Crete, was already associated with deer hunting, as shown, for example, on a Mycenaean seal that shows the goddess aiming her arrow at a deer (Evans 1925: 21, fig. 24).

mentions the golden and rapid chariot of Artemis pulled by deer (*Hymns and Epigrams*: iii, 'Hymn to Artemis', 105–115). A similar chariot is depicted on an interior frieze of the temple of Apollo Epicurius in Bassae, from the 5th century BC, where Apollo is shown riding together with his sister (Richter 1930: fig. 146).

In the Roman world it was customary to offer a sacrifice for the 'mistress of animals' before the hunt to ensure its success, and afterwards as gratitude. Since, for the Romans, hunting took place not only to supply animals to the arena, for amusement, or for the realisation of *virtus*, but also for food, Artemis can also be seen as a goddess who ensures prosperity. Artemis appears in many hunting mosaics, and some of them also depict sacrifices in her honour, e.g. the mosaic of 'the little hunt', from Piazza Armerina, Sicily, and other hunting mosaics of Antioch and North Africa (Dunbabin 1999: 133, 135, fig. 137, 164–165, figs 169–170). During the Roman period there are many depictions of Diana with a stag, for example, an early Imperial-period statue showing Diana with a gazelle, whose style combines classical and Archaic characteristics (Zanker 1988: 251, fig. 197).

Goats

The religious significance ascribed to the goat probably originated from its fertility and sexual potency. These qualities associated it with Zeus, Dionysus, Aphrodite, as well as Artemis (Bevan 1986: 180). In Greek mythology the nymph Amalthea, who, with her cornucopia, symbolised generosity and wondrous deeds, suckled the infant-god Zeus in a Cretan cave (Callimachus, *Hymns and Epigrams*, i, 'Hymn to Zeus', 48–49; Diodorus Siculus, *Bibliotheca historica*: V.70; Virgil, *Georgics*: IV, 150). But the goat is mainly associated with Dionysus, who often appeared in its form (Prieur 1988: 112). It was customary to sacrifice a goat to Bacchus to atone for a crime (Pausanias, *Description of Greece*: IX.8.1). Goats were also sacrificed to Dionysus to preserve the memory of the myth in which Zeus turned Dionysus into a young goat in order to protect him from Hera, and then was transferred by Hermes to Mount Nysa in Asia Minor, where he was raised by the nymphs, as well as to ensure the revival of vine growing every year and the ripening grapes (Gersht 2007: 95).The satyrs forming part of Dionysus's entourage have ears, horns and goat legs. The shepherds' god, Pan, possessed these features from birth, together with a goatee (Aristophanes, *Frogs*: 229–230).As a companion of Dionysus, he symbolised masculinity and reckless behaviour. Pan is occasionally depicted with his crook (pedum), playing the flute or syrinx in front of a goat ('Pan', *New Larousse Encyclopedia of Mythology* 1989 (1968): 161). In two wall-paintings from Herculaneum and Pompeii, a sports competition between a goat and the god Pan is shown (Reinach 1922: 100, nos 4, 6). Some Archaic rituals continued during the Roman period. For example Ovid records the Lupercalia festival, in which the priests wore goat skins, in Pan's likeness, to promote fertility (*Fasti*: II, 445–448).In Rome goats were sacrificed to rural deities, such as Faunnus and Silvannus, and to spring goddesses, such as Flora. Aphrodite is sometimes illustrated sitting on the back of a goat, after her epithet *Epitragia* (Pausanias, *Description of Greece*: VI.25.1). The goat appears as early as the Mycenaean and Geometric periods, but animal became especially popular in the 6th and beginning of the 5th centuries BC. A bronze statuette of a goat, from the beginning of the 5th century BC, in the Archaeological Museum of Florence is typical of the end of the Archaic period, from which have survived many similar statuettes that show the animal in a variety of postures and depictions, stylish as well as naturalistic. A typical example of a goat depiction from the Hellenistic period is an antefix from the Metropolitan Museum, with the heads of two fighting goats emerging from acanthus leaves (Richter 1930: 25–27, figs 124, 135).

A carnelian gem from the Israel Museum bears a representation of a satyr intimately petting a goat which stands between his legs, one hand under her neck and the other holding her chest hair (Figures 10a and b). This gem was mistakenly considered as being ancient, but dates to the 18th century. A similar gem, also dating to the 18th century, is held in the Fitzwilliam Museum and portrays a satyr lifting a goat's hoofs as if encouraging it to dance on its hind legs (Henig 1994: no. 691). Another similar gem from the catalogue of Lippold, which also dates to the 18th century, shows Silenus caressing a goat (Lippold 1923: Taf. CIX, 7). The posture of the figures is the same: on both gems the satyrs are seated, in right profile, extending their hands to caress the goat standing in front of them under its chin.

Figure 10a. Satyr petting a goat, carnelian, 17 x 15 mm, 18th century. The Israel Museum Jerusalem, The Harry Stern Collection, bequeathed by Dr Kurt Stern, London. In memory of his parents and his brother who perished at Sobibor. IMJ76.42.2427 ©Photo: The Israel Museum, Jerusalem, by Vladimir Naikhin.

Figure 10b. Impression of the carnelian stone.
©Photo: The Israel Museum, Jerusalem, by Vladimir
Naikhin.

Although most of the Roman gems showing this theme are less intimate (Henig 1994: 330), the carnelian gems from the Fitzwilliam Museum that feature a sitting satyr, holding a thyrsus and erotically caressing a goat, are dated by Henig to the era of Augustus (31 BC–AD 14) (Henig 1994: 102, nos 186, 187). Gem no. 186 is very similar stylistically to many other on which satyrs are depicted in the 'Wheel Style' (Maaskant-Kleibrink 1978: 170–172, nos 335–343; Sena-Chiesa 1966: nos 791, 794, 796; Walters 1926: no. 1612; Zwierlein-Diehl 1973: vol I, no. 297, vol. II, no. 1104).

On a red jasper gem from the collection of the Israel Museum a goat is seen standing on its hind legs and browsing from a tree (Figures 11a and b). It dates to the 2nd century AD, since red jasper was particularly popular during this period (Guiraud 1996: 95; Maaskant-Kleibrink 1978: 251–285; Richter 1956: 61; Sena-Chiesa 1966: 60), and also on a stylistic basis, being made in the 'Imperial Small Grooves Style', as defined by Maaskant-Kleibrink (Maaskant-Kleibrink 1978: 251–252, 268, no. 727). The motif of two goats standing on both sides of a palm tree is ancient, symbolising fertility and renewal (Vollenweider 1967: vol. I, no. 58 (a Kassite cylinder-seal); for gems see Gramatopol 1974: no. 520; Kibaltchitch 1910: no. 262). It appears already in the 3rd millennium BC in Mesopotamia and is very common in the 1st millennium among the Arameans, Phoenicians and Hebrews. The palm tree is identified in the mythologies of the ancient East with the 'Tree of Life'. Some believe that its shape and meaning are embodied in the Menorah of the Temple, which became the symbol of Judaism.

A similar gem kept in the Fitzwilliam Museum, dating from the 1st century AD, shows two goats standing on their hind legs, one on each side of a tree (Henig 1994: 170, no. 365). Additional gems exhibiting the same iconography are, inter alia, an example of a Roman gem from Dover that dates to the 2nd – beginning of the 3rd century AD (Philp and Henig 1985: 463–465, pl. CIII.e), and a Roman gem from Lippold's catalogue, both featuring a goat standing on its hind legs and climbing a palm tree (Lippold 1923: Taf. XCI, 8). Goats are also depicted standing on their hind legs and browsing from a tree in other media, such as a Roman terracotta lamp from the British Museum (White 1970, pl. 71) and sarcophagi (Gerke 1948, pls. 18; 24, figs 3, 4, cf. Toynbee 1963: 166). At first glance, gems on which goats are depicted seem to belong to the genre of idyllic rural descriptions, but the palm tree is known as a symbol of Imperial victory, and, also, as noted above, it has fertility, renewal and life associations (Philp and Henig 1985: 464, pl. e). A tree depicted between two goats, like on an amethyst

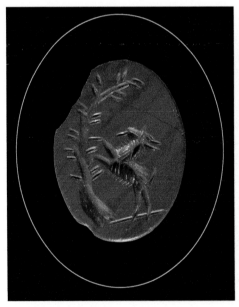

Figure 11a. Goat browsing from a tree, red jasper, 17 x 13 x 2 mm, 2nd century AD. The Israel Museum Jerusalem, Bequest of Mr. Adolphe Doreen, Paris. IMJ70.62.383. ©Photo: The Israel Museum, Jerusalem, by Vladimir Naikhin.

Figure 11b. Impression of the red jasper stone. ©Photo: The Israel Museum, Jerusalem, by Vladimir Naikhin

gem from Roman Wroxeter, or a tree depicted between two peacocks, such as on the Roman Tripontium buckle could originate from the Mesopotamian 'Tree of Life' (Hawkes 1972: 152; Maxwell-Hyslop 1976: 263–276, cf. Henig 1977: 362).

A granite gem from the Israel Museum shows at the bottom a pair of clasped hands and in the centre an ear of corn enclosed between a pair of goats, while above there is a leaping goat (Figure 12). According to Henig, such a depiction has been linked to prosperity, and he mentions a similar carnelian gem which portrays a handshake, but above them both a krater enclosed between two cornucopias and in the upper part appear three eagles (Henig 1981: 273–275, pl. VIII C). The Israel Museum gem is made in the 'Wheel Style' and therefore dates to the 1st century BC to AD 30 (see Maaskant-Kleibrink 1978, 154–155).

Figure 12. Pair of clasped hands, ear of corn and goats, impression of a granite stone, 14.5 x 14 x 2 mm, 1st century BC-AD 30.
The Israel Museum Jerusalem, Bequest of Mr. Adolphe Doreen, Paris. IMJ70.62.373.
©Photo: The Israel Museum, Jerusalem.

Hands clasped in Dextrarum Iunctio/Dexiôsis (a right handshake between man and woman), are symbols of harmony, or, more specifically, an engagement or marriage union, and express harmony between the couple, i.e. on a pair of sardonyx cameo rings from the Content collection, featuring clasped hands and below them the inscription 'harmony' or 'congratulations' (Molensworth and Henig 2011: 181, pls. 8, 11). Depictions of handshakes on Roman sarcophagi, such as on the sarcophagus from the Palazzo Massimo alla terme, had the added meaning of symbolising the ultimate reunion of the couple in the Afterlife. The ear of corn on the gem from the Israel Museum is also known as a symbol of the Afterlife (Henig 1977: 361–362).

On an amethyst gem from the Israel Museum, dated by Henig to the 1st century AD, two goats leap back to back on either side of an amphora, from which grow an ear of corn and another plant, possibly an olive tree (Figure 13). A similar Roman gem appears in Lippold's catalogue (1923: Taf. XCVIII,11), portraying two goats facing each other and leaping over a skyphos. This depiction is related to the 'Tree of Life' symbolism, and the interpretation is related to prosperity, where the amphora containing wine represents the 'life fluid'.

Figure 13. Two goats on either side of an amphora, impression
of an amethyst stone, 14.5 x 14 x 2 mm, 1st century AD.
The Israel Museum Jerusalem, Bequest of Mr. Adolphe Doreen,
Paris. IMJ70.62.385. ©Photo: The Israel Museum, Jerusalem.

A carnelian gem from the Israel Museum shows a countryman milking a goat under a tree (Figure 14). The herdsman's hair resembles a hat tightly fitted to the head. This detail places the intaglio in the 'Imperial Cap-With-Rim Style', as defined by Maaskant-Kleibrink, and dates to the end of the 1st–2nd century AD (Maaskant-Kleibrink 1978: 302).

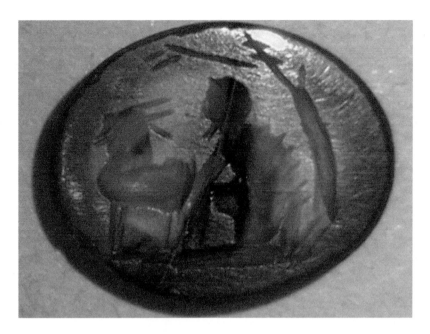

Figure 14. Countryman milking a goat, carnelian, end of the 1st–2nd century AD.
The Israel Museum Jerusalem, Bezalel Collection, IMJ77.31.978.
©Photo: The Israel Museum, Jerusalem.

On two gems, one from Bath and the other from Asthall in Britain, similar depictions appear (Henig 1997: 99–100, pl. 4.2, Asthall). The chalcedony gem from Bath dates to the end of the 1st century AD, and portrays a herdsman dressed in a leather cloak sitting in profile to the left under a tree and a milking a goat (Henig 1978: 250, pl. XVI, no. 503; Henig 1988: 32, no. 21). The gem from Asthall, dating from the middle of the 2nd century AD, features a shepherd sitting on the ground and milking a goat (but without a tree) (Henig 1997: 99–100, pl. 4.2, Asthall, the intaglio). The Caesarea collection includes two gems depicting herdsmen milking goats, and Walters and Richter also describe a number of gems with pastoral scenes of shepherds, or satyrs, alongside goats (Hamburger 1968: nos 148–150; Richter 1971: pl. LV: 452; Walters 1926: pl. XXII: 1611, 1612, 1614, 1616). Such depictions evoke a sense of fecundity and plenty, a subject that also appeared frequently in the Flavian period, mainly on the coins of Vespasian and Titus from 77–78 AD, to symbolise recovery and renewal after civil strife (Henig 1997: 48; Mattingly 1930: xli, 40, no. 220 (pl. 6, 17) and 42, no. 230 (pl. 7, 4). Scenes of shepherds milking goats are also common in various media of later Roman art as part of pastoral depictions, evoking a sense of heavenly paradise, for example on a 3rd-century AD sarcophagus from the Museo Nazionale in Rome and a mosaic from the Great Palace in Constantinople (Toynbee 1963: 165, pls. 79, 81).

On a chrome chalcedony gem from the Israel Museum (Figure 15) a shepherd appears dressed in an animal skin cloak, with a dog lying beside him and a nursing goat. The gem should be dated to the 1st century AD, mainly because the chrome chalcedony (which originated in Asia Minor) dates to this period. A gem whose depiction is almost identical, and which is identified as plasma, is held at the J. Paul Getty Museum in California (Spier 1992: no. 290). A similar scene from the 1st century AD is also represented on a gem in the Fitzwilliam Museum (Henig 1994: no. 340). Such themes are interpreted as depictions of rural abundance.

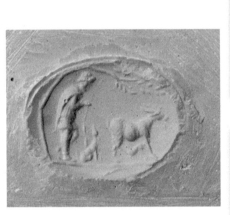

Figure 15. Shepherd with a dog and a nursing goat, chrome chalcedony, intaglio and impression, 1st century AD.
The Harry Stern Collection, bequeathed by Dr Kurt Stern, London. In memory of his parents and his brother who perished at Sobibor. IMJ76.42.2428. ©Photo: The Israel Museum, Jerusalem.

Furtwängler, in his monumental work, was the first scholar to point out a group of intense green-coloured gemstones distinguished from the other chrome chalcedony gems. He separated these stones into a group he called 'kleine parser' and dated them from the end of the 1st century BC to the beginning of the 2nd century AD (Furtwängler 1900: 309). Catalogues of museums have confused the names used for green gemstones: among these can be found the terms plasma (actually a wrong term), prase, chrysoprase, and others (Platz-Horster 2010: 179–181; Zwierlein-Diehl 1992: 43–47; Spier 1992: 5). Among all these terms for the rare green chalcedony gems, lies the chrome chalcedony group, the rarest of them all – with its geological origin only recently found. This material is extremely rare in gem use, and its green colour is due to a large amount of chromium. Maaskant-Kleibrink's study confirmed Furtwängler's dating of chrome chalcedony gemstones to the 1st century AD (Maaskant-Kleibrink 1975: 168). The depictions on chrome chalcedony were unique and included copies of well-known statues, heads of gods, portraits, and rural scenes. It was only in the 1970s that a chrome chalcedony mine was discovered in the central Anatolia and which might have been the ancient Roman source (Platz-Horster 2010: 179–181, 184, 186, 187, 191, 195–197).

Horses

The horse probably first arrived in Crete and Greece from the Mesopotamian east during the Minoan period. Images of horses denoted aristocratic status, a warrior's character and victory in battle, as well as wealth. Homer illustrates the wealth of King Erichthonius by describing his many horses (*Iliad*: 20.219–229). The pride of horses is a regular theme in the poetry of Homer and remained associated with heroic excellence in Greek art through the ages (*Iliad*: 7.38, 22.161, 24.804). In Classical Greece the horse was mainly a status symbol for kings and nobles, who are seen hunting, in battle, chariot racing, and mounted at ceremonial processions (Richter 1930: 14). In the *Iliad* (11.698) there is an allusion that already in the Mycenaean period there were quadriga races at Olympia. Pausanias notes the beginning of quadriga races at the Olympic Games of 680 BC (*Description of Greece*: 5.8.7), and in 408 BC the inclusion of two-horse chariot races (biga) also began there (*Description of Greece*: 5.8.10).A victorious quadriga is depicted, for example, on a *dekadrachm* of Syracuse dating from 480 BC, referring to an Olympic victory by tyrants (Harris 1972: 159, pl. 65). Although the most important use of the horse was as in battle, the cavalry was not the most important unit in ancient conflicts. The infantry remained as the most effective force – the Greek hoplites, the Macedonian phalanx, and the Roman legions. The cavalry was important at the beginning of a battle and in the final charges – as demonstrated by Alexander the Great – and as a measure against enemy cavalry. But although the cavalry did not play a dominant role in battle, it did have an important role in society – and the spheres of politics and economics – in both Greece and Rome. Thus, in both these two countries the word 'cavalry' was used to define a class marked by criteria of wealth, responsibility, and rights, beyond those given to poorer citizens (Harris 1972: 152-153). In the 3rd century BC there was a change in the ancient tendency to show gods, kings and princes sitting or standing within chariots, but on horseback instead.

Aelian refers to the horse as having a moral sense, and also attributes to it a strong loyalty for its owner, provided it was well treated, an example being Bucephalus, the horse of Alexander the Great (*De natura animalium*: IV. 7, VI. 44). In the *Iliad* (17.437-440) he horse is said to be endowed with intelligence and feelings similar to those of humans: Achilles' horse actually weeps, and the hero even conducts a dialogue with his horse Xanthos (19.400-424); Patroclus' horses cry at the time of his death (23.283-284); Pliny notes that King Nicomedes' horse mourns the death of its owner and ended his own life by not eating (*Natural History*: VIII.64); Caligula was also attached to his horse (Suetonius, *De vita caesarum: Caligula*: xlv). The horse is also perceived as a mediator between humans and gods; knowing the future it elevates thoughts from the realm of mortals to that of the gods. The *Iliad* (19.408-410) refers to this aspect of the horse's character when the two horses of Achilles, Xanthos and Balios, remind him that his moment of death will soon be nigh (See also Frère 1997: 431-433). According to Plato, the horse is a symbol of the human spirit, which ascends to heaven, and he includes this celestial aspect of the horse within the metaphysical perception of the soul in the Universe, in *Phaedrus*, when he discusses the ideal image of the horse, within the context of the ideal image of a chariot and a charioteer (*Phaedrus*: 246 A).

During the Geometric period in Greece, representations of the horse in art were schematic and in the Archaic period the horse is stylised and expressionless – yet naturalistic details such as the mane and hooves can be identified (Richter 1930: 15, figs 49, 50, 52). In the second half of the 6th century BC, the design is still rigid and stylish, but the lines are more flowing and the proportions more naturalistic. As examples from the 5th century BC of horse depictions it is worth mentioning a chalcedony gem from the Museum of Fine Arts in Boston, featuring a racehorse with loose reins, and the refined and noble marble sculptures from the Acropolis Museum (Richter 1930: 16, figs 53–60). The horses from the Demareteion tetradrachm of Syracuse (now in the British Museum), and the great bronze statue from the Metropolitan Museum of Art, are fine examples from the middle of the 5th century BC (Richter 1930: figs 61, 62). From the 5th century BC onwards, there is progress towards naturalism, as can be seen in the horses portrayed on the eastern pediment of the Temple of

Zeus at Olympia, and those on the frieze in the monument at Xanthos (Richter 1930: figs 64–66). The horses on the western, northern and southern friezes of the Parthenon, and those of Helios and Selena on both sides of the eastern pediment from the second half of the 5th century, are portrayed with much vitality and marked by close observation (Richter 1930: 16–17, figs 67, 69). These depictions correspond to those of the neighing horses mentioned by Xenophon (*De re equestri* (*On Horsemanship*): X.3 f, XI.8–9). From the 4th century, a galloping horse on a carved gold ring in the British Museum, and the horse from the Halicarnassus Mausoleum frieze, perhaps made by Skopas, are typical examples. In both cases, the fervour and simplicity of their predecessors is still evident, while the other horses on the mausoleum sculptures, especially those from the chariot group on the top of the building, are not characterised by the previous refinement (Richter 1930: 18, figs. 73, 76, 77). The horses of the 'Alexander Sarcophagus' from the last quarter of the 4th century BC (now in the Archaeological Museum in Istanbul), and those of the bronze heads from the Archaeological Museum in Florence, regarded as precursors of Renaissance work, represent later interpretations of a more naturalistic character and a further refinement of detail (Richter 1930: figs. 78–80). This refinement is

Figure 16. Front torso of a galloping horse, garnet, intaglio and impression, 16 x 14 mm, 2nd century BC. The Harry Stern Collection, bequeathed by Dr Kurt Stern, London. In memory of his parents and his brother who perished at Sobibor. IMJ76.42.2415. ©Photo: The Israel Museum, Jerusalem.

greatly emphasised later, in the Late Hellenistic period. Light and shade are now strongly contrasted, and the former quiet sense of simplicity disappears. Nevertheless, the former atmosphere of a sense of 'good taste never disappears completely, in other words, naturalism is now subordinated to general organised design, as reflected on the garnet gem from the Israel Museum (Figure 16), where the front torso of a galloping horse is seen. The gem is dated to the 2nd century BC, according to the material from which it is made (garnet), which becomes more popular during the Hellenistic period, and also by its cabochon shape, a convex style that was typical of this gemstone (the ancient name is *carbunculus*) (Adams 2011: 12).

The horse arrived in the Roman world mainly from the Peloponnese, Thessaly and Apulia (Varro, *De re rustica*: II,1, 6, 7, 15). In Rome, chariot racing, together with other sports, was public entertainment, with the Romans adopting it from the Greeks or Etruscans. According to tradition, the Circus Maximus was first established in the era of the Tarquinian kings, who were Etruscans. Julius Caesar rebuilt it and by the middle of the 1st century AD it could contain a vast crowd of 250,000. At the end of their careers, the charioteers would build monuments detailing their winnings, and some even added lists of their horses, including details of name, breed, colour, etc. (Harris 1972: 185–194).

A 1st-century AD gem from the Israel Museum (Figure 17) features a grazing horse, to its right the head of a ram (?) or the Greek letter Epsilon (?), and to its left a lion (?) or the Greek letter Pi (?). According to Henig, this combination of signs can be related to the name of the owner. Glyptic devices sometimes had a particular reference, i.e. as a family badge, such as Pompey's lion with sword (Plutarch, *Pompey*: LXXX, 5; see also Henig 1997: 48). In addition, it is dated to the 1st century AD, since it is similar to an engraved gem from the Dover excavations, on which a similar racehorse appears (M. Henig, personal communication, September 2011). On a gem from the Fitzwilliam Museum, and another from Middleton's catalogue, a horse appears standing to the right, its head bent as if to graze, and the left leg raised. Above the horse a star within a crescent is featured (Henig 1994: 119, on. 223; Middleton 1891: xviii, no. 73). It may be a portrait of a favourite racehorse, branded with the star and crescent – the symbols of its owner (Middleton 1891: xix, no. 73). In light of this, it is possible that the gem from the Israel Museum also depicts a much-loved racehorse, and that the symbols on both sides are the symbols of the owner.

On a *globolo*-style Etruscan scarab, made of carnelian (Figure 18) and which dates to 300 BC, a horse galloping to the right with a palm-branch is depicted, the latter, of course, being a symbol of victory. A similar horse appears on a gem from Lippold's catalogue, where the winner in the race is portrayed with a palm-branch tied with a ribbon (Lippold 1923: Taf. LXXXIX, 4).

Figure 17. Grazing horse, agate, intaglio
and impression, 14 x 8 mm,
1st century AD.
The Harry Stern Collection, bequeathed
by Dr Kurt Stern, London. In memory
of his parents and his brother who
perished at Sobibor. IMJ76.42.2417.
©Photo: The Israel Museum, Jerusalem.

Figure 18. Horse with a palm-branch,
impression of a carnelian stone,
12 x 9 x 6 mm, an Etruscan 'globolo' style
scarab, 300 BC.
The Israel Museum Jerusalem, The Harry
Stern Collection, bequeathed by Dr Kurt
Stern, London. In memory of his parents
and his brother who perished at Sobibor.
IMJ76.42.2387.
©Photo: The Israel Museum, Jerusalem.

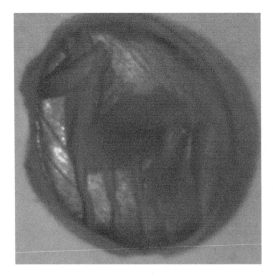

Figure 19a. Horse in profile, carnelian, 3 x 9 x 11 mm, 2nd century AD. The Israel Museum Jerusalem, Bequest of Mr. Adolphe Doreen, Paris. IMJ70.62.348. ©Photo: The Israel Museum, Jerusalem.

Figure 19b. Horse in profile, drawing. ©Drawing: The Israel Museum, Jerusalem, by Pnina Arad.

Another carnelian gem from the Israel Museum (Figures 19a and b) illustrates a horse in profile to the right. It seems that this gem can be dated to the 2nd century AD, it being carved in the 'Plain Grooves Style', as defined by Maaskant-Kleibrink (Maaskant-Kleibrink 1978: 311).

Two gems from the Israel Museum feature quadrigas: a heliotrope is apparently drawn by a representation of Nike/Victory (Figure 20), and a carnelian shows the car being drawn by Helios/Sol (Figures 21a and b). The quadriga often appears on gems, and other media, as the chariot of the gods Helios/Sol and Nike/Victory (Prieur 1988: 145). Emperors are also depicted riding ceremonial quadrigas, mainly on coins. The quadriga was also adopted in Roman chariot racing. Each of these figures has its own attributes to help enable its identification: Helios/Sol has a radiated solar crown and a whip; Nike/Victoria is winged and bears a wreath – an emperor would usually have a laurel crown and a decorated chariot, while a charioteer would have a helmet without crest feathers, typical coloured clothing, and would often appear holding a palm-branch, as represented on a heliotrope gem from the Archaeological Museum of Napoli (Pannuti 1983: vol.1, no. 159).[6] The depiction on gem no. 70.62.386

---

[6] Depictions of charioteers on gems are quite common, see, e.g., Humphrey 1986: 204–207; Zazoff 1970: nos 86, 138–139; Lippold 1923: Taf. xxxiii, 4, 6. In other media detailed depictions appear

Figure 20. Nike/Victory riding a quadriga, heliotrope,
2.5 x 10.5 x 13 mm, 2nd century AD.
The Israel Museum Jerusalem, Bequest of Mr. Adolphe
Doreen, Paris. IMJ70.62.386.
©Photo: The Israel Museum, Jerusalem.

can be interpreted as Nike/Victory, as the goddess is frequently shown riding a quadriga on 2nd-century AD gems (Hamburger 1968: 10, no. 69; Walters 1926: pl. XXIII: 1723). In addition, heliotrope was used during the Late Roman period, although not very commonly. The Greeks, however, hardly used it as a seal-stone, thus also helping the dating to Late Roman times (Middleton 1891: 146). The engraving on the Nike/Victoria Jerusalem gem was made with rounded drills and no details were added except for some grooves. In addition, the prominent hair-roll around the head is also suggestive of the 'Imperial Cap-With-Rim Style', as defined by Maaskant-Kleibrink, and dates to the end of the 2nd century AD (Maaskant-Kleibrink 1978: 302). A gem in the Rijksmuseum van Oudheden, Leiden (formerly in The Hague Collection) is very similar in iconography and date (Maaskant-Kleibrink 1978: 302, 305, no. 892).

Gems featuring deities were believed to confer protection and beneficial powers upon the wearer. The goddess of victory, Nike/Victory, was particularly popular among the Roman army, but her contexts expanded beyond the military world as well: she also symbolised the triumph of the soul over death (Goodenough 1953–1968: vol. 7, 135–171). In addition, the victorious horse (or team) in chariot races

of racing charioteers, e.g. on the 4th-century mosaics discovered in Piazza Armerina (Carandini, Ricci and de Vos 1982: figs 19–21, 202–205).

symbolises victory in life; thus the charioteer is sometimes Nike/Victoria herself rather than a mortal (Henig 1997: 51). Boardman also suggests that the image of Nike/Victory on gems alludes to success in a race, for example, but then restricts it immediately by noting that her image has become so trite in many works of art, and thus not every Nike/Victory can depict a specific victory (Boardman 1980: 106).

The Helios/Sol Jerusalem gem features the god riding a quadriga with a radiated solar crown and a whip. It is made in the 'Plain Grooves Style', as defined by Maaskant-Kleibrink, and dates to the 2nd century AD (Maaskant-Kleibrink 1978: 311). Similar representations appear, for example, on gems in the Fitzwilliam Museum and the Caesarea Antiquity Museum (Hamburger 1968: no. 21; Henig 1994: no. 266). From the 2nd century AD onwards, the frontal depiction of Helios in his chariot becomes more popular than his usual profile figure on wall-paintings, mosaics and gems. The triumphant iconography of emperors adopted and developed the motif of the frontal chariot in the portrayals of the emperor as world ruler (Dunbabin 1982: 71–72).

Figure 21a. Helios/ Sol riding a quadriga, carnelian, 2nd century AD. The Israel Museum Jerusalem, Bequest of Mr. Adolphe Doreen, Paris. IMJ70.62.345. ©Photo: The Israel Museum, Jerusalem.

Figure 21b. Helios/Sol riding a quadriga, drawing. ©Drawing: The Israel Museum, Jerusalem, by Pnina Arad.

The horse is the animal that canonically pulls the chariot, a vehicle attributed to the sun in most cultures of the Middle East, with the horse being closely to the worship of the sun (Prieur 1988: 142). Helios, the sun-god, is conventionally depicted driving a quadriga. In Greek ceramics Helios is depicted driving his chariot from the 5th century BC onwards. From then on, the motif was a familiar one in Greco-Roman art and appears, for example, on the Augustus breastplate relief Prima Porta, the Jupiter column of Mayence, various sarcophagi, and as late as the Arch of Constantine, which dates to the 4th century AD (Prieur 1988: 145). This depiction has no magical meaning; it is a customary motif in the Hellenistic and Roman eras. It was only at the end of the Roman period that this motif was given magical meaning, either by adding unique iconographic schemes typical of magical gems, or by inscribing on them magical names or signs (Bonner 1950: 148).

Athena driving a turning biga, a two-horse chariot, is depicted on a carnelian gem in the Israel Museum (Figures 22a and b). The deity is shown standing and

Figure 22a. Athena driving a biga, carnelian, 18 x 14 mm, 18th century.
The Israel Museum Jerusalem, The Harry Stern Collection, bequeathed by Dr Kurt Stern, London. In memory of his parents and his brother who perished at Sobibor. (previously in Streafelld Collection). IMJ76.42.2454.
©Photo: The Israel Museum, Jerusalem.

Figure 22b. Impression of the carnelian stone.
©Photo: The Israel Museum, Jerusalem.

holding the reins, clad in helmet and breast-armour, the aegis, and driving a turning chariot with a pair of galloping horses. Boardman mentions a very similar styled gem, which dates to the Classic period, featuring a turning biga, although driven by a mortal charioteer (Boardman 1970: pl. 561). However, this engraved gem from the Israel Museum, mistakenly considered as ancient, is dated to the 18th century on stylistic grounds. These gems of the 18th century were copies of ancient ones and part of the neo-Classical vogue of the day. Close examination of the face and the horse's mane, as well as other engraving details, all indicate a treatment unknown in the ancient world.

According to Homer, the war goddess Athena, a superb charioteer, was equipped with a pair of horses, in addition to a helmet and her aegis (*Iliad*: 5.835–841).She invented the harness, tamed horses (including Pegasus), and her relationship with horses was reflected in one of her epithets – Athena Hippia (Homer, *Iliad*: I.30.4; Pausanias, *Description of Greece*: I.31.3). On the Israel Museum gem, Athena is shown wearing a long *chiton*, similar to the 'Charioteer of Delphi', the typical garment of Greek charioteers, called *xystis*, while in the Roman world charioteers are seen in short tunics, as depicted on a Roman ivory statuette (Harris 1972: 162, pls. 63, 66, 71, 72).

Achilles, Penthesilea, and her horse are all depicted on a carnelian gem inlaid in an 18th-century gold ring in the collection of the Israel Museum (Figures 23a and b). It can be challenging to decide whether an engraved gem is ancient or neo-Classical. Nonetheless, it is fairly certain that this example dates to the end of the 1st century BC (the Augustan period) (M. Henig, personal communication, September 2011). The ring is inscribed with words that can be translated as: 'Eleonora D... the actress in Florence'. Achilles is depicted nude, wearing a helmet, and the folds of his cloak flap as he turns his head away from Penthesilea, while supporting the falling Amazon queen under her right arm. The dying queen sinks to her knees, her head is bowed in profile to the right; she is naked too. On the altar can be seen a leaning spear, the one by which Penthesilea was slain. Penthesilea's horse is shown looking anxiously towards her, raising his right leg as if about to bolt. The shield of Penthesilea, the *pelte*, can be seen behind her.

The flapping cloak of Achilles on the Jerusalem gem is comparable to that of Theseus on a gem attributed to Philemon (Vollenweider 1966: Taf 40.3). There is also a resemblance to the depiction on the famous 'Dioskourides' gem at Chatsworth, where Diomedes is portrayed taking the palladium (Vollenweider 1966: Taf 62).This gem indeed appears to date from the 1st century BC (and not from the 18th), as opposed to other depictions which are neo-Classical (Vollenweider 1966: Taf 39.4). The artist of the gem in the Israel Museum

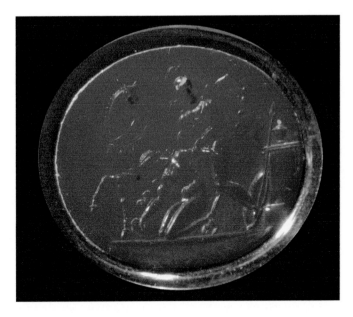

Figure 23a. Achilles, Penthesilea, and her horse, carnelian,
20 x 18 mm, the end of the 1st century BC, The Israel
Museum Jerusalem, The Harry Stern Collection, bequeathed
by Dr Kurt Stern, London. In memory of his parents and his
brother who perished at Sobibor. IMJ76.42.2433.
©Photo: The Israel Museum, Jerusalem, by Vladimir Naikhin.

Figure 23b. Impression of the carnelian stone.
©Photo: The Israel Museum, Jerusalem, by Vladimir Naikhin.

deliberately contrasts the softness of the female body form and the masculinity of the warrior. These engraved gems were tiny personal jewels that could be enjoyed privately. Erotic scenes were favourite subjects on small carved gemstones, as well as on precious cameos. A cameo from the Metropolitan Museum dating to the Imperial period bears a surprisingly similar representation of a nude Amazon supporting her naked and wounded comrade by the shoulders; behind them, a horse turns to the right (Devambez, s.v. 'Amazones', in *LIMC*, vol. I (2), (1981): 632, pl. 738; Richter 1956: 127, no. 632, pl. 71). However, this version of the subject omits Achilles and replaces him with an Amazon comrade, as is also depicted on a Campana relief in the Museés Royaux d'Art et d'Histoire, Bruxelles (Devambez, s.v. 'Amazones', in *LIMC*, vol. I (2), (1981): 631, pl. 734). This genre of ancient art (engraved gems and cameos) was much more private and intimate than larger and more public vases, sarcophagi, paintings, and large-scale marble and bronze statues. In other media, Penthesilea generally features in this scene wearing her typical helmet and clothes, although there are also some representations closer to the gem under discussion, for example, on a Campana relief in the Louvre, dating from the 2nd century AD, in which Achilles is also depicted as supporting the dying, nude Amazon, his cloak flapping behind him, and he looks away from her while she still holds her weapon in her right hand with her *pelte* at her feet (Devambez, s.v. 'Amazones', in *LIMC*, vol. I (2), (1981): 587, 601, pl. 223a). The horse does not appear on this relief, but since it is broken, it is impossible to know for sure what the complete depiction looked like. On a similar gem from the Nissan-lez-Ensérune Museum in southern France, the artist creates a drama and an atmosphere of tension when depicting Achilles supporting the body of the Amazon queen. The tension between the kneeling, nude body on the left and the shield on the right highlights the hero, who remains standing, in a flexible, slightly diagonal line (Guiraud 1996: 45, fig. 24). The warrior is actually lifting the fallen woman. In other media as well, such as reliefs depicting the battle between the Greeks and the Amazons, only Achilles performs this gesture, alluding to his late and vain love with the beautiful queen (Guiraud 1996: 105). The Amazonomachy was a popular motif in the 6th and, especially, the 5th centuries BC, and persisted into Roman Imperial times. According to the myth, shortly after the funeral of Hector, Penthesilea, the queen of the Amazons, led her fighting sisters against the Achaeans. Achilles killed Penthesilea but, immediately on removing her helmet, he was dazzled by her beauty and fell in love with her, full of remorse for his deed. This scene was particularly attractive to artists, vase-painters, sculptors and gem-engravers, leaving a variety of representations (Devambez, s.v. 'Amazones', *LIMC*, vol. I (2), (1981): pls. 168–229). The Greek hero is shown either in the act of killing the Amazon queen, or, especially on later monuments, supporting her stricken body. In the ancient literature there is little evidence of the relationship between Achilles and Penthesilea: there is a summary in *Chrestomathia*, by Proklos, of the relevant passage in Arktinos's *Aithiopis* (Kinkel, *Epicorum Graecorum Fragmenta* 1877: 33, cf. Glynn 1982: 169). Similar information is found in Apollodorus (*Bibliotheca, Epitome*: 5.1) and in Quintus Smyranaeus (*The Fall of Troy*: 1.671–674), while later sources expand the story, adding the rather unpleasant details of the indignities suffered by the body at the hands of Thersites (Schol. Sophocles, *Philoktetes*: 445; Schol. Lycophron 999, cf. Glynn 1982: 169). The 6th-century artist was concerned with a simple statement of the death of Penthesilea, without romantic overtones, and there are no illustrations extant of Achilles regretting his action, being enchanted by the Amazon at the very moment he strikes the death-blow. By the middle of the 5th century, depictions of Achilles supporting the body of the dead queen start to appear, such as that on the throne in the temple of Zeus at Olympia, undertaken by the artist Panainos (a relative of the sculptor Pheidias) (Pausanias, *Description of Greece*: 1.11.6). Another example is an Etruscan agate scarab in the British Museum, on which Achilles supports the dying Amazon as she sinks to her knees. Both are still wearing their helmets and clothes: Achilles with a leather cuirass, a chitoniskos, and greaves; Penthesilea with a short chiton and a pair of laced boots, the hoplite shield strapped to her left arm by the porpax, the hand having fallen free from its grip. On the left are shown her spear and double-axe, the *bipennis* (Glynn 1982: 171, figs 1–4; Walters 1926: 77, pl. 11 no. 634; Zazoff 1968: 46–8, pl. 15 no. 48). Achilles is seen glancing away, similar to his representation on the Jerusalem gem and the Campana relief. According to Zazoff, relating to the ancient literature, the warrior behaves in this manner because Thersites is close, mocking him, and Achilles' gaze is in response to those taunts (Glynn 1982: 172). Two vases of the mid 4th century BC from south Italy echo strongly the representation on the Etruscan scarab (Trendall 1967: 410, no. 335). In addition, there are a few copies of a sculptural group of the Hellenistic period, in which Achilles, catching the collapsing body of the Amazon, turns his head away from her and lift his gaze heavenwards, as if expressing despair and remorse at his deed (Glynn 1982: 174). This group is found time and again, with only slight variations, on many Roman Amazon sarcophagi, such as those from Palazzo Borghese and Villa Pamphili (Robert 1890: vol. 2, 76–77, 108–129, nos 88–89). These represent Penthesilea either still alive, apparently walking alongside Achilles, although she is weak and puts her arm around his neck for support, or, as in the free-standing group, collapsing to her knees (Glynn 1982: 174).

A late 1st century AD carnelian gem from the Israel Museum (Figures 24a and b) shows a pair of horses with heads bowed, standing in front of a pillar. Since the gem is chipped at the edge, it is difficult to identify the depiction with certainty. However, a similar gem was found in Bath, and, based on the comparison between them, it can be ascertained (Henig 1978: 588; Henig 1988: 32, 53, no. 25). On the Bath gem, an amphora-like vessel is depicted above the pillar. The horses seem to bow their heads, as if to lick up the drops of wine that have fallen from the amphora. In another similar gem, a herm is shown in front of the horses, instead of a pillar (Furtwängler 1900: no. 2499, cf. Henig 1988: 32, no. 25).

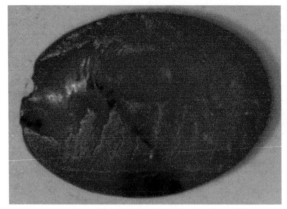

Figure 24a. Pair of horses in front of a pillar,
carnelian, 11.5 x 8 x 2.5 mm, Late 1st century AD.
The Israel Museum Jerusalem, previously in the
Bezalel Collection, IMJ77.31.1069.
©Photo: The Israel Museum, Jerusalem.

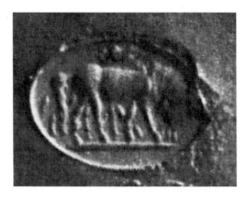

Figure 24b. Impression of the carnelian stone.
©Photo: The Israel Museum, Jerusalem.

The horseman was one of the most common images in Roman Imperial iconography. Rider figures appear in sculpture in the round, in relief, and in painting and the minor arts, including on engraved gems.

Four engraved gemstones in the collection of the Israel Museum, Jerusalem, depict riders. The first example is a carnelian intaglio, set in an original gold

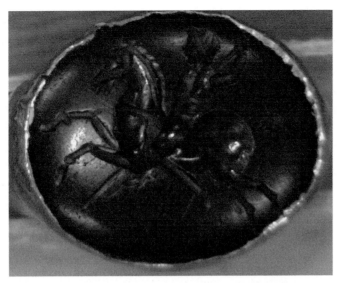

Figure 25a. horseman on a galloping horse, carnelian, 16 x 12
mm, end of the 1st–2nd century AD.
The Israel Museum Jerusalem, The Harry Stern Collection,
bequeathed by Dr Kurt Stern, London. In memory of
his parents and his brother who perished at Sobibor.
IMJ76.42.2430.

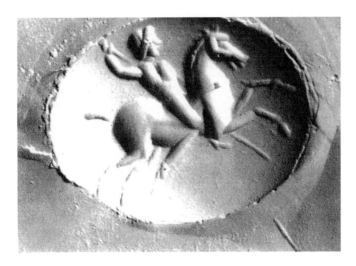

Figure 25b. Impression of the carnelian stone.
©Photo: The Israel Museum, Jerusalem.

frame (Figures 25a and b), showing a horseman on a galloping horse and holding
a spear in his right hand. The second is a carnelian intaglio (Figure 26) bearing a

representation of a rider on a galloping horse, facing a tree and holding a spear in his right hand, with an animal apparently being trampled beneath them.

A closer look at the carving technique of these two gems shows them to have been modelled with a rounded drill. The hair on the heads of the figures resembles a hat tightly fitted to the head, and their legs are pointed and lumpy. These details place the Israel Museum intaglios in the 'Imperial Cap-With-Rim Style', as defined by M. Maaskant-Kleibrink, and date to the end of the 1st–2nd century AD (Maaskant-Kleibrink 1978: 302).

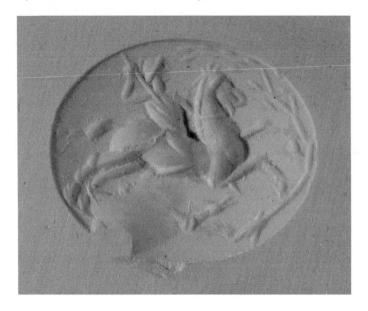

Figure 26. Rider on a galloping horse, impression of carnelian stone, 15 x 12 x 4 mm, end of the 1st–2nd century AD.
The Israel Museum Jerusalem, Bequest of Mr. Adolphe Doreen, Paris. IMJ70.62.372.
©Photo: The Israel Museum, Jerusalem, by Vladimir Naikhin.

These visual depictions of horsemen draw basically upon Greek imagery. In Greek art, the development of the rider figure depended not on a divine iconography but on the human and heroic. Greek gods were described as riding in a chariot, and not mounted on a horse. Gods depicted as riders were very rare. The Dioscouri, too, were usually depicted standing by their horses rather than mounted on them. Cavalry figures begin to appear on vases from the mid 8th century BC (Anderson 1961: 10). During the Archaic period, riders began to feature on funerary monuments (Kurtz and Boardman 1971: 86, 221, pl. 50, fig. 15), although fighting horsemen start to be seen on burial reliefs only during the 5th century BC (Woysch-Meautis 1982: 25). The rider motif, echoing mounted mythological heroes, such as Bellerophon, probably served to commemorate cavalrymen who had died in battle, while also symbolising their bravery and courage.

The Hellenistic period saw a new approach, influenced by Alexander the Great, and the art and iconography that were developed for him appear to have altered and raised the status of the rider. These were the first monuments to have as their subject a living and identifiable individual, as opposed to a generalised ideal (Mackintosh 1995: 3–4). With Alexander, too, the distinction between gods and humans began to be blurred. Alexander's successors imitated him, as can be seen from the fragments of an equestrian statue of Demetrios Poliorketes, a life-size, or slightly over life-size, gilded equestrian statue (Houser 1982: 230).

The third carnelian intaglio from the Israel Museum (Figure 27), depicting a rider with his chlamys fluttering behind as he gallops, dates to 240–228 BC, according

Figure 27. Rider with his chlamys fluttering, carnelian, intaglio and impression, 14 x 10 mm, 240–228 BC.
The Israel Museum Jerusalem, The Harry Stern Collection, bequeathed by Dr Kurt Stern, London. In memory of his parents and his brother who perished at Sobibor. IMJ76.42.2429. ©Photo: The Israel Museum, Jerusalem.

to its resemblance to a Vlasto coin (no. 943) from Tarentum. Hellenistic kings were often depicted on coins wearing this type of helmet, to which was added a crest of feathers, in a way similar to the helmet depicted on the Israel Museum gem (Snodgrass 1967: fig. 59).[7]

During the Roman Empire, the emperor, who was the new divine figure, adopted the habit of commissioning colossal rider statues. For example the equestrian statue of Domitian, erected in the Forum Romanum in 91 AD, was the subject of a poem by Statius (cf. Hannestad 1986: 139) extolling its virtue as the visualization of Imperial invincibility. Originally a portrait of Domitian, the head was replaced later by that of Nerva. It was dedicated at the shrine of the Augustales, the priests of the Imperial cult. The Domitian cuirass with Flavian symbols was left in place. It is the only galloping equestrian bronze statue that is known to have survived.

Octavian was represented in sculpture at the beginning of his career as a rider astride a horse, to generate public recognition of his services to the state and abilities as a military commander. The first of these statues was dedicated to him by the Senate and the Roman people in 43 BC, when he was only 19 years old. The statue stood in the most visible place in Rome, suggesting that Caesar's successor would have great political power. This statue of Octavian is also depicted on coins (Zanker 1988: fig. 29a). Before him, Sulla, Pompey the Great, and Julius Caesar had also been presented in this way as horsemen, and the placement of Octavian's sculpture was intended to exceed them in its shared honours. Later on, Octavian was displayed on sculptures in a similar way to that of the Dioscouri – as an omnipotent rescuer and saviour (Zanker 1988: 37–39, fig. 30).

On gems from the Israel Museum the spears which the riders are holding enable their identification as warriors or heroes. Depictions of cavalrymen holding spears, unconnected with the image of any god, are known from sarcophagi, gravestones, monuments, and Imperial gems. In most cases those riders are depicted galloping during battle. There are also several examples of gems featuring a rider, beneath whose horse is a kneeling or lying captive, such as on a gem from the Munich Museum (Brandt 1972: no. 1671). In other cases the depiction of a rider on a horse indicates a hunter setting out for the chase. Those depictions are common on Roman sarcophagi, and no less so on gems. The second carnelian gem from the Israel Museum appears to be of this type

---

[7] The type of helmet which appears on the gemstone from the Israel Museum is identified as a Boeotic one, which became widely used from the late 3rd century BC. Xenophon recommends this type of helmet for the cavalry, as it causes minimum inconvenience to the sight and hearing of its wearer (*De re equestri*: xii.3).

(Figure 26), but since it is somewhat damaged it is difficult to discern what is depicted beneath the horse. This is probably a rider-hunter with his prey, similar to the depiction on a gem from Dalmatia (Middleton 1991: App. 12a+b), and another item from Berlin (Zwierlein-Diehl 1970: fig. 538), on which the rider is depicted killing a lion (Middleton 1991: App. 12a+b). Another example is that of a gem from the Royal Coin Cabinet, The Hague (now in the Rijksmuseum van Outheden in Leiden) (Maaskant-Kleibrink 1978: 302, 305, no. 890), with a helmeted warrior astride a horse and galloping to the right, while attacking a lion, with a spear held in his right hand.

Henig engaged with the question of the meaning of the motif of the rider when he published a gem discovered at Aldborough, England, dated by him to the 1st or early 2nd century AD. The gem depicts a soldier riding a horse, holding a spear and with two javelins behind him. It is easy to interpret this horseman as an auxiliary of the Roman army, mainly because the site at which the gem was discovered was once a Roman fortress. However, it is unclear what the protective or spiritual role of such a self-portrait might be. Henig assumed that the rider was perceived by the gem engraver and owner as a god or hero (Henig 1973: 180, pl. 2). Dimitrova, too, has argued that the horseman presents iconographical convention for a god/hero, and that this iconography is borrowed from Greek art (2002: 209).

Depictions of what has been termed the 'Heros Equitans' are very similar to depictions of the rider on such gems. The imagery of the 'Heros Equitans' presented a mounted warrior, frequently holding a spear. During their lives these heroes were perceived as the best and first of mortals, and typified by physical strength, courage, and an awe-inspiring appearance. Such heroes often defended a particular area, where they were admired. Upon death, the heroes were worshiped and their burial place became sacred. 'Heros Equitans' is often identified on votive reliefs with various divinities (e.g. Apollo, Asclepius, Dionysus, the Dioscouri). Perhaps the figure of 'Heros Equitans', which was very common in the Greek east,[8] is that which inspired the depictions of emperors and horsemen on gems (Cermanović-Kuzmanović 1992: 1019–1081).

The 'Heros Equitans' is extensively associated with the Underworld and is therefore a chthonic figure: stelae bearing his depiction have been found on graves and grave-mounds (Kazarow 1918: 1133, 1140); he is sometimes depicted in the company of an heroicised dead figure (Cermanović-Kuzmanović 1992: 56–60, 388–395, 565–570, 603, 638–639), and very frequently shown in connection with serpents, whose chthonic associations are well known (Cermanović-

---

[8] The majority of such reliefs come from the Black Sea region, Thrace, and Asia Minor.

Kuzmanović 1992: nos 104–108, 113–126, 145, 148–154, 166–185, 204–213, 240–249).[9]

These rider-hero depictions were particularly common in Thrace, where one can find reliefs with their images on gravestones and votive plaques, and also from the Roman Imperial period, like the example in the National Archaeological Museum, Sofia, which dates to the 2nd century AD (Dimitrova 2002: 212, fig 1). Furthermore, on a great many reliefs the 'Thracian Horseman' is shown as a hunter. Such images of the 'Thracian Horseman' as hunter are often accompanied by representations of wild animals (boars, hares, deer, etc.) near altars, no doubt as a sign that they are about to be sacrificed. 'Thracian Rider' reliefs function as dedicatory, in view of the Thracian belief in the immortalisation of the dead (Dimitrova 2002: 227). Oppermann sees the 'Thracian Horseman' as an indigenous, protective divinity (Oppermann 2006: 276), whereas Boteva contends rather that the snake was thought of as divine, while the horseman was simply an envoy, a mediator between mortals and immortals (Boteva 2011: 101).

As previously discussed, the rider was apparently perceived by this gem's engraver and owner as some god or hero.[10] However, since no altar, snake, or special gesture feature on this Israel Museum gem, the identification of its rider with an 'Heros Equitans' is equivocal, and it is probably a Roman military rider or rider-hunter with his prey.

The fourth gem showing a rider is a carnelian intaglio set in an original gold Roman ring (Figure 28). It depicts a naked horseman with long spiky hair, holding a long shield, here truncated at both ends, and of a type associated with the Gauls.

There are quite a number of Celtic/Gaulish horsemen featuring on gems (Henig and MacGregor 2004: nrs. 7.26, 7.27 and 7.29, although these are helmeted; Henig and Whiting 1987: no. 286; Maaskant-Kleibrink 1978: no. 402; Zazoff 1975: no. 388 and the battle scene in no. 390). The horse seems to be stumbling, as though an extract from a Celtomachy. Its origin may lie in the defeat of the Gauls at Pergamum in Hellenistic times. It is probable that people wore such gems as a reminder of the iconic defeat of the northern barbarians by the Attalids, as well as more recent Roman victories (over the Teutons and the Cimbri by Marius in 102–101 BC, and over several Gallic tribes in 50 BC by Caesar in the Gallic Wars). In addition, the style and engraving technique of this intaglio from the Israel Museum is compatible with the styles of the end of the Republic, as defined by

---

[9] For further discussion, see Liapis 2011: 102–103.
[10] The second carnelian gem from the Israel Museum (Figure 26).

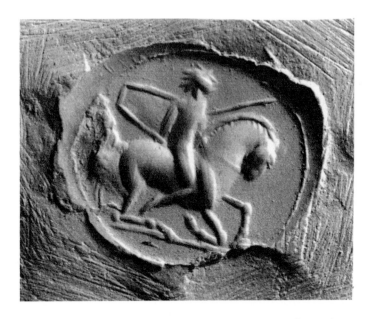

Figure 28. A Celtic/Gaulish horseman, impression of carnelian
stone, 11 x 12 mm, the first half of the 1st century BC.
The Israel Museum Jerusalem, The Harry Stern Collection,
bequeathed by Dr Kurt Stern, London. In memory of
his parents and his brother who perished at Sobibor.
IMJ76.42.2431. ©Photo: The Israel Museum, Jerusalem.

Maaskant-Kleibrink; hence, a dating of the first half of the 1st century BC is
probable (Maaskant-Kleibrink 1978: 179–180).[11]

In summary, horsemen frequently appear as images on intaglios. The Roman
engraved gems drew their inspiration from established Greek rider imagery.
Under the Roman Empire, the rider image became the preserve of that new
divine figure, the Emperor. The Imperial rider combined the attributes of a
Bellerophon, or the Dioscouri of the Classical period, with those of an Alexander
of the Hellenistic period.

Figures of Gauls, too, are fairly common in art and there are quite a number
of Celtic/Gaulish horsemen on gems. As mentioned above, presumably, people
wore such gems as a reminder of the iconic defeat of the northern barbarians
by the Attalids, as well as more recent Roman triumphs.

---

[11] The 'Flat Bouterolle Style', one of the styles from the end of the Republic, is noted for an
exaggeration in the use of the large blunted drill for engraving the larger shapes, such as bodies
and heads. The limited detailing is done with rounded wheel grooves.

In addition, there are several examples of gems featuring a rider with a lion, or other animal, trampled beneath his horse's hooves. It is likely that such riders were perceived by the gem engraver and owner as gods or heroes. Since these depictions of cavalrymen on gems are similar to the 'Heros Equitans' image, they were possibly inspired by it, as were the depictions of the emperors.

Boars and sows

On a carnelian Classical-Phoenician scarab, dated mid 5th century BC, in the Israel Museum (Figures 29a and b), a sow is shown in profile to the right with a prominent crest of bristles down the back and a beaded shoulder line (Boardman 2003: 126, pl. 43/22).[12] She is full-bodied with heavy udders.The representation of a sow, which was very common for Archaic Greek seals, had a symbolic value and, according to Vollenweider, corresponded with a sense of prosperity and fertility (Henig 1997: 45). Boardman suggests a similar hypothesis, but immediately dismisses it, claiming that it is difficult to justify such symbolism of fertility in other works (Boardman 1970: Ch. XIII; Boardman 1980: 104). Male or female wild boars, sometimes with piglets, were a popular theme in the 6th and 5th centuries BC. The 6th-century wild boars are usually thin and long-legged compared to those from the end of the Archaic period and 5th century, which are fleshy (Boardman 1968: 146). A series of fine, plump boars and sows are shown on some scarabs and scaraboids of the mid 5th century BC (Boardman 1968: 152, pls. 533–555, especially pls. 546 and 554). The bristles on the backs of these creatures are broken at the centre, a feature of eastern Greek boars, not unknown elsewhere, as on Athenian vases (Boardman 1968: 152). Their kin are seen on a number of eastern Greek coins, and in Lycia, especially, we see the dotted shoulder line (as on pl. 546), as well as the Jerusalem scarab (Boardman 1968: 152). In the 6th and 5th centuries BC, boars and sow figurines appear as offerings in temples, on the metopes of the Sikionian treasury, on sarcophagi, and often also on gems and coins (Richter 1930: 23–24, figs 107, 108). For example an electrum stater of the Ionic Revolt of 500 BC features a sow, while a Boston chalcedony scaraboid from the second half of the 5th century BC represents a sow with two piglets (Boardman 1968: 149, pl. 554; Richter 1930: figs 112, 113). Other similar gems, in which the bristles are broken at the centre, can be found at the Fitzwilliam Museum in Cambridge, where a wild boar is depicted on an Archaic scarab from the beginning of the 5th century BC (Henig 1994: 488, no. 1073); there are other examples showing a sow from Oxford and Lippold's catalogue (Lippold 1923: Taf. XCIII, 1,3,7; Zazoff 1983: Taf. 36, 2).

---

[12] This scarab belongs to a group of scarabs featuring the same subjects as the 'Classical Phoenician scarabs' listed above, although in other materials; these appear to be of the same period and from the same sites, but not the same workshops.

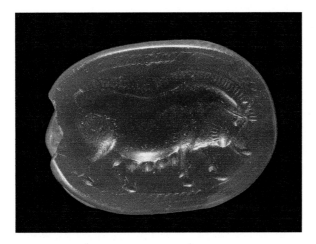

Figure 29a. Sow, carnelian, 16.5 x 12 x 9.5 mm, a
Classical-Phoenician scarab, mid 5th century BC.
The Israel Museum Jerusalem, The Harry Stern
Collection, bequeathed by Dr Kurt Stern, London. In
memory of his parents and his brother who perished
at Sobibor. IMJ76.42.2377. ©Photo: The Israel
Museum, Jerusalem, by Vladimir Naikhin.

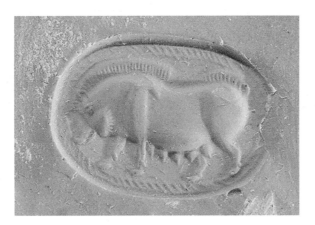

Figure 29b. Impression of the carnelian scarab.
©Photo: The Israel Museum, Jerusalem, by Vladimir
Naikhin.

Regarding the interpretation of prosperity and fertility, boars and sows were
associated with Demeter and Persephone, and, according to Clement of
Alexandria, the swine of Eubouleus were consumed by the earth at the same

time as Kore/Persephone was abducted by Hades/Pluto (Clement of Alexandria, *Exhortation to the Heathen*: 14–17, 176; v. II, 14–17). Eubouleus is sometimes considered as the brother of Triptolemus, in whose hands Demeter deposited the first ear of grain (Pausanias, *Description of Greece*: I.14.2). In European folklore the pig is the embodiment of the corn spirit (Frazer 1951(1890): vol. II, 16. cf. Bevan, 1986: 69). A divine sow was later anthropomorphised and merged into Demeter's image (Frazer 1951(1890): 16–21). The piglet was an important sacrifice during the Eleusinian mysteries because it was considered especially suitable for the gods of the Underworld according to Aelian (*De natura animalium*: X, 16). The ceremony of the *Thesmophoria* involved depositing sacrifices into the earth by night and retrieving the decaying remains of pigs that had been placed the previous year in the *megara* of Demeter, trenches and pits or natural clefts in rock. As snakes were known to congregate in such pits, women would shout to scare away any that might be lurking there. After prayers the fetid remains of the pigs from the previous year were mixed with seeds and planted, which promised a fruitful crop (Frazer 1951 (1890): 16–18; Pausanias, *Description of Greece*: IX.8.1). A myth involving the transformation of Demeter or Persephone into sows did not survive, but Ovid mentions that Demeter failed to find her daughter because the girl's traces were erased by those of a sow, and it is possible that this extract from Ovid echoes such a myth (*Fasti*: IV, 461–466). The rituals of *Thesmophoria* were linked to the fertility of the earth, and were intended to ensure the success of the sowing of the grain. The pig is probably closer to the soil than other animals, as it burrows and digs into the ground in its search for food. It also gives birth to many offspring in one litter, more than cows, sheep or goats. The fertility of the pig and its proximity to the soil made it suitable for sacrifice and a symbol of Demeter, a deity of the harvest and agriculture, who presided over grain and the fertility of the earth, as well as her daughter Kore, a vegetation goddess associated with regeneration (Bevan 1986: 79).

Various heroic myths are associated with overcoming wild boars: Heracles subdues the wild boar of Arimanthus during one of his labours; Odysseus, Theseus, or Meleager kill others; the Calydonian boar was a monstrous beast, and Homer points out that many heroes were needed to hunt him (*Iliad*: 9.533–546). Theseus killed the Krommyonian sow, a wild and cruel creature (Diodorus Siculus, *Bibliotheca historica*: IV, 59.4; Pausanias, *Description of Greece*: 1.27.9; Plutarch, *Lives*: vol. 1,*Theseus*: 9). The wild boar that Odysseus slew left a scar on his leg, which his old nurse recognised him by on his return home from his wanderings (*Odyssey*: 19.439–466), and the wild boar hunted by Adonis was the one who caused his death (Apollodorus, *Bibliotheca*: III, 14.4; Orphic Hymns, Hymn 56: to Adonis, 46–47). These myths reflect early attempts to save the country from the destruction caused by this wild beast (Richter 1930: 23). It is not surprising, then, that tusks of wild boars used to decorate warriors' helmets

(Homer, *Iliad*: 10.263–265). Pausanias notes that the great terror which these creatures caused drove people to assign sending them below, to their gods, in order to punish mortals (*Description of Greece*: 1.27.9). Thus, for example, Artemis sent the Calydonian boar to destroy the region in order to punish King Oeneus (Homer, *Iliad*: 9.533–546), and Apollodorus refers to the death of Adonis being due to the same deity (Apollodorus, *Bibliotheca*: III, 14.4).

The strength and powers of the wild boar are recorded in the *Iliad* (17.21, 725; V, 783). Plato uses the wild boar image as an allegory of the belligerent fervour of the *thumos*. For Plato, swine wallowing in the mire came at times to symbolise lust. On the other hand, sometimes the positive aspects of the boar are emphasised: its energy, zeal and boldness come close to those of the lion and tiger (*Euthydemus*: 294D; *Laches*: 196E–197B; see also Frère 1997: 428–429). Those positive qualities of the boar may also account for the selection of its image on private intaglios during the Archaic period.

Predatory animals

Panthers

A nicolo engraved gem (a special variety of two-layered agate, in which the lower layer is usually of black or brown non-translucent agate and the upper layer thin and whitish or bluish in colour) from the Israel Museum, shows a female panther with a thyrsus in her left forepaw, a yoke attached to her neck, walking, with right forepaw raised and head looking back (Figure 30). It is thought to date from the end of the 2nd – beginning of the 3rd century AD, since gems of nicolo were widespread mainly in the 2nd century AD (Henig 2007: 31; Maaskant-Kleibrink 1978: 251–285). This depiction clearly belongs to a series of renderings of felines as the mounts, draught animals, and companions of Dionysus/Bacchus, and of the personages connected with him.

Lions, panthers and leopards are among the attributes of the god Bacchus and a part of his *thiasos* (retinue). In Euripides's *Bacchae* (1017, 405 BC) the chorus turns to Dionysus and asks him to appear in the form of a lion breathing fire; and Pliny (AD 23–79) mentions the building of a temple to Dionysus in a place where a man had saved a lion from dying (*Natural History*: VIII.21.56–58). The wild nature of these felines matched the unbridled character of the Dionysian cult. The panther, according to some scholars, was not the only wild animal to accompany Dionysus, and his favourite, but the creature has also been linked to the initiation rites of the god's followers. It was even maintained that the panther had a great love of wine. As Philostratus (*c.* AD 190 –*c.* AD 230) tells us, the panther leaps as gracefully and lightly as a Bacchante, and this is the reason the

Figure 30. Female panther with a thyrsus, nicolo, 12 x 10 x 3 mm, the end
of the 2nd – beginning of the 3rd century AD.
The Israel Museum Jerusalem, Bequest of Mr. Adolphe Doreen, Paris.
IMJ70.62.339. ©Photo: The Israel Museum, Jerusalem.

god loves him so (*Imagines*: I.19.4 (322k)). Of all the felines devoted to Dionysus, it
was not only the most graceful and enthralling, but also the most ferocious and
bloodthirsty. The panther's agility and graceful movements – evolved for killing
– exhibit the same union of beauty and lethal menace found in the maenads
who accompany Dionysus (Kerenyi 1996: 373–377; Otto 1993: 110–112). Among
the most impressive Hellenistic forerunners of Roman representations of the
god riding on a leopard's back are the pebble mosaics of the late 4th century BC
found in the 'House of Dionysus' at Pella, and the well-known floor mosaic from
c. 100 BC in the 'House of the Masks' on Delos (Bruneau 1974: 24; Toynbee 1973:
84). The tiger remained unknown to the Greeks until the time of Alexander the
Great. Seleukos I is considered to have been the first to bring a tiger to Athens,
where it aroused great interest (Keller 1887: 137). A figure riding a tiger appears
on Hellenistic mosaics in the Casa del Fauno at Pompeii, and in the 'House of
Dionysus' at Delos (Dunbabin 1999: 33, 44, fig. 43). The panther, leopard, lion, and
tiger – male and female – also appear in countless Roman depictions of the god
astride their backs, or feature as harnessed to his wagon. Pliny claims that the
first leopard to appear in Rome was a tame one in a cage, and was presented by

Augustus in 11 BC when the theatre was dedicated to Marcellus (Toynbee 1973: 70). Martial (*c.* AD 38 –*c.* AD 102) refers to harnessed leopards and tigers, and then documents in great detail how, when Emperor Domitian returned from the war against the Sarmatians in AD 93, several tigers pulled chariots in the arena. He compares this scene with the Indian Triumph of Dionysus/Bacchus (Martial, I, 104, 2, 3, VIII, 26). Virgil (70–19 BC), in one section of the *Eclogues* (V, 29, 30), implies that tigers pulled the chariot of Dionysus during the Dionysian victory. This is well illustrated in the Saragossa (Zaragoza) mosaic, now in the Museo Arqueológico Nacional de Madrid, which shows two tigresses harnessed to the chariot of the victorious god, as well as in the well-known mosaic from El-Djem (Thysdrus) in Tunisia, both from the late 2nd – early 3rd century AD. (Toynbee 1973: 70). On the mosaic from La Maison de la Procession Dionysiaque at El-Djem, the infant Dionysus, with thyrsus and cantharus, is depicted riding a tigress, and Dionysus astride a lion is represented on the mosaic of the Triumph of Dionysus from Sousse (Hadrumetum) (early 3rd century AD). Several of those mosaics have a strong ritual element and are most unlikely to have been chosen simply as decoration without thought for their religious content. There is little doubt that their subjects were chosen by followers of the Dionysiac cult, who desired the decoration of their floors to allude in a specific way to the ceremony of initiation that they had undergone, or to the basic principles of their belief (Dunbabin 1978: 176–178, pl. 176). The central figure on a Roman marble sarcophagus (presumably found in Rome, and purchased by the Third Duke of Beaufort from Cardinal Giulio Alberoni (1664–1752) in Rome) depicting the Triumph of Dionysus and the Seasons, dating to *c.* AD 260–270 and now in the Metropolitan Museum, is that of the god Dionysus holding a thyrsus and seated on a panther (Toynbee 1973: 85). A panther and thyrsus also appear on engraved gems in different collections, such as on an amethyst from The Hague (now in the Rijksmuseum van Oudheden, Leiden) and a gem from the Ham hill-fort in Somerset, in Henig's British Corpus, both dating to the 1st century AD (Brandt 1970: no. 909; Henig 2007: 33; Maaskant-Kleibrink 1978: 221, no. 492; other examples include: Sena-Chiesa 1966: nos 1179–1181; Zwierlein-Diehl 1973: no. 368).

Like the large feline, the thyrsus is also an attribute of the god Dionysus. It was held by Dionysus and his entourage during the festivities and dancing, and was sometimes used to stimulate the excited crowd to a frenzy of ecstasy. The ability of the thyrsus to fertilise the soil (by placing it in the ground) thus made it a symbol of prosperity. The thyrsus in the *Bacchae*, for example, caused the flowing of water and wine from the ground (Euripides, *Bacchae*: 704). It also had magical connotations. The Orphic doctrines and the mysteries of Eleusis dedicated to Dionysus played an important role in Roman funerary beliefs, and the thyrsus is thus sometimes depicted in the hands of the deceased to ensure them the pleasures of the Afterlife. It became a symbol of the mysteries of Dionysus (*Anthologia Graeca*: IX.524.8; Nonnos, *Dionysiaca*: XVII, 147; XXV, 108; XLVII, 504; XXII, 135–140).

This gem thus indicates that its owner belonged to the cult of Bacchus. It was probably considered to confer protection by the god. The gem would also have acted as a reminder to the initiate of the sacred ritual of the Bacchic religion. Its wearer would almost certainly have participated in the Bacchic mysteries, believing that this would ensure immortality. It should be remembered that Bacchus was the most powerful of the saviour deities of Rome. The analogy between the female panther and the Bacchantes would suggest that this gem probably belonged to a female initiate.

Lions

On a Classical-Phoenician scarab from the Israel Museum, dated to 400 BC and made of green jasper, a lion is portrayed seated, with head turned towards its tail (Figure 31) (Boardman 2003: 115, pl. 38/30). This scarab is similar to a carnelian example dated to the end of the 6th – beginning of the 5th century BC, featuring a lion in a similar way, looking at its tail (Boardman 1968: 126, pl. XXVII, fig. 380), and also to another Greco-Egyptian scarab, made of green glazed faience, from the end of the 6th century BC and displaying strong Greek influence (Henig 1994: 2, no. 3).

Figure 31. Seated lion, impression of green jasper stone, 13.5 x 9.5 x 6 mm, a Classical-Phoenician scarab, 400 BC. The Israel Museum Jerusalem, The Harry Stern Collection, bequeathed by Dr Kurt Stern, London. In memory of his parents and his brother who perished at Sobibor. IMJ76.42.2381. ©Photo: The Israel Museum, Jerusalem.

Boardman classifies the Jerusalem scarab as 'Miscellaneous' with an overlapping of categories (Egyptianising, Levantine and Hellenising subjects) (Boardman 2003: 10). The motifs shown on Classical-Phoenician scarabs are mainly Egyptianising (Gorton 1996: 1, 43, 55), but they often have Greek characteristics, for example in the shortening of the representations of the lions (Boardman 2003: 17–18). In addition, most styles of lion depictions on these scarabs are Egyptian (Boardman 2003: 114).

The most important feature of the lion motif is its solar association. Whenever a star and a crescent are presented in addition to the lion, then the lion can be interpreted as a solar animal (Bonner 1950: 36; Budge 2004 (1904): vol. 2, 360; Henig 1994: 168, no. 358). Stars and Daimons are identical, so gem engravers were obsessed with carving solar deities (Henig 1994: 219). The lion cult existed in Egypt from ancient times, and spread during the Old Kingdom. The lion was worshiped because of his great strength and courage, and was usually associated with the sun-god, Horus or Rā, and with other solar deities (Budge 2004 (1904): vol. 2, 360): there was even a city in Egypt called after it – Leontopolis (Aelian, *De natura animalium*, XII. 7). In Egyptian mythology the lion has an important role, and one of the earliest lion deities is the god Aker, believed to keep the gateway to the dawn, through which the sun-god passes every morning. Aker is also mentioned in the *Pyramid Texts* ('The Pyramid of Unas' 1968: lines 498, 614). According to Aelian, the Egyptians believed that the lion is always awake and therefore they attributed it to the sun, because the sun never wearies either (*De natura animalium*: V. 39). Since the Egyptians believed that the gates of the morning and evening were kept by lion-gods, they placed statues of lions at the entrances to temples and tombs to protect both the living and the dead, and to prevent evil spirits and mortal enemies from entering and harming those inside. Keeper-lions were occasionally given human heads (either male or female), that the Greeks called 'sphinxes' (Budge 2004 (1904): vol. 2, 361). The Egyptians worshiped the lion and decorated temple doorways with gigantic lion heads, predominantly because the Nile overflows when the sun reaches a connection with Leo (Plutarch, *Moralia*, vol. V, 'Isis and Osiris': 366.38). The Egyptians believed that the sun dwelt in Leo, and when it arrived its zenith in summer, it approaches Leo (Aelian, *De natura animalium*: XII.7). In addition, the lion was also venerated in the Greek and Roman world due to its attributes of strength and courage (Pliny, *Natural History*: VIII.19), and also because of its alleged wisdom, as implicit in a quotation from Aelian, who cites Homer (*De natura animalium*: V. 39). The solar symbolism of the lion spread to Greece from the East, and, as an animal associated with the sun-god it was also linked to Apollo (Bevan 1986: 233). Herodotus notes that Croesus sent a golden lion to Apollo's temple at Delphi, and after a fire broke out in the temple it was stored in the Corinthian treasury (*Historiae*: I, 50).

In the *Iliad* (12.41–48, XXIV, 39–45; XX, 164–175; XXI, 571–575; VII, 228) the lion symbolises the heroism of the warrior in battle, but at the same time also its cruelty and thirst for blood, and it is mentioned as the fiery-tempered and proud possessor of a 'hero's-heart'. The image of the brave and proud lion also appears in various *Dialogues* of Plato, and is especially mentioned in the *Republic*. In the Tenth book, Plato (*c.* 380 BC) discusses the issue of the re-incarnation of the soul as an animal. He gives as an example the Homeric hero Ajax, who after the incident in which the armour of the deceased Achilles was delivered to someone else, slaughtered a herd of sheep, and, having experienced humiliation, he despised his own existence as a human and preferred reincarnation as a lion. Ajax's militant temper, explains Plato, was re-embodied in the belligerent nature of the lion (*Republic*: X, 620 B). In the Ninth book, Plato defines the part of the human soul he calls the *thumos*. The thought, which creates an image of the soul, first conjures up an image of a fantastic monster, such as the Chimaera or Cerberus, which is a symbol of the desires. The shapes of a lion and of a man are then formed, which will be the symbols of the *thumos* and *nous*. When these three images are combined into a single image, which incorporates Cerberus, the lion, and the man, an overall image of the human being is obtained (*zoon anthrôpon*) (Plato, *Republic*: IX, 588 B–E). The inner man can choose whether to connect to the Cerberus within him, or to restrain it and connect to the lion within him, and he will accordingly produce the correct actions and speech. Thus, for Plato, the lion represents a more peaceful figure than the passionate warrior in battle (such as Ajax), and also an image of that part of the soul, the *thumos*, which acts as an intermediary between the inner being and Cerberus (*Republic*: IX, 589 A–B. see also: Frère 1997: 427). Perceived in this way, representations of lions on engraved gems could have been intended to imbue the person wearing them with strength and courage (Guiraud 1996: 139; Henig 1997: 47)

The agate engraved gem from the Israel Museum (Figure 32) features a lion treading on a supine human, with one paw on his throat. This gem can be dated to the second half of the first century and the early years of the second century AD because the gold ring is Type II (see: Henig 2007, fig. 1, 9-12). Gems with depictions of a lion treading on another animal, or on a man, were apparently used as amulets to protect their owners from harm (Bonner 1950: 36). This depiction resembles the theme of the gladiator, which is rarely depicted on gems, and indicates *memento mori*. Henig mentions a bronze key-handle showing a lion with an impressive mane, its front paws treading on a man, its mouth wide open as if to devour him. Although the human victim can be considered as *damnatus ad bestias*, these representations might better be considered as apotropaic, bearing the meaning of protection against evil forces, rather than referring to the arena. Such gems could also have functioned as *memento mori*, a reminder that death can suddenly come upon each of us, just like the leap of a wild lion. One should thus interpret their appearance on gems as having a protective meaning, against the death that awaits everybody (Henig 1977: 356–357; Henig 1984a: 407–408, fig. 14, pl. LVII; Henig 1997: 45–88). Other examples of this theme can be found, for example, on several Fitzwilliam Museum gems (Henig 1994: 168–169, nos 357, 358).

In Roman sepulchral art the lion has its place as a symbol of the ravening power of death and of man's victory over it. This notion was even older, however, for the lion had also been regarded as a powerful guardian in Mesopotamia and lions were sculpted symmetrically on either side of the doors of palaces, temples, and tombs (Prieur 1988: 17). In Greece the lion symbolised heroism, courage, and triumph rather than being a symbol of a particular god, although there are cases in which gods took on the shape of a lion. Indeed, while a god or a goddess flanked by two lions is an ancient motif, the lion in Greece is, above all a symbol of victory. Interestingly, the lion statues erected to mark victories

Figure 32. Lion treading on a supine human, agate, intaglio and impression, 12 x 9 mm, the second half of the 1st century - beginning of the 2nd century AD.
The Israel Museum Jerusalem, The Harry Stern Collection, bequeathed by Dr Kurt Stern, London. In memory of his parents and his brother who perished at Sobibor. IMJ76.42.2426. ©Photo: The Israel Museum, Jerusalem.

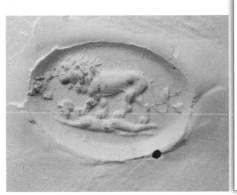

were usually those of lionesses, which were considered braver than their male counterparts.

In Archaic Greek art the earliest known lion tomb, dated to 600 BC, is the 'Menekrates Tomb', housed in the Archaeological Museum of Corfu (Αρχαιολογικό Μουσείο Κέρκυρας). Other examples from the Archaic period are those of two seated lions from Miletus in Anatolia. In an epitaph written by Simonides (c. 556 –c. 468 BC), the lion explains why he was elected as the favoured tomb guardian, and in this case the name of the deceased too is Leon:

> 'I am the most powerful of the animals, as was he, whose grave I'm going to keep in stone, among mortals. But if Leon had not had my spirit, as well as my name, I would not put my feet on his grave.' (Peek 1955: 1173; cf. Kurtz and Boardman 1971: 239).

In the Classical period, sculpted lions are often depicted crouching with their forelegs upright, as on the tombstone memorial for the battle of Chaeronea in 338 BC (Kurtz and Boardman 1971: 238–239, pls. 64–67). The Hellenistic period produced the 'lion tomb' from Knidos, which bore at the top of its pyramid a colossal lion statue, currently housed in the British Museum. This funerary monument was apparently modelled on the mausoleum at Halicarnassus, whose construction was completed in 349 BC, and which also bore atop it a lion sculpture as part of the sculptural programme (Fletcher 1987: 138–139; Lawrence 1996: 147, 197, fig. 108, ill. 229).

In Roman funerary art lions are also fairly common. A large Augustan tomb re-erected beside a modern street in Aquileia has lions poised on two of the corners of its enclosure wall; and in the Danubian, German, and British provinces lions appear as tomb groups (Toynbee 1973: 67).

A yellow jasper engraved gem from the Israel Museum (Figures 33a and b), which dates to the 2nd century AD, shows a lion attacking a deer, leaping on its neck, with a six-pointed star above them. This gem can be dated to the 2nd century AD since it can be assigned to the 'Small Grooves Style', typified by rounded wheel grooves employed for detailing (see Maaskant-Kleibrink 1978: 251–252). A similar Fitzwilliam Museum gem, from the end of the 1st century AD, features a lion trampling a supine deer and biting its neck. Here, the victim has managed to rotate its head toward its relentless assailant with its last remaining strength (Henig 1994: 169, no. 359). Other examples of this theme can be found, for example, on several Metropolitan Museum gems, as well as on some from the Royal Coin Cabinet at The Hague, and now in the Rijksmuseum van Oudheden, Leiden (Maaskant-Kleibrink 1978: nos 640, 717; Richter 1956: no. 505; Richter 1971: no. 368).

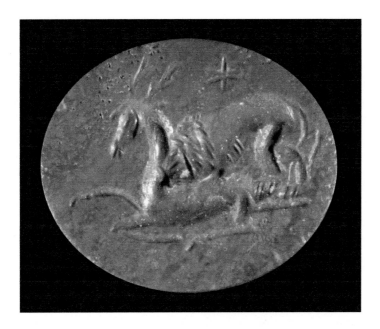

Figure 33a. Lion attacking a deer, yellow jasper,
12.5 x 10.5 x 2.5 mm, 2nd century AD.
The Israel Museum Jerusalem. Bezalel Collection. IMJ77.31.976.
©Photo: The Israel Museum, Jerusalem, by Vladimir Naikhin.

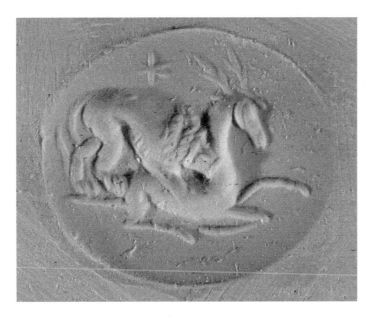

Figure 33b. Impression of the yellow jasper stone.
©Photo: The Israel Museum, Jerusalem.

Another yellow jasper engraved gem from the Israel Museum (Figures 34a and b), second-third century AD, depicts a lion leaping upon the back of a goat, with both rearing up on their hind legs. This gem can be dated to the second-third century AD since it is made of yellow jasper which was popular in the late Roman period. Yellow jasper was often used for these kinds of lion depictions, and the stone itself was attributed magical meaning, being known as 'the stone with the colour of a lion's pelt' (according to a reference in the lapidary of Sokrates and Dionysios, which was pointed out by A.A. Barb. See Bonner 1950, 8–9; Henig 1980, 331; Henig 1994: 168, 175, nos 358, 381; Middleton 1891: 145; Richter 1956: xx). Very similar in iconography are several yellow jasper Roman gems from Caesarea and Aquileia (Hamburger 1968: nos 108, 109; Sena-Chiesa 1966: nos 1142, 1145–1147, 1153, 1154). Engraved gems made of yellow jasper bearing a depiction of a lion attacking another animal were designed to protect their wearer, through both their material and iconography (Guiraud 1996: 139).

Figure 34a. Lion attacking a goat, yellow jasper, 15 x 11.5 x 3 mm, 2nd-3rd century AD. The Israel Museum Jerusalem, Bequest of Mr. Adolphe Doreen, Paris. IMJ70.62.115. ©Photo: The Israel Museum, Jerusalem.

Figure 34b. Lion attacking a goat, drawing. ©Drawing: The Israel Museum, Jerusalem, by Pnina Arad.

The theme of the lion devouring another animal, usually a bull or a deer, re-entered the Greek world from the East in the 8th century. It was known already in the Bronze Age, as on gems from the Mycenaean period (dated to 1450–1300 BC), now in the British Museum (Boardman 1968: 121; Higgins 1967: 180–184, ills. 224–230). The motif of a lion devouring its prey is interpreted by most scholars as an allegory of the victory of the soul over death (Henig 1977: 356; Toynbee 1973: 65–68). From the second quarter of the 6th century BC these scenes of a lion attacking animals – especially wild boars and goats – became more prevalent. A particularly prominent example of such depictions can be seen on the fine limestone groups from pediments on the Athenian Acropolis (Boardman 1968: 121). The motif of an attacking lion was popular during the Archaic period, when the prey could have been a bull, a deer, or a human. This motif appears for instance on the Siphnian Treasury north frieze, which dates to 525 BC, on a relief from 450 BC housed in the Louvre, and on coins from Akanthos from 500–400 BC (Richter 1930: 5–6, figs 8, 13). By the second half of the 5th century BC, the lion was no longer as popular in Greek art as it had been earlier; and on a later gem from the British Museum, showing a lion attacking a deer, this theme is represented very naturalistically compared to the earlier depictions (Richter 1930: 7–8, fig. 21). During the 4th century BC Greek sculpture became increasingly realistic, but limitations deriving from the artists' unfamiliarity with this animal is felt more acutely compared to depictions of horses, for example, which the artists were able to study closely. The reason for the popularity of lion depictions during the Archaic period is not clear, but might be linked to a renewed interest in Oriental themes and styles, which could have inspired the new series of archaic Greek scarabs that acquired a similar symbolic significance as that in the Orient (Richter 1930: 8, 121, figs 28–29). Representations of a lion attacking another animal bore an important symbolic connotation in the East. During the Achaemenid period (550–330 BC) depictions of a lion attacking a bull appear on the Persepolis relief and on cylinder seals (Delaporte 1923: pls. 107.27–29). According to one proposed interpretation, the lion, which symbolises the sun, is devouring the bull, signifying the earth; and this is a metaphor of the arrival of spring, as well as the victory of light over darkness, or of life over death. The lion was not a familiar creature in Greece, except in its artistic manifestations, and therefore should be treated as almost a 'real' monster, like the sphinx or griffin. It is thus possible that the attacking lion theme that appears on gems has the same connotation of divine power, borrowed or adopted by a human being (Boardman 1980: 103).

In Roman funerary art the lion devouring its prey is also a familiar theme, symbolising victory over death. A fragment of a sarcophagus in the Musei Capitolini dating to the 3rd century AD bears a depiction of a lion pouncing forcefully upon its prey (Toynbee 1973: 65–66). Tombstones discovered in Colchester and

Cambridge feature lions devouring an animal or human being (Henig 1977: 356). On a marble statue of a lion devouring a goat (the Corbridge Lion) from the 2nd–3rd century AD, which may have adorned a tomb in the past, the predator has a massive head and mane, its forepaws are extended, its jaws gaping, and it is trampling on the goat with all four paws (Toynbee 1973: 65–67, fig. 18). A lion devouring a man is depicted on sculptures from Chelmsford and Silchester, as well as on gems from Gestingthorpe, Essex and Bath (Henig 1977: pl. 15.Vb.). Using amulets showing an image of a lion treading on another animal's head bore specific meaning for their owners, and were intended to confer power upon that person, such as that of the lion's power over other animals (Bonner 1950: 36). Such depictions also had an apotropaic meaning of protecting the gem's owner from evil forces. Gems with depictions of a lion attacking another animal were apparently regarded as amulets and as protecting their owners from harm. An engraved gem featuring a lion was believed to protect its wearer in the same way that lions protected tombs. On magical gems the depictions of a lion overpowering a supine figure symbolised the sun-god, with the meaning of overcoming the fate of mortals and achieving immortality for the gem owner (Michel 2004: 86–87). A famous 2nd-century AD mosaic from Verulamium showing a lion holding in its maw the head of an antlered stag, apparently bears the same meaning, although the *canthari* on the decorative border soften the grim message, promising that the death of the body is but a prelude to the eternal world of paradise (Henig 1984a: 408, fig. 14, pl. LVII; Toynbee 1973: 68, pl. 16; Henig 1977: 358). The star depicted on the yellow jasper gem alludes to the *aeternitas* of the heavens, thus providing supporting evidence that the devices portrayed on these gems were primarily concerned with victory over death. We cannot, of course, be entirely sure that the owner of this gem, or of any of the others mentioned here, indeed thought along these lines, but a clear anxiety concerning death and the Afterlife is to be discerned in the beliefs of ordinary people of that 'Age of Anxiety', the Middle Empire (Dodds 1965: 3–4). Petronius (c. AD 27 –c. AD66) mocks this anxiety when he has Trimalchio note during the feast that even wine outlasts humans and therefore one has to rejoice before dying. Petronius also orders his slave to bring him a silver skeleton in order to demonstrate to the revellers more tangibly what awaits them after their death, and to indicate that they should live well and enjoy life. It is possible to see the manifestation of this anxiety also reflected in jewellery and other objects owned by women of this period (Petronius, *Satyricon*, XXXIV. see also Henig 1977: 351; Henig 1984b: 246).

The second-third century AD red jasper intaglio from the Israel Museum (Figure 35) features Heracles' first labour: that of killing the Nemean Lion. The muscular naked hero is shown strangling the predator bare-handed, his club upright in the background. The lion places its left front paw on Heracles' foot, while its right front paw, with its tail twirling round it, rests on the ground.

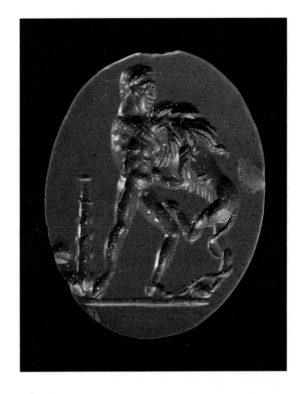

Figure 35. Heracles battling the Nemean lion, red jasper, 21 x 15 mm, 2nd-3rd century AD. The Israel Museum Jerusalem, Clark Collection (YMCA) purchased by Carmen and Louis Warschaw Fund for Archaeological Acquisition. IMJ90.24.403.
©Photo: The Israel Museum, Jerusalem, by Vladimir Naikhin.

Red jasper, which was particularly prevalent from the 2nd century AD onwards (Guiraud 1996: 95; Maaskant-Kleibrink 1978: 251–285; Richter 1956: 61; Sena-Chiesa 1966: 60),[13] was valued as amulet, believed to have occult virtues and attributed with magical qualities (Bonner 1950: 8–9; Middleton 1891: 145; Walters 1926: lv), as well as the ability of curing diseases (Pliny, *Natural History*: XXXVII.169–170). The red colour resembled blood in all its contexts: energy, dynamism, strength, and even life itself (Andrews 1990: 37; Mastrocinque 2011).

It was widely believed that an image of Heracles battling the Nemean Lion, as depicted on this Roman red jasper gem, would protect a warrior in battle (Soeda 1987: 186). Gems on which this theme appear were also related to the healing of colic, a painful disease of the lower intestine.

Medical references in the essay 'On Stones' (Theophrastus (*c.* 371–287 BC), De Lapidibus) confirm an early interest of Classical medicine in stones. By the end of the 1st century AD, this had become fully developed, as can be seen in the 'Materia Medica', a pharmacology essay by Dioscorides of Anazarbus (AD 50–70) from Cilicia in southern Asia Minor. The Fifth book of 'Materia Medica'

---

[13] The Jerusalem red jasper Heracles gem is also carved in the 'Small Grooves Style' and therefore dated to the 2nd century AD (Maaskant-Kleibrink 1978: 251–252).

deals mainly with the medicinal properties of gems. The stones, even when not decorated, were believed to have some innate curative or other power. For example hematite was recommended for healing eye diseases, sapphire against scorpion stings; all types of jasper were recommended as amulets that allowed a swift labour for women, and so on.

According to Dasen, in ancient times there was a connection between magic and medicine. There is evidence that pills and ointments bore images of divine or magical characters, with the figure of Heracles, for example, being prevalent on Greco-Roman surgical tools (Dasen 2011: 69). His presence is explained by several factors: the glory attributed to his prowess and stamina; his talent and ability to repel evil (he is described as *alexikakos*), and, finally, the genealogy of Hippocrates. It was believed that the physician Hippocrates (*c.* 460 BC – *c.* 370 BC) was a descendant of Asclepius through his father and of Heracles through his mother. An apocryphal letter to Abraxas compares Hippocrates, who fought 'wild' diseases, to Heracles, who defeated dangerous animals (Jouanna 1992: 32–33; Letter II; *Littré* IX, 314–315; Pliny, *Natural History*: VII.56, 123; cf. Dasen 2011: 69, note 2. Heracles' image on medical instruments was believed to 'tame' pain, just as he had tamed wild animals, and to increase the endurance and resilience of the patient (Dasen 2011: 69). The connection between Heracles and Hippocrates intensifies the efficacy of the depiction of the hero on healing amulets.

This scene of Heracles fighting the Nemean Lion was attributed with healing power. In the 6th century AD, a Greek physician named Alexander of Tralles gave the following instructions to those of his patients suffering from colic: 'On a Median stone engrave Heracles standing upright and throttling a lion. Set it in a gold ring and give it to the patient to wear' (Alexander of Tralles, *Therapeutica*: 2.579; cf. Bonner 1950: 62; see also Faraone 2011: 52, note 28; Michel 2001: 248–249; Nagy 2012: 79, note 25). The precise identification of the 'Median stone' mentioned in the text is uncertain and it may have been a form of hematite or magnetite. Alexander's prescription, however, matches the depiction that appears in a common series of opaque, red stone amulets (almost always red jasper): Heracles' struggle with the lion. For example such a depiction of Heracles standing upright and battling the Nemean Lion appears on three Roman gems of red jasper in the British Museum (Faraone 2011: 52, pls. 5-7), as well as on a red jasper gem from the Cabinet des médailles, Paris (Mastrocinque 2014: 150, no. 398). Alexander points out that an amulet of this kind has two important components: a special stone and a special image. However most of the existing gems of this type, as well as the above mentioned, include an additional component – an inscription of the Greek letter kappa three times on the reverse of the gem (Faraone 2011: 53), the K may be the initial of κωλική, 'colic' (Mastrocinque 2014: 150). Variants of this type include other inscriptions, for example a gem in the Rijksmuseum van Oudheden, Leiden (GS–01115) which bears a magic formula that alludes to colic and contains three K letters: κολοκερ κολοφο.[14] Another Roman gem made of red jasper, and also in the Cabinet des médailles, Paris, substantiates that these gems were indeed used in the treatment of intestinal disease centuries before Alexander of Tralles wrote his prescription, for around the image of Heracles and the lion appears the inscription: 'Withdraw colic! The divine one pursues you' (Faraone 2011: 53, pl. 8; Mastrocinque 2014: 152, no. 403). On this gem the inscription of kappa letters (with pentagram) appears at the foot of the fighting couple, while on the other side of the gem appears a tri-form Hecate with the magical names Iao above and Abrasax below, which is another common magical image. The purpose of the depiction of Heracles' famous labour on this gem in Paris is easily interpreted: the image of the dangerous lion being strangled by a powerful hero is designed to scare away the intestinal disease and chase it far from the wearer. This particular inscription has been found only on this gem, and is part of a far more ancient Greek tradition of protective incantations. It is more probable that on most of these kinds of gems the lion, with its sharp claws, represented the sharp stomach pains of the intestinal disease, which by a process of evincive magic was intended to be 'strangled' and eliminated, just as Heracles had strangled the lion (Faraone 2011: 53).

A number of scholars have suggested that the definition of magical gems is problematic due to its reducing nature (Nagy 2012: 106; 2002: 153–179), and owing to its assumption that only inscribed examples can be regarded as such (Hamburger 1968: 3–4). Kotansky posits that "the figure of Herakles strangling the lion on gem-stones served as a general, apotropaic device, especially since we know that Herakles was often referred to as alexikakos, 'averter of evil'" (Kotansky 1982: 111). Nagy has suggested that it is better to regard magical gems as 'Hellenised' versions of amulets (Nagy 2012: 84–87, 106; 2002: 153–156, 169–170). We know from ancient sources, e.g. the *Lithika*, and magical papyri, that there existed a much larger range of gems with magical properties, for example with regard to healing diseases (Dasen 2014: 178, note 1; Nagy 2002: 153–179; 2011; 2012: 85–87). Bonner cites several specimens of uninscribed gems along with their inscribed counterparts, and points out that sometimes the lack of an inscription does not invalidate their magical use. Furthermore, he points out that certain gems, which bear no inscription of a magical character, may, nevertheless, have been worn as amulets (Bonner 1950: 14, cf. Hamburger 1968: 3). Faraone has noted that if we use Alexander's two criteria for colic amulets, gems which have the correct medium (a red stone) and the right image (Heracles and the Lion), could presumably serve for this purpose. However, according to

[14] See Matrocinque 2014: 150, note 509, regarding the inscription and similar examples.

modern scholarship, they are merely ornaments, as they lack the triple kappas on the reverse (Faraone 2011: 53). However, according to Faraone, the image of Heracles and the Lion was very old, being imported from the East, and thought to have inherent powers of its own; in addition 'the text is clearly the last to arrive of the three important features of magical gems (1. a potent medium 2. a powerful image and 3. a magical symbol or text)' (Faraone 2011: 54, 57).

A red jasper intaglio from the Israel Museum (2nd–3rd century AD)[15] features Eros astride a galloping lion and holding a whip in his hands (Figures 36a and b).

Figure 36a. Eros galloping on a lion, red jasper, 14 x 11 x 3 mm, 2nd-3rd century AD. The Israel Museum Jerusalem, Bequest of Mr. Adolphe Doreen, Paris. IMJ70.62.344. ©Photo: The Israel Museum, Jerusalem.

Figure 36b. Eros galloping on a lion, drawing. ©Drawing: The Israel Museum, Jerusalem, by Pnina Arad.

---

[15] As noted above, red jasper was particularly prevalent in the 2nd–3rd centuries AD (Maaskant-Kleibrink 1978: 251–285; Guiraud 1996: 95; Richter 1956: 61).

The motif of Eros riding a lion is fairly common on engraved gems from the Roman period and appears with slight variations (Brandt 1972: fig. 2288; Walters 1926: no. 1486, pl. 20; nos 2852–2854, pl. 30). For example Eros might be depicted without a whip, or all four of the lion's paws might be represented touching the ground, as in the gem from The Hague (Maaskant-Kleibrink 1978: 368, no. 1160). This visual motif was very popular in Antiquity, as demonstrated by an onyx cameo from the Hellenistic period in the Museo Archeologico Nazionale, Florence, and signed by Protarchos (Furtwängler, pl. LVII. 1; Lippold 1923, Taf. XXIX, 8; Vollenweider 1966, fig. 12.1). It is also mentioned in the written sources, and Pliny refers to a statue of cupids playing with a lioness, as if it were a pet, not a fierce predator (*Natural History*: XXXVI.41); while an epigram from the *Anthologia Graeca* (9.221) tells of a signet ring bearing the motif of a lion harnessed to a chariot driven by Eros:

'I see upon the signet-ring Love, whom none can escape, driving a chariot drawn by mighty lions. One hand menaces their necks with the whip, the other guides the reins; about him is shed abundant bloom of grace. I shudder as I look on the destroyer of men, for he who can tame wild beasts will not show the least mercy to mortals.'

The earliest representations of Eros riding a lion are terracotta statuettes from the 2nd–3rd centuries BC.[16] The motif is also depicted in other media throughout the Hellenistic and Roman periods, including coins, such as a silver find (dated AD 209–212) from Pessinus in Galatia depicting Eros astride a lion, holding a whip in one hand and the lion's mane in the other (Hermary, Cassimatis and Volkommer 1981: 266, 269). The motif is prevalent on mosaics, such as one in Cologne (Colonia Claudia Ara Agrippinensium) featuring Eros on a lion and holding a *thyrsus*, as part of a Dionysian representation, which includes the drunken Dionysos, surrounded by Eros, satyrs, and dancers (Blanc and Gury 1981: 335). When Eros is riding a lion, he usually leads the Dionysian procession, as seen on the mosaic from Sousse (Stuveras 1969: fig. 23). The theme of Eros on a lion is also related to sepulchral iconography, following the belief that the lion is a protector and a symbol of the power of death, and of the human triumph over it (Toynbee 1973: 65).

This gem was probably intended to encourage love. It needed to be given to the other person, either overtly or in secret, or worn by the owner of the object. If a gem depicting Eros – in a ring or amulet – was worn by someone seeking to

[16] However, depictions of Eros riding on a lion originate from red-figure vases from the 4th century BC, on which Eros appears as one of the companions of Dionysos. He is easily recognisable by his wings, and he is riding a leopard rather than a lion (see Hermary, Cassimatis and Vollkommer 1981: 257–258).

attract a lover, it is probable that the intention was for it to affect the target due to the latter's belief in the god Eros, and not merely through its amuletic or magical power. Nonetheless, people would sometimes rub an amulet or an image on a ring. An amber ring carved with the bust of Minerva from Carlisle had clearly been rubbed by its owner.[17]

The figure of Eros is rarely simply a decorative motif (Platt 2007: 89). Hesiod indicates in the *Theogony* (116–129) that Eros was one of the primordial forces of nature, represented along with Chaos, Gea and Tartaros as one of the most ancient deities who existed at the genesis of the cosmos. His role was to arrange the elements that constituted the Universe. He brought harmony to chaos and enabled life to evolve. The power of Eros, the god of love, was regarded as immense, as illustrated in the anthropomorphic myths associated with him (Boardman 1978: 20).

Birds, Birds of Prey, and Fowl

Eagles

Three gems from the Israel Museum feature an eagle: the first is a yellow jasper gem (Figure 37), which is made of yellow jasper and dates to the 2nd century AD,[18] with an eagle standing on a pedestal between two military standards (*vexilla*), holding a wreath in its beak; the second (Figure 38), dating from the 1st century AD,[19] bears a similar representation of an eagle standing on an elevated pedestal between two military standards; and the third, made of nicolo and dating to the 2nd century AD, illustrates an eagle standing on a pedestal, holding a wreath, and at its feet a laurel and a palm-branch (Figure 39).[20] Similar gems on which an eagle is shown between two standards can be found in many collections, for example in the collection of gems from Gadara, Jordan (Henig and Whiting 1987: pls. 330, 332). A similar depiction of an eagle between two standards also appears on coins (Guiraud 1996: 98). Similar gems featuring an eagle standing on an altar and holding a wreath are quite common on gemstones (Brandt 1972: no. 2438; Gramatopol 1974: nos 554–565; Henig 1978: nos 689–697; Henig, Whiting 1987: nos 336–341; Maaskant-Kleibrink 1978: nos 688, 759; Sena-Chiesa 1966: nos 1259–1280; Vollenweider 1984: no. 118).

---

[17] I am indebted to Revd Dr Martin Henig for this helpful information.

[18] It is thought to date to the 2nd century AD, since gems of yellow jasper were widespread mainly in this period (Henig 2007: 31; Maaskant-Kleibrink 1978: 251–285).

[19] Since it is made in the 'Imperial Small Grooves Style', as defined by Maaskant-Kleibrink (Maaskant-Kleibrink 1978: 251–252).

[20] It is thought to date to the 2nd century AD, since gems of nicolo were common mainly for this time (Henig 2007: 31; Maaskant-Kleibrink 1978: 251–285).

Figure 37. Eagle standing on a pedestal
between two military standards (*vexilla*),
drawing of yellow jasper stone,
2 x 9.5 x 1.51 mm, 2nd century AD.
The Israel Museum Jerusalem, Bequest of
Mr. Adolphe Doreen, Paris. IMJ70.62.355.
©Drawing: The Israel Museum, Jerusalem,
by Pnina Arad.

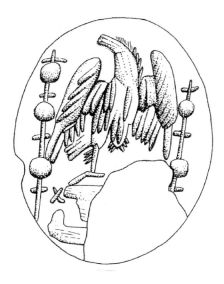

Figure 38. Eagle standing on a
pedestal between two military
standards (*vexilla*), drawing of
carnelian stone, 12.5 x 10.5 x 2.5 mm,
1st century AD,The Israel Museum
Jerusalem, Bequest of Mr. Adolphe
Doreen, Paris. IMJ70.62.335.
©Drawing: The Israel Museum,
Jerusalem, by Pnina Arad.

Figure 39. Eagle standing on a pedestal and
holding a wreath, drawing of nicolo stone,
12 x 10 x 3.5 mm, 2nd century AD.
The Israel Museum Jerusalem, Bequest of
Mr. Adolphe Doreen, Paris. IMJ70.62.358.
©Drawing: The Israel Museum, Jerusalem, by
Pnina Arad.

Eagles were symbols of Imperial Rome, a symbol of victory and power, and
especially of its legions, quoting Tacitus: 'Romanae aves, propria legionum
numina' (*The Annals of Tacitus*: ii, 17). Furthermore, an eagle between two
military standards was a generic reference to legions, a point established
by the discovery of an eagle and standards gem in Cyprus inscribed 'Leg XV
Apollinari' (*AJA*, LXXIV (1970): 74 and pl. xxiii, 16. cf. Henig 1978: 105). During

the Republic, the eagle often appears in the context of the great marshals, such as Scipio Africanus, while voyaging to Africa, eagles guided his ships (Silius Italicus, *Punica*: XVII, 52 ff). The coin symbols of cities are featured by the eagle, which served as the attribute of Zeus/Jupiter. The theme was familiar among Hellenistic rulers and later adopted by Roman emperors as an administrative and Imperial symbol (Dvorzetsky 2007: 105).

On coins from Caesarea, for example, the Roman eagle is depicted holding a wreath, and within it are inscribed the letters SPQR (*Senatus Populusque Romanus* – 'The Senate and People of Rome'). On an AD 219 Elagabalus coin from Emmaus-Nicopolis there is a winged eagle with a wreath, inscribed 'Nicopolis – the city of Victory'. These kinds of inscriptions are found on coins minted in Rome on the order of the Senate (Dvorzetsky 2007: 127–128).

The military symbol of the eagle between two standards (*vexilla*) represented the Roman legions in general, as well as the luck of the military unit, and it was admired by the army and apparently became a magical icon (Hamburger 1968: 14; Henig 1997: 49). Before the time of Marius, the eagle was one of the five symbols of the legion, in addition to the wolf, Minotaur, horse and boar. Of all these symbols Marius retained only the eagle, and the eagle standard (*aquila*) became a collective symbol for the entire legionary forces, although the individual legions had their own emblems (*signa*) (Pliny, *Natural History*: X.4–5). The eagle, which was initially made of silver, and later gold, stood on a thunderbolt with its wings spread out and was carried at the top of a long pole. In camps during wars, and permanent fortresses, the eagle was established in a special chapel in the headquarters building and was revered as the personal divine protector of the legion (*proprium legionis numen*) (Tacitus, *The Annals of Tacitus*: II, 17, 2). The greatest disaster that could befall any legion was the loss of its standard. In every legion there was a soldier whose job was to carry the standard (*aquilifer*), and it is known that they defended him fiercely in battle (Julius Caesar, *De bello Gallico* (*The Gallic War*): IV, 25). In 27 BC coins were minted in Asia Minor in honour of Augustus, and on them the eagle of Jupiter holds the *corona civica* in its talons, which gradually became a symbol of power (Zanker 1988: 93, fig. 76b). This impressive image was created in Rome, where it first appeared on a cameo now kept in Vienna (Zanker 1988: 93–94, fig. 77). The eagle, whose colour is brown against a white background, is depicted frontally, and its head is directed towards the viewer's right. It stands on a palm-branch and in its left claw holds a wreath, identified as the *corona civica*. Pliny wrote at length about the *corona civica*, very much linking it to the army (*Natural History*: XVI.5, 4).

In general the eagle is involved in the dynastic stories of emperors, guiding them up during their Apotheosis. It is perceived as the one who leads the soul of the deceased, and the emperor who passed Apotheosis is sometimes presented straddling an eagle in flight. During the funeral ceremony of an emperor it was customary to release an eagle from the top of the pyre to symbolise his soul making its way to heaven (Toynbee 1963: 242). Some Roman emperors appeared disguised as Jupiter, such as Augustus on the Gemma Augustea, in which he is shown sitting on the throne and at his feet the eagle (Zanker 1988: 231, fig. 182).

Walters mentions a gem which bears a representation of an eagle between standards, together with Fortuna (Walters 1926: pls. XXIII: 1731). The standard does not appear alone on the gems, but the eagle can appear alone and in various combinations (Walters 1926: pls. XXXII: 3387–3388). Sometimes the eagle is accompanied by two other symbols of victory – the wreath and palm-branch (Bonner 1950: 49, 64ff).

Parrots

A red jasper gem from the Israel museum features Eros riding a chariot harnessed to two parrots (Figures 40a and b). It is made in the 'Plain Grooves Style', as defined by Maaskant-Kleibrink, and dates to the 2nd century AD (Maaskant-Kleibrink 1978: 311). In addition, red jasper was particularly prevalent in the 2nd century AD onwards (Guiraud 1996: 95; Maaskant-Kleibrink 1978: 251–285; Richter 1956: 61; Sena-Chiesa 1966: 60). A similar iconography and date appear, for example, on a gem from Dalmatia (Middleton 1991: fig. 82). Representations of Eros driving an animal-chariot are common in the Roman world, as on the Casa dei Vettii Pompeian wall-paintings, where the god is depicted several times as a charioteer driving a chariot pulled by deer and swans. These representations are in accordance with ancient literary sources (Propertius, *Elegies*: 3.1). This motif is also common on gems, where Eros is shown riding various animal-chariots, among them lions and deer (McCann 1978: fig. 25), tigers, goats, horses and birds (Mollard-Besques 1963: fig. 76.b; Walters 1926: fig. 1484; Zwierlein-Diehl 1970: fig. 448, pl. 79), various kinds of fowl, such as roosters and swans (Walters 1926: fig. 1484), and even butterflies (Maaskant-Kleibrink 1978: fig. 210a).

In Rome parrots were thought to be of Indian origin and were known as *psittacus torqualus*. On wall-painting they can be identified by their green colouring, and a band of red-gold feathers creating a collar around their necks (Aristotle, *Historia animalium*: 8.12.597B; Pliny, *Natural History*: X.58, 117). A similar collar, though not so colourful, appears on the Israel Museum gem, as well as others, such as the nicolo and agate gems in the Royal Coin Cabinet, The Hague, and now in the Rijksmuseum van Oudheden, Leiden (Maaskant-Kleibrink 1978: fig. 565a–b, 731a). The Indian parrot was not familiar in Greece before the time of Alexander the Great, and was considered in Greece as an exotic and rare animal, yet there is

Figure 40a. Eros riding a chariot harnessed to two parrots, impression of red jasper stone, 13 x 11 x 2.5 mm, 2nd century AD. The Israel Museum Jerusalem, Bequest of Mr. Adolphe Doreen, Paris. IMJ70.62.362. ©Photo: The Israel Museum, Jerusalem.

Figure 40b. Eros riding a chariot harnessed to two parrots, drawing.
©Drawing: The Israel Museum, Jerusalem, by Pnina Arad.

a detailed depiction of it on a Greco-Persian gem in New York, from which it is possible to conclude that the Greek artist must have seen the bird in Persia at the end of the 5th century BC (Richter 1930: 38, fig. 210). A bronze statuette of a parrot found in Samsun (ancient *Amisos*), and kept in Berlin, is realistically made, with its feathers portrayed in detail (Richter 1930: 38–39, fig. 211). Aristotle calls it the 'Indian bird', noting its talent for mimicry, and adds that this bird 'becomes even more brazen after drinking wine' (*Historia animalium*: 8.12). Varro notes that parrots sometimes took part in public performances (*De re rustica*: III, 9, 17). They are mentioned in various contexts of Latin literature, for example as pets of personalities who taught them to speak, and mourned their death as that of a close friend (Ovid, *Amores*: II, 6; Statius, *Silvae*: II, 4). Statius describes his friend's beloved parrot as 'the Emperor with the emerald colour from the East', which greeted kings and said the name of Julius Caesar (*Silvae*: II, 4).The parrot in one of the mosaics from the Pergamene palace, dated to the mid 2nd century BC and now in the Pergamon Museum in Berlin, is one of the earliest depictions of parrots in

Greco-Roman art (Altertümer von Pergamon V, I, 61, pl. 15; cf. Toynbee 1973: 249; Kunze 1992: 72, Taf. 6). In Pompeii the birds appear on celebrated wall-paintings and mosaics (Hinks 1933: 26, no. 48; 28, fig. 28; Keller 1963: I, II, fig. 19), and one was copied in a famous work by Sosus (which did not survive), as described by Pliny (*Natural History*: XXXVI: 184).The parrot was also a favourite subject among gem engravers (Jereb, s.v. 'Papagei', in *RE*, Bd. 18.3 (1949): cols. 933, 934). Depictions of birds, including parrots, drawing carts were a source of amusement in the Roman world (Toynbee 1973: 280), and the same is true of other animals, especially larger ones, harnessed to *bigae*, and performing in circus events. For example a wall-painting from Herculaneum features a green parrot pulling a cart driven by a grasshopper (Reinach 1922: 365, no. 8). This motif originated in the Hellenistic period (Stuveras 1969: 96), and is common in the tombs of Myrina, where numerous figurines of animal-drawn carts were discovered, in the context of Eros Psychopompos (Mollard-Besques 1963: vol. II, fig. 76.a). However, this depiction gradually became part of the chariot-race motif, and Eros begun to appear as a charioteer (Stuveras 1969: 96). Many of the animals pulling carriages have a Dionysian context, including parrots, which were considered as a symbol of Dionysus (because of their Indian origin), and associating them with the god's journey to India (Middleton 1991: 66).

In the harnessing of animals to a chariot, and thus controlling them, we encounter Eros, the dominant god. He not only controls wild beasts but, indeed, all animals, demonstrating his immense powers, with which he also dominates the souls of men.

Roosters

A carnelian gem from the Israel Museum, which dates to 100 BC, depicts a rooster walking with a raised head (Figure 41). Roosters were a popular theme in Greek sculpture. They appear on a frieze from the end of the Archaic period from Xanthos, now in the British Museum, and in other works of art which emphasise its characteristics: it walks slowly with head up, and sometimes searches for food with his head bowed (Richter 1930: 39, fig. 213). A Hellenistic bronze statuette (perhaps a Roman copy) from the Metropolitan Museum features the rooster in a naturalistic way (Richter 1930: 40, fig. 215).

The rooster symbolised masculinity, and its enthusiasm for mating led him to be associated with fertility and love deities: it was identified with Priapus, Eros/Amor and Hermes/Mercury. Hermes' origins are as a Herm, a phallic stone column. The tradition of associating Hermes with the rooster is an ancient one, and had several meanings, based on rituals and the phallic associations of the rooster. There are gemstones which portray Hermes/Mercury as a human-

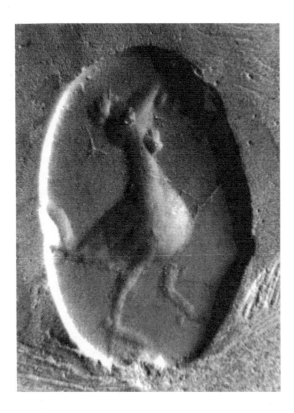

Figure 41. Rooster, impression of carnelian stone,
12 x 8 x 6.5 mm, 100 BC.
The Israel Museum Jerusalem,
The Harry Stern Collection,
bequeathed by Dr Kurt Stern,
London. In memory of his
parents and his brother
who perished at Sobibor.
IMJ76.42.2380. ©Photo: The
Israel Museum, Jerusalem.

headed rooster. Hermes as a rooster is also shown on other media, for example on a 1st-century AD bronze statue in the British Museum, and associated with phallic amulets hung in Roman houses (Furtwängler 1896: no. 7084; Spier 2010: 246–247, figs 3, 4). Priapus is sometimes depicted as a rooster as well, having a rooster's head, or holding a rooster (Baird 1982: 81–82, 85). The rooster was also ascribed with eschatological meanings since Antiquity, and identified with Hermes through his role as Psychopompos, because it woke the sleeping to their working day and the deceased for a new life, and was identified with and sacred to Demeter and Persephone as well, as one of the chthonic deities associated with the world of the dead (Goodenough 1953–1968: vol. III, 63, 66–67; Michaeli 2006: 360–376; Toynbee 1973: 257; Orth, s.v. 'Huhn', In *RE*, Bd. 8.2 (1913): cols. 2532–2533). An example of this can be seen in two terracotta reliefs from Persephone's temple in Locri Epizephirii, and now in the Archaeological Museum of Reggio Di Calabria. One represents Hermes holding a rooster in his right hand, and the other Persephone sitting next to Hades with a rooster beneath them (Goodenough 1953–1968: vol. III, 66–67, figs 36, 40; Michaeli 1998: 162). Already in Egypt the rooster has been identified with the gods Anubis and Osiris, deities related to the deceased and their rebirth (Gray, s.v. 'Cock', in Hastings, J. (ed.), *Encyclopedia of Religion and Ethics*, VIII, 1951), 694). The rooster had a dual meaning in Greece and Rome: he was associated with solar deities, with the rise of dawn and with light, and concurrently with the removal of darkness: therefore it is the companion of Apollo and Helios (Baird 1982: vols. 7–8, 81–82; Goodenough 1953–1968: vol. III, 60; Gray, 'Cock', 969; Cooper 1992: 54). Roosters were also raised in a temple erected in honour of Heracles and Hebe, as noted by Aelian (*De natura animalium*: XVII. 46). Roosters which lived in Heracles' compound used to cross the river that separates the two banks in order to mate with the hens which lived on Hebe's side. The relationship between fertility and birth, death and resurrection, is embodied in this literary depiction as well. The rooster's association with childbirth is specifically mentioned in Aelian, who specifies how the bird stood beside Leto when she gave birth to her twins – Apollo and Artemis (*De natura animalium*: IV. 29). Since then it was accepted as a bird assisting a woman in childbirth.

A quartz gem (Figure 42) in the Israel Museum bears a representation of a pair of roosters engaged in a cockfight. It is made in the 'Wheel Style', a style typified by parallel and short grooves, hence dates to the 1st century BC–AD 30 (Maaskant-Kleibrink 1978: 154–155).

Roosters were admired by the Greeks for their courage and fighting ability (Boardman 1968: 125). In Italy, they were reared already by the 2nd century BC, as Lucilius points out (*Carminum Reliquiae*, vol. I, Prolegomena and Text: 22, 300, 301). A depiction of two fighting roosters appears on a Greek-Persian gem in Leipzig from the end of the 5th century BC, engaging fiercely, with their heads down, beaks open, and neck feathers bristling (Richter 1930: 40, fig. 216). This is an early example, foreshadowing the later famous groups of cockfights carved on the chair of Dionysus' priest in the Athens Theater (Risom, Le Siège du prêtre de Dionysos, In A. Picard (ed.), *Mélanges Holleaux* (1913): pls. IX–XI; cf. Richter 1930: 40). The theme of the cockfight was common on engraved gems, for example a Roman gem from Lippold's catalogue (1923: Taf. XCVI, 6), where

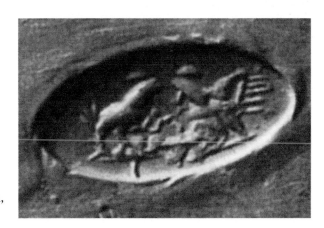

Figure 42. Pair of roosters engaged in a cockfight, impression of quartz stone, 20 x 11 x 5 mm, 1st century BC–AD 30.
The Israel Museum Jerusalem, Bequest of Mr. Adolphe Doreen, Paris.
IMJ70.62.370.
©Photo: The Israel Museum, Jerusalem.

a pair of roosters stand facing each other, among them a pilaster, and at their feet palm-branches.

In addition, it was associated with homosexual relations in ancient Greece, and was also considered an appropriate gift of love from older men to boys (Baird 1982: 83–84; Neils 1992: 37). Even though the primary meaning attributed to the rooster was erotic, it was also considered a symbol of victory (Saglio, s.v. 'Alektryonon agones', in Daremberg and Saglio (eds), *DAGR*, t. I, 1: 180–181; Schneider, s.v. 'Hahnenkämpfe', in *RE*, Bd. 7.2: cols. 2210–2215). Victory in cockfight was interpreted as a victory over death, since chthonic creatures such as the rooster and the mouse had a funerary meaning of protection against death, as in the Roman gem from Giroux that illustrates a pair of roosters in combat positions and between them a mouse (Guiraud 1996: 139–140, fig. 93). Many wall-paintings from ancient Greece depict cockfights, some of which may have taken place in the wrestling area where the men exercised, then bathed, put oil on their bodies and rested. It is not surprising, therefore, that the rooster, a fowl that inhabited spaces where men lived, and was perceived as a symbol of masculinity, was also considered an appropriate gift of love in homosexual relationships (Klinger 1999: 25). As illustrated by a red-figure kylix (Klinger 1999: ill. 53*), and according to many studies on the subject (Hoffmann 1974: 195–220; Koch-Harnack 1983), the rooster is usually held by the older suitor, often bearded, the *erastes*, and he brings it to his young lover, the *eromenos* The erotic significance of these depictions is probably the reason for the popularity of the rooster's appearances on small pottery objects, such as a Corinthian alabastron, from around 600 BC, and similar vessels that contained fragrant oils that were often used by young men during their erotic encounters (Klinger 1999: 25, ill. 54).

Columella notes that in his time there were professional trainers of roosters (*lanistae*), and that betting would take place on cockfights (*De re rustica (On Agriculture)*: VIII, 2, 5; Varro, *De re rustica*: III, 9, 5). A relief from the Greco-Roman period (now in the Evangelical School in Smyrna, Turkey) bears a representation of a victorious rooster walking arrogantly to the left and holding a large palm-branch (Keller 1963 (1909): I, II, 132, fig. 34). A cockfight with four participants, three defeated roosters on the left, while the winner stands on a golden goblet on the right, is depicted in a mural from 'Casa dei Vetti' in Pompeii (Nappo 2000: 133, fig. 133; P. Ducati: 1942, pl. 103). On a small table behind the roosters sacred objects are shown, an athlete's or a god's figurine and a palm-branch; another palm-branch is seen behind the winning rooster. In another work from Pompeii, a mosaic from the 'House of the Labyrinth', two roosters are depicted, with a palm-branch, a pouch and a *caduceus* of Hermes/Mercury on the table behind the fowls, so there may have been some religious significance to the mosaic.

Figure 43. rooster and a scorpion, impression of carnelian
stone, 3rd century AD.
The Israel Museum Jerusalem, Bequest of Mr. Adolphe Doreen,
Paris. IMJ70.62.396. ©Photo: The Israel Museum, Jerusalem.

In another gem from the Israel Museum (Figure 43), a rooster stands in the
foreground, about to attack a scorpion of equal size. The gem is made of carnelian
and is cut in an octagonal form, dating accordingly from the 3rd century AD
(M. Henig, personal communication, September 2011). It is interpreted as
the triumph of light and good (the rooster) over evil (the scorpion). In most
cultures of the Near East, the rooster is considered to possess solar significance,
as it is dedicated to the sun, which it welcomes at dawn – thus expelling night's
forces, and, metaphorically, death itself. The rooster was also considered to
have apotropaic powers (Bonner 1950: 125–127).

Two gems from the Israel Museum feature a rooster with a mouse: the first – in
red jasper one, dates to the end of the 2nd century AD (Figures 44a and b) and
portrays a rooster preying upon a mouse; the second example dates to the third
century AD[21] and is made of carnelian (Figure 45); it bears a representation of a
mouse riding a rooster and whipping it. A pair of gems from the Sa'd collection

---

[21] The red jasper gem (Figures 44a and b) is engraved in the 'Small Grooves Style' and is therefore
dated to the 2nd century AD (Maaskant-Kleibrink 1978: 251–252). In addition, red jasper was
particularly prevalent in the 2nd century AD (Guiraud 1996: 95; Maaskant-Kleibrink 1978: 251–
285). The carnelian gem (Figure 45) is cut in an octagonal form and dates accordingly to the 3rd
century AD (M. Henig, personal communication, September 2011). See also Goldman 2014: 164.

of Gadara in Transjordan (today near the Jordanian town of Um-Qais) bear a
similar iconography and date (Henig and Whiting 1987: pls. 382–383).

Figure 44a. Rooster preying
upon a mouse, red jasper,
13 x 9.5 x 3 mm, 2nd century AD.
The Israel Museum Jerusalem.
Bequest of Mr. Adolphe Doreen,
Paris. IMJ70.62.330.
© Photo: The Israel Museum,
Jerusalem.

Figure 44b. Rooster preying
upon a mouse, drawing.
©Drawing: The Israel
Museum, Jerusalem, by Pnina
Arad.

Figure 45. Mouse riding on a
rooster, carnelian,
12.5 x 10 x 3.5 mm,
3rd century AD.
The Israel Museum Jerusalem.
Bequest of Mr. Adolphe
Doreen, Paris. IMJ70.62.363.
©Photo: The Israel Museum,
Jerusalem.

The rooster, as mentioned, was associated with daybreak, with light (Gray 1951: 969; Bonner 1950: 125–127; Orth 1913: cols. 2532–2533), while a mouse, in contrast, was considered a chthonic creature (Aelian, *De natura animalium*: XII. 5). Consequently, this depiction of a rooster preying upon a mouse was perceived as the victory of good over evil and of life overcoming darkness (Henig 1997: 47). The second gem, bearing a representation of a mouse riding a rooster, is considered as apotropaic, since, according to Plutarch, whatever is curious was thought to attract and neutralise the baleful stare of the 'evil-eye' away from the wearer (*Moralia*, vol. VIII, 'Quaestiones convivales': V.7.681; see also Henig 1977: 47). Similar gems featuring a mouse riding a chariot drawn by a pair of roosters are found in the Sa'd collection and in Lippold's catalogue (1923: Taf. XCVI, 12; Henig and Whiting 1987: pls. 380–381). Some of the gems bearing curious depictions probably had additional cryptic meanings: mice, for example, being considered chthonic creatures, could therefore indicate the power of life and productivity, in coming from the realm of Demeter, and perhaps even implying the mysteries of Eleusis and hence rebirth, as noted by Henig. In addition, these gems could also have been used as love charms: mice are both nocturnal and domestic, and therefore could remind the gem wearer of his beloved, whom he would meet in his home at night (Henig 1997: 47–48); the rooster has phallic associations and is linked to love and fertility deities (Aelian, *De natura animalium*: XVII. 46; IV. 29; Baird 1982-1982: 81–82, 85; Spier 2010: 246–247, figs 3, 4).

Geese

A carnelian gem from the Israel Museum (Figures 46a and b) bears a representation of Juno holding a sceptre in her right hand, and in her left a small vase handed down to the goose standing beside her with open wings. This gem is an 18th-century copy of ancient depictions of this motif (M. Henig, personal communication, September 2011).

A flying goose appears, for example on an onyx gem which dates to the second half of the 5th century BC (Richter 1930: 81, fig. 195). This modern gemstone mimics a classical composition appearing, for instance, on a cylinder-shaped carnelian in the Ashmolean Museum in Oxford, which features a woman with a heron (Boardman 1970: pl. 640). The geese were considered sacred to Juno, the goddess of marriage and childbirth. No doubt pet animals on gems, such as geese for instance, allude to fecundity (Henig 2006: 63, fig. 12). In Henig's opinion, these were mostly gifts of love, or marriage, and were used as jewellery rather than seals (Henig 2006: 57–66). Thus, for example, a naked Aphrodite with a goose appear on a sardonyx in the Metropolitan Museum, a Roman copy of a Hellenistic gem that dates to the 1st century BC – 2nd century AD.

Figure 46A. Juno and a goose, carnelian, 13 x
15 mm, 18th century.
The Israel Museum Jerusalem, The Harry
Stern Collection, bequeathed by Dr Kurt
Stern, London. In memory of his parents
and his brother who perished at Sobibor.
IMJ76.42.2480. ©Photo: The Israel Museum,
Jerusalem, by Vladimir Naikhin.

Figure 46b. Impression of the
carnelian stone.
©Photo: The Israel Museum, Jerusalem,
by Vladimir Naikhin.

Therefore, the meaning behind these miniature objects is personal to their
wearer, and impregnated with human passions and emotions. The epigrams
written by Posidippus in the 3rd century BC reinforce Henig's argument, since
they deal with gemstones and their personal significance for humans (*Posidippi
Pellaei quae supersunt omnia*: Poems 1–20).

Swans

On a 1st-century AD chrome chalcedony gem from the Israel Museum,[22] inlaid
in a Roman gold ring, a nude Leda is depicted standing with a large swan that is
coupling with her (Figure 47). The myth of Leda and the Swan is related to love,
and is common on gems, apparently as a gift of love or marriage (Henig 2006:
64). Myths engaging with deities and animals constituted an endless source of
inspiration for gem devices, as well as other media. Some common myths, for

---

[22] This material is very rare in gem use; its green colour is due to a large amount of chromium. In
her study, Maaskant-Kleibrink confirmed Furtwängler's dating of the chrome chalcedony to the
1st century AD (Maaskant-Kleibrink 1975: 168). See 'kleine Praser', Furtwängler 1900: vol. 3, 309.

example, include Europa riding on the back of the bull Zeus; Zeus taking the form of a swan to seduce Leda (as on this gem); Artemis turning Actaeon into a stag; and Athena turning Arachne into a spider.

Leda, the daughter of the Etolian King Thestius, and wife of King Tyndareos of Sparta, was mentioned in legend as the mother of Clytemnestra and other heroines, but she is much better known as the mother of the Dioscouri and Helen. In early Greek myths, Helen was regarded as the daughter of Nemesis; Leda was initially only a nurse to the famous beauty. It was said that Nemesis once transformed herself into a goose and in this shape was seduced by Zeus, who had taken the shape of a swan for the occasion. The result of this coupling was a large egg. Leda found the egg and took care of it, and Helen emerged from it subsequently. A carnelian gem (50 BC–AD 50) in the Kestner Museum, Hanover, features this version of Leda discovering Helen hatching from the egg of Nemesis (Maaskant-Kleibrink 1999: 19, fig.1). The story in which Zeus, in the shape of a swan, seduced Leda, seems to be of later date and it is thought that it only became popular as a result of Euripides' famous play about Helen (Maaskant-Kleibrink 1999: 19). Over time a story was introduced in which not only Helen but also her brothers, the Dioscouri, were hatched from eggs. However, the seduction scene is almost

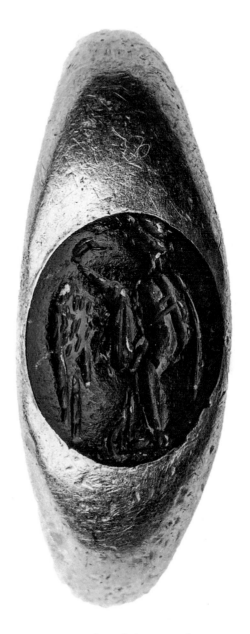

Figure 47. Leda and the swan, chrome chalcedony, 13 x 15 mm, 1st century AD. The Israel Museum Jerusalem, The Harry Stern Collection, bequeathed by Dr Kurt Stern, London. In memory of his parents and his brother who perished at Sobibor. IMJ76.42.2441. ©Photo: The Israel Museum, Jerusalem.

entirely absent from Classical iconography, except for an askos, dating from 400 BC, where a swan is seen approaching Leda, who is sitting on a rock, while a vase of the 4th century BC features a swan approaching a seated woman as she lifts her mantle (Kahil, s.v. 'Leda', *LIMC*, (1992): VI). The motif of Leda and the Swan first appears in statues from the end of the 5th century BC and continues throughout the 4th century BC; some scholars believe that the gems on which the subject is depicted mimic these sculptures (Dierichs 1990: 37–50). Nevertheless, the dominant theme in the representations of the statues is that of a swan who seeks protection under Leda's garment, and the seduction is either non-existent or merely subtly implied. In addition, while in the sculptures the emphasis is on the depiction of the draperies, and also the swan is relatively small, on gems the swan is larger and the contrast between its sharp beak and feathery wings and the smooth body of the naked Leda is evident. The portrayals of Leda on gems are also very reminiscent of how Aphrodite is depicted. These differences in the representation of the subject in sculpture versus gems become clear in light of the purpose of the rings on which the subject appears: they were given as gifts of love and thus their erotic and sensual content can be explained. In addition, it should be remembered that the sculptures were designed for temples or public places, whereas the gems were personal objects (Maaskant-Kleibrink 1999: 19). An important change in the concept of this motif of the swan being sheltered by Leda began in the Hellenistic period, when the swan started to be portrayed as larger, and clearly coupling with the heroine, as demonstrated in a Greek bronze mirror in Berkeley and dated to the 4th century BC (Kahil, s.v. 'Leda', *LIMC*, (1992): no. 19), and also a Roman copy of a sculpture in the Correr Museum, Venice (Prieur 1988: 61). Many gems dating from the Republic and Imperial periods are influenced by this Hellenistic invention of a standing, nude woman coupling with a swan of the same size as herself. In these gems the posture of Leda usually looks awkward, because she has to bend her body to the swan (Maaskant-Kleibrink 1999: 20). This is exactly the case with the gem from the Israel Museum as well. Other renderings of the motif on intaglios include a crouching and bathing Leda with swan; Leda reclining, coupling with a swan; and Leda with swan in a sanctuary (Maaskant-Kleibrink 1999: 20–22, figs. 4–12). In addition, it is interesting to note that at Lons-le Saunier a proportionally large amount of costly green ringstones were found. Guiraud denotes that the stones are small and set in gold rings which belonged to women. Similar very small green stones are listed in Furtwängler's catalogue under 'kleine Praser' (Maaskant-Kleibrink 1999: 21). The motif of Leda coupling with the swan continues into Late Antiquity and the Medieval Christian West. There is evidence that a large number of Medieval rulers and high dignitaries of the Church adopted ancient gems as their personal seals. The Deacon André of Soisson, for example, sealed his documents with an intaglio of Leda and the Swan (Soeda 1987: 185). Clement of Alexandria severely criticises the use of such 'immoral' subjects as classical figures and strongly attacked those with signet rings showing the image of Leda and the Swan (*Paedagogus*: III, 9). However, it is tempting to regard them as symbols of the 'immaculate conception', as suggested by the authors of the *LIMC* entry on Leda (Kahil, s.v. 'Leda', *LIMC*, (1992): 246; cf. Maaskant-Kleibrink 1999: 22).

Insects

Ants

Two gems from the Israel Museum bear a representation of an ant: the first is made of carnelian and dates to the 2nd century AD; it portrays Ceres wearing a thin cloth, holding ears of corn and a cake, with a star to her right and an ant below (Figure 48). The second example is made of agate and shows an ant with a grain of wheat in its mouth; this dates to the 1st–2nd century AD (Figures 49a and b). The gems were dated stylistically according to the classification developed by Marianne Maaskant-Kleibrink (1978), as their archaeological context is unknown.[23] A close look at the carving technique of gem no. 70.62.352 shows it to have been modelled with a rounded drill. The rather schematised

Figure 48. Ceres holding ears of corn, with an ant below, impression of carnelian stone, 2nd century AD. The Israel Museum Jerusalem, Bequest of Mr. Adolphe Doreen, Paris. IMJ70.62.352. ©Photo: The Israel Museum, Jerusalem.

---

[23] Maaskant-Kleibrink classified the gems according to style and engraving technique rather than workshop, as it was clear that they had been executed in different provinces. In addition, the material and the shape of the stones themselves have helped in establishing the correct date, or at least an approximate one, since different materials were typical of different periods. These features were highly dependent on changes in 'fashion' and related to different shapes of finger-rings (Maaskant-Kleibrink 1978: 59–61).

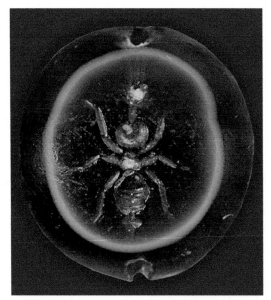

Figure 49a. Ant with a grain of
wheat, agate, 11.5 x 11 x 3.5 mm,
1st–2nd century AD.
The Israel Museum Jerusalem,
Bequest of Mr. Adolphe Doreen,
Paris. IMJ70.62.361.
©Photo: The Israel Museum,
Jerusalem, by Vladimir Naikhin.

Figure 49b. Impression of the agate
stone.
©Photo: The Israel Museum,
Jerusalem, by Vladimir Naikhin.

style, and especially the prominent hair-roll around the head, are suggestive of
the 'Imperial Cap-With-Rim Style', as defined by Maaskant-Kleibrink, and date
such gems to the end of the 1st–2nd centuryAD (Maaskant-Kleibrink 1978: 302).
However, since the goddess Ceres began to appear on gems only from the 2nd
century AD (Henig 1978: 32), the Jerusalem gem is dated to this era.

The second gem (Figures 49a and b) is made in the 'Imperial Classicising Style', and
hence dated to the 1st–2nd century AD (Maaskant-Kleibrink 1978: 194–197). Very
similar in iconography and date are gems showing ants in the Fitzwilliam Museum
(Henig 1994: 174, no. 378) and the Ashmolean Museum (Boardman and Vollenweider

1978: vol. 1, cat. 339). The ant was associated with Ceres/Demeter, probably because these insects inhabit fields of cereals, as illustrated on a gem from the Metropolitan Museum featuring the goddess in a field with a large ant (Richter 1956: Pl. XLV: 346). An ant with a grain of wheat in its mouth being a distinct symbol of Ceres/Demeter, it is therefore most likely that the designs of both gems were chosen by their owners as means of divine protection by the goddess associated with good harvests, the renewal of nature, and fertility. The ant is a symbol of diligence and productivity, and therefore of abundance, good luck and prosperity (Aelian, *De natura animalium*: II. 25, VI. 43; Keller 1963 (1909): ii, 416 ff). Ants could also represent wealth achieved through hard work, as recounted in the myth of Midas, whereby they brought him bean pods as a child, and thus predicted his future riches (Fronto, Marcus Cornelius, *The Correspondence, Ad Verum*: 2, 8).

Marine creatures

Dolphins

The dolphin is considered the monarch of the Mediterranean, leading humans on their sea voyages, helping them predict the weather, and in times of danger even carrying them to the shore and saving their lives. Pliny attributes human qualities to dolphins, such as intelligence, loyalty, determination, and love for music (*Natural History*: IX.8). Plutarch also mentions a number of cases in which dolphins saved people from drowning, or helped them in other ways (*Moralia, vol. XII*, 'The E at Delphi': 984A–985C).

Aristotle is fascinated by the speed of the dolphin (*Historia animalium*: 48), and Oppian notes that the dolphin is more divine than all other creatures (*Halieutica*: I, 648, 660–663). According to Aelian, dolphins treat their dying companions with great affection and will not abandon them at the time of death, sometimes even bringing their dead ashore, trusting that humans will give them a proper burial (*De natura animalium*: XII. 6).

A carnelian gem from the Israel Museum bears a representation of Eros riding a dolphin and holding a trident in his hand (Figure 50). It is carved in the 'Imperial Cap-With-Rim Style' and hence dated to the 1st century AD (Maaskant-Kleibrink 1978: 302). On gemstones cupids are often portrayed riding on the backs of dolphins.[24] Very similar in iconography and date is a plasma gem once kept at the Royal Coin Cabinet, The Hague, and now in the Rijksmuseum van Oudheden, Leiden (Maaskant-Kleibrink 1978: fig. 510a–b). Representations of Eros with a dolphin on engraved gems can be found from the 5th century BC onwards (Boardman 1970: pl. 691).

---

[24] Roman examples are many, to name a few: Henig 1994: 149, cat. 305; Zwierlein-Diehl 1973: vol. 1, fig. 198, pl. 33; Walters 1926: fig. 1493; Sena-Chiesa, 1966: figs 280, 281.

This motif first appeared on red-figure vases, for example on a cup dated to 520 BC in Palermo (Greifenhagen 1957: fig. 26). Later, these depictions of Eros riding

Figure 50. Eros riding a dolphin, carnelian, intaglio and impression, 11.5 x 10 x 2 mm, 1st century AD. The Israel Museum Jerusalem, Bequest of Mr. Adolphe Doreen, Paris. IMJ70.62.393. ©Photo: The Israel Museum, Jerusalem.

a dolphin also include some of Eros' first representations as a child (Hoorn 1951: fig. 370). One of the early portrayals (5th century BC) of this latter scene on intaglios appears in a silver ring from Rhodes, now in the British Museum (Furtwängler 1900: vol. 1, pl. 13.31). This theme is also known in various media. For example the famous Delos mosaic, from the end of the Hellenistic period, showing the god riding on two dolphins (Hermary, Cassimatis and Vollkommer, s.v. 'Eros', In *LIMC* (1981): III, 164). The subject is also depicted on coins, mainly from coastal cities, such as those of Carteia in Spain, and Paestum in southern Italy (Plant 1979: nos 1713, 1717). Important sources for the depictions of the subject are terracotta figurines, usually found in tombs, especially in Myrina in Asia Minor (Mollard-Besques 1963: fig. 76.d). This leads to a discussion of the meaning of Eros riding a dolphin motif as a funerary image. In this context, there is an analogy between Pegasus, who carries souls to heaven, and the dolphin leading them to the Islands of the Blessed (Stuveras 1969: 159; Toynbee 1973: 207). During the Hellenistic period the role of the dolphin is strengthened as a funerary symbol and is interpreted as a carrier of the deceased. Eros, who is commonly seen riding a dolphin during this period, is integrated within the funerary symbolism (Toynbee 1973: 206).

In Roman art, cupids riding on dolphins are also common themes, for example on a wall-painting from Herculaneum, in which Galatea's message to Polyphemus is conveyed by a cupid riding a dolphin (Reinach 1922: 172, no.3). Two cupids are shown riding dolphins in the 'Villa of the Nile' mosaic in Leptis Magna (Aurigemma 1960: pls. 87, 88), and a cupid riding a dolphin is the central panel of a mosaic (160 AD) at Fishbourne Roman palace, near Chichester (Cunliffe 1971: colour plate I). The funerary aspect is prevalent during the Roman period as well, especially after the 2nd century AD, when the depiction of cupid riding a dolphin frequently appears on sarcophagi, especially those of children (Huskinson 1996: 4.2, pl. 10.1). As can be seen on one of these sarcophagi, the journey to the Underworld, or the Islands of the Blessed, is depicted (Stuveras 1969: fig. 74). Two Erotes riding on dolphins are shown; and also Hermes Psychopompos, the leader of souls, identified by his caduceus. Since Eros represents the soul, Eros riding a dolphin represents the soul's journey to the Islands of the Blessed (Henig 1978: 44). The dolphin could be regarded as a symbol of rebirth into the Afterlife, and the creature stands for life and good fortune (Henig 1977: 348; 1997: 48).

When examining the appearance of this motif in the Roman period, the new images created by the Battle of Actium and Octavian's victory should be noted. Dolphins, hippocamps and other marine creatures became allusions to the victory at Actium. They appeared in both public and private works of art, including many seals (Zanker 1988: 12–13, 61, 82–84, figs 10, 47). But in later periods the significance of these symbols became more personal for the wearer, probably the journey over the sea to the Islands of the Blessed (Henig 1997: 52). The maritime victory is expressed in the statue of Augustus from Prima Porta, where Eros riding a dolphin is seen at the foot of the Emperor, also used as a support. The dolphin in this case is certainly used to mark the victory at Actium, and therefore is a political symbol. However, specifically here, Eros is more important than the dolphin, as he indicates that the originator of the Julio-Claudian dynasty, i.e. Augustus, is descended from the goddess Venus (Zanker 1988: 189, fig. 100). The Julii claimed a divine origin for their family, directly from Venus and Anchises, the father of Aeneas. In the 1st century BC, Augustus assigned Virgil to write the epic *Aeneid*, relating it to the foundation of Rome, and to connect the family to its divine ancestors, including Venus herself. Hence the importance of Eros (or Cupid in his popular Roman name) is well understood as the son of Venus as well as Mars (Zanker 1988: 193–195).

The dolphin is also associated with Apollo, confirmed by his epithet 'delphinios': in the Homeric hymn to Apollo, the god appeared to the sailors of the Cretan ship as a dolphin and ordered them to set up a temple in his honour in Delphi (*Homeric Hymns*, 'To Apollo': III, 391 ff). Apollo and the dolphin share their love for music (Aristophanes, *Frogs*: 1317–1318; Euripides, *Electra*: 435–436) and this is also the reason, according to Plutarch, that it is the god's favourite (*Moralia*, vol. XII, 'The E at Delphi': 984B–C). In addition, the myth of Arion is a well known, whereby a dolphin rescues the musician Arion from the pirates who plotted to kill him (Herodotus, *Historiae*: I.23–24; Pausanias, *Description of Greece*: III.25.7; Pliny, *Natural History*: IX.8, 27–28).

However, dolphins are first and foremost the companions of Venus, who is sometimes portrayed as Venus Marina, accompanied by Erotes on dolphins, as on a famous fresco from Pompeii from the 1st century AD. Another depiction appears in the 2nd-century AD statue of Aphrodite of Nysa-Scythpolis (Beth Shean), where Eros, riding a dolphin, serves as a support for the goddess (Foerster 2005: 3–14). Eros is seen here as a plump, winged child sitting on a dolphin, his left hand holding his fin, and his right hand holding the whip. For the love goddess, as Hesiod tells us, was born from the foam of the sea (*Theogonia*: 188–202). Hence the goddess is also deeply associated with dolphins and other marine creatures (Stebbins 1929: 83–84). The ancient sources also mention dolphins as servants of Venus (Gellius, Aulus, Noctes Atticae: VII, 8; Stuveras 1969: 159, n. 2, fig. 42). It was the presence of Eros during the birth of Venus (Hesiod, *Theogonia*: 201) that also connects him to the sea.[25] The representation

---

[25] The figure of Eros is rarely simply a decorative motif (Platt 2007: 89). Hesiod indicates in the *Theogony* (II. 116–129) that Eros was one of the primordial forces of nature, represented along

of Eros on a dolphin indicates that the young god is, among other things, his mother's servant and representative (Hermary, Cassimatis and Vollkommer, s.v. 'Eros', In *LIMC* (1981): III, 940). The connection between Eros and the dolphin can be summarised as signifying the control that the god exerts over the sea, as an epigram from the *Anthologia Graeca* (16.207) tells us:

'... [A]nd it is not without reason that he (Love) holds in his hands a dolphin and a flower, for in one hand he holds the earth, in the other – the sea.'

Those gems featuring cupids riding on the backs of dolphins could have been used as love charms, intended to evoke love (especially when also keeping in mind the dolphin allusion to friendship) (Henig 1997: 48). These gems needed to be given to the other person, either overtly or in secret, or worn by the owner of the object. If a gem depicting Eros – in a ring or an amulet – was worn by someone seeking to attract a lover, it is probable that the intention was for it to affect the target due to the latter's belief in the god Eros, and not merely through its amuletic or magical power. Nevertheless, sometimes people would rub or even kiss an amulet or an image on a ring (Marshman 2017: 142–146). An amber ring carved with the bust of Minerva from Carlisle had clearly been rubbed by its owner.[26]

Seashells

A gem of nicolo,[27] from the Israel Museum and dated to the 2nd century AD, shows an elephant emerging from a sea-shell (Figure 51). It is made in the 'Small Grooves Style' and hence dated to the 2nd century AD (Maaskant-Kleibrink 1978: 251–252). In addition, nicolo intaglios were chosen with special frequency by 2nd-century gem engravers (Henig 1984b: 244; Maaskant-Kleibrink 1978: 251–285).

There are other similar Roman gems depicting a shell from which an animal emerges: for example a gem from the Fitzwilliam Museum in Cambridge, which also dates to the 2nd century AD, features a shell with a rooster springing from it and catching a mouse (Henig 1994: 165, cat. 349); another example, from France, depicts a dog leaping from a shell (Guiraud 1996: 139, no. 94).

---

with Chaos, Gea and Tartaros as one of the most ancient deities that existed at the genesis of the Cosmos. His role was to arrange the elements that constituted the Universe. He brought harmony to chaos and enabled life to evolve. The power of Eros, the god of love, was regarded as immense, and was illustrated in the anthropomorphic myths associated with him (Boardman 1978: 20).
[26] I am indebted to Revd Dr Martin Henig for this helpful information.
[27] a Roman sardonyx with a bluish-white top layer and dark-blue/black bottom layer.

Figure 51. Elephant emerging from a sea-shell, nicolo, 2nd century AD.
The Israel Museum Jerusalem. Bequest of Mr. Adolphe Doreen, Paris.
IMJ70.62.371.
© Photo: The Israel Museum, Jerusalem.

The motif of an elephant emerging from a shell is a familiar one. This theme appears on engraved gems in various collections, while other objects, like a torch, a palm-branch, or a sheaf of wheat, are occasionally added with the elephant. All of these gems have been dated to the Imperial period, the end of the 1st – beginning of the 3rd century AD (Henig 1984b: 243–247, fig. 1a). Such depictions of the elephant and shell probably served an apotropaic function, similar to that of 'combination gems' (Henig 1984b: 244). Furthermore, both shells and elephants had a symbolic significance in Antiquity. The sea-shell represented the *uterus* from which life arises, and therefore constituted a powerful symbol of fertility and rebirth. An elephant emerging from a shell presents an apt symbol of rebirth, due both to its renowned longevity and to its being favoured by the sun-god (Henig 1978: 102; Henig 1984b: 244, 246). The *Caelestia Animalia* mentioned in an inscription dated AD 216, from Banasa in Mauretania, are thought to have been elephants (Scullard 1974: 254–259, cf. Henig 1984b: 244, note 8).

Hybrids

Sphinx

Sphinxes are depicted on four gems from the Israel Museum. Three feature a winged sphinx seated in profile in the foreground with unique hairstyles (Figures 52-54); and another has a naked sphinx seen leaping upon a nude warrior (Figure 55).

The agate gem (Figures 52a and b) is made in the 'Italic-Republic Pellet Style', dated accordingly to the 2nd– 1st centuries BC and marked by the stylistic

Figure 52a. Winged sphinx seated in profile, agate, 15X10 mm, 2nd – 1st century BC.
The Israel Museum Jerusalem, The Harry Stern Collection, bequeathed by Dr Kurt Stern, London. In memory of his parents and his brother who perished at Sobibor. IMJ76.42.2424. © Photo: The Israel Museum, Jerusalem, by Vladimir Naikhin.

Figure 52b. Impression of the agate stone. ©Photo: The Israel Museum, Jerusalem, by Vladimir Naikhin.

feature of numerous small pellets in the design (Maaskant-Kleibrink 1978: 131–132). Very similar in iconography, date and style is an onyx gem from the Merseyside Museum, Liverpool (Henig 1988: 253–254, fig. 2). Another agate gem (Figures 53a and b) originates from Chios and is inset in a modern ring. It dates to the 1st century BC by its circular shape, material and style. Banded agate gems were very popular in the 1st century BC, as well as the 'Wheel Style', noted for the short parallel grooves used to depict details such as hair and the folds of garments (Maaskant-Kleibrink 1978: 154–155).

Banded onyx and agate were especially popular from the 3rd century BC onwards, and particularly in the 1st century BC. Artists used to place the white stripe in the dark stone in the centre of the ring, exactly as it is seen in these gems (Figures 52a and b and 53a and b) from the Israel Museum. Also, the oval shape of the gem portrayed in figs. 52a and b and the round shape of figs. 53a

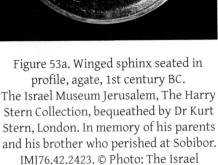

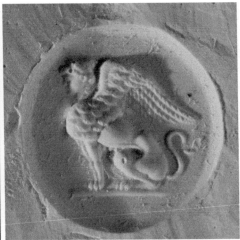

Figure 53a. Winged sphinx seated in profile, agate, 1st century BC. The Israel Museum Jerusalem, The Harry Stern Collection, bequeathed by Dr Kurt Stern, London. In memory of his parents and his brother who perished at Sobibor. IMJ76.42.2423. © Photo: The Israel Museum, Jerusalem, by Vladimir Naikhin.

Figure 53b. Impression of the agate stone. ©Photo: The Israel Museum, Jerusalem, by Vladimir Naikhin.

and b are forms which were favoured starting from the 1st century BC. The Archaistic style of the first gem (Figures 52a and b) can be explained in the context of a gem artist who deliberately worked in this style and used a motif that was familiar to him from contemporary sculptures and reliefs (Glynn 1982: 174–175). It is also possible to compare those gems to an Augustan gem from the Fitzwilliam Museum, also made in an Archaistic style (Henig 1994: 106–107, no. 195).

The winged sphinx on a carnelian gem has a headdress with diagonal lines across it, and feathers are seen above the forehead (Figures 54a and b), probably a remnant of the headdress sometimes used to characterise Egyptian sphinxes. A similar gem is held in the Archaeological Museum at Michigan State University, although its style is different (Bonner 1954: 145). Another example is an Augustan gem from the Fitzwilliam Museum, portraying a similar sphinx (Henig 1994: 121, no. 229). The gem from the Israel Museum is made in the 'Wheel Style', hence it is dated to the 1st century BC (Maaskant-Kleibrink 1978: 154–155).

The two gems from the Israel Museum (Figures 53a and b and figs. 54a and b) depict sphinxes, with wings drawn back, thus linking them to the type

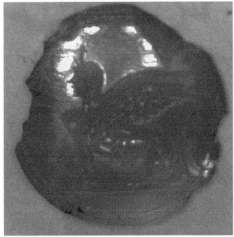 

Figure 54a. Winged sphinx seated in profile, carnelian, 1st century BC. The Israel Museum Jerusalem. Bequest of Mr. Adolphe Doreen, Paris. IMJ70.62.392. © Photo: The Israel Museum, Jerusalem.

Figure 54b. Impression of the carnelian stone. ©Photo: The Israel Museum, Jerusalem.

associated with the first seal of Augustus. Henig mentions a coin from England, on one side of which there is a sleeping dog (inscribed VERI for Verica), and on the reverse a sphinx with wings drawn back, a depiction associated with the first seal of Augustus, the origin of which was a coin, or, more likely, a gem (Henig 1988: 253).

The sphinx is depicted in the visual arts as a hybrid with a human head and a lion-like body. This figure first appeared in Egypt in the 3rd millennium BC and resembled a lion-like creature without wings and with a bearded, human head. It is mentioned in the *Pyramid Texts* under the name 'Lion-God', and is related to Atum, a connection that is also referenced in the *Book of the Dead*. The lion-god is interpreted as a guardian deity, just as the Great Sphinx of Giza guards the Kingdom of the Dead, or the pyramid of Pharaoh Khephren (Budge 2004 (1904): 361; Prieur 1988: 111). In the Eastern Mediterranean, the sphinx appeared less monumental than in Egypt and is more common on cylinder seals and amulets. Even though in Egypt the sphinx was depicted not only in a monumental context, but also as a favoured decorative motif on small objects such as beads, talismans and small bronze sculptures from earlier periods. The earliest sphinx amulet dates to 2134–2040 BC and is made of gold (Cherry 1995: 110).

From Egypt, the image of the sphinx spread to the Levant and the countries of the Eastern Mediterranean, and in the 14th century BC it spread throughout the

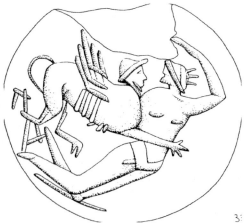

Figure 55a. Sphinx attacking a warrior, impression, late 2nd–3rd century AD. The Israel Museum Jerusalem. Bequest of Mr. Adolphe Doreen, Paris. IMJ70.62.331. © Photo: The Israel Museum, Jerusalem.

Figure 55b. sphinx attacking a warrior, drawing. ©Drawing: The Israel Museum, Jerusalem, by Pnina Arad.

Near East and Greece, but was slightly differently portrayed from its Egyptian image, and wings were added to it, which continued to characterise it later in Asia and the Classical world. Another innovation was a female sphinx, whose figure is depicted, for example, in frescoes from the palace of Zimri-Lim in Mari (18th century BC) and on carved-ivory plaques from Acham Huyuk, Anatolia (19th or 18th centuries BC) (Cherry 1995: 106). In Mesopotamia, representations of sphinxes are known from the first half of the 3rd millennium BC on cylinder seals. Later they appear on ivory, and in the first millennium BC they enclose the entrances to the palaces of the kings, although in a different form than the Egyptian sphinx (Cherry 1995: 112–113). In the Minoan period the sphinx was known, and is shown, for example, on a green jasper seal found by Sir Arthur Evans. Sphinx seals were also found at Mycenaean sites (Cherry 1995: 116). In Minoan and Mycenaean art, sphinxes also appear on vases, murals, figurines, bronzes and ivory plaques (Brodrick 1972: 102, fig. 47a; Higgins 1974 (1967): 130, 134, ills. 162, 163; Tsiafakis 2003: 93, 102, 116, 169, ills. 101, 134).

The sphinx arrived in Greece from Egypt in the 8th century BC, mediated by the Phoenicians who brought artefacts (on which sphinxes were depicted) by sea, although there is evidence of sphinx depictions on works of art from Crete as early as the 13th century BC (Klingender 1971: 63). Greek sphinxes began to appear in funerary contexts and as votive offerings in sacred precincts, and unlike the Egyptian sphinxes, they were winged and with a woman's head and breasts (Bevan 1986: 293–297, 302–303, 312–314; Cherry 1995: 118). The sphinxes in Greece were regarded as temple keepers and in the funerary context they functioned as grave-guardians and protectors of the dead (Tsiafakis 2003: 82). Since the sphinx preserved temples and tombs, it is possible to assume that a gem engraved with a sphinx was believed to protect its wearer (Henig 1997: 45, 48). The funerary importance of the sphinx is related to its demonic aspect, that is, its apotropaic function. The sphinx repelled the 'Evil Eye' by forcing the observer to keep a distance. This prophylactic role is implied in its use on warriors' helmets for example (Kourou, Komvou, Raftopoulou, Krauskopf and Katakis, s.v. 'Sphinx', In *LIMC*, vol. VIII (1), (1997): 1152–1153, nos 8, 38, pl. 794).

The depictions of the sphinx in Rome are probably copies from a Greek source from the Classical period that was the height of a standing man. The appearance of the motif so frequently in miniature art reinforces the assumption that the original was a famous monument. Perhaps it was even one of the statues given by Augustus as a gift to the temple of Apollo on the Palatine Hill. In this case it should be seen as a deliberate and intelligent political image (Zanker 1988: 271–272, figs. 212, 213). In 30 BC, when Egypt became a Roman province, the cult of Isis and Osiris became more popular and important than ever before, and as a result Egyptian monuments and artefacts became very popular in Rome (Cherry 1995: 119–121). On a sphinx represented on coins from this period, such as a coin from Pergamon, one can see a declaration of a new era in the Augustan period, with the sphinx becoming a symbol of hope (Zanker 1988: 48, fig. 36b). But as early as 42 BC, Augustus began to use the sphinx as his seal, a symbol of the *regnum Apollinis*, which the sibyl had predicted to him (Pliny, *Natural History*: XXXVII.1, 10; Suetonius, *De vita caesarum: Augustus*: 50; Virgil, *Eclogues*: 4). According to Pliny, at the beginning of his career Augustus found among his mother's rings two identical seals on which sphinxes were carved. During the civil wars his personal advisers used one of them in his absence, to sign letters and proclamations, which the circumstances demanded be sent in his name. In later years Augustus replaced the sphinx device with that of Alexander the Great (Pliny, *Natural History*: XXXVII.1, 10). In any event, the sphinx soon became a common motif for various media of Augustan art, as shown, for example, on furniture, as well as on a gem from Hanover (Zanker 1988: 50, fig. 38, 269–273, figs 211a and b).

The fourth gem bears a representation of a sphinx attacking a warrior, both of them nude (Figures 55a and b). It is reasonable to assume that such a depiction is derived from Archaic gems, such as the London one, showing a similar iconography (Boardman 1968: 251). An Augustan gem from the Fitzwilliam Museum features a sphinx standing on its hind legs and placing its front paws against the chest of a naked young man who kneels before her (Henig 1994:

106–107, no. 195). Unlike the Jerusalem gem, the young man does not appear to be so threatened, and the riddling between Oedipus and the sphinx is probably depicted here. The Israel Museum gem is made in the 'Chin-Mouth-Nose Style', belonging to the 'Imperial Coarse Styles' (late 2nd–3rd century AD), as defined by Maaskant-Kleibrink (Maaskant-Kleibrink 1978: 294, 320–325, nos 978–980). In this style the figures are engraved in a very slapdash manner. The figures consist of only a few lines that are often incoherently joined together. The attributes of the figures are usually represented by no more than a line or scratch. Many of the designs on these ringstones are impossible to make out unless one has recourse to similar designs on better-quality intaglios. It therefore seems that the Jerusalem gem can be dated to the 2nd–3rd centuries AD.

In the 7th century BC, the Greek artists first began to depict the sphinx in a narrative context, rather than as part of animal friezes. Two of the earlier representations of sphinxes in the context of death of youth are a Laconian ivory comb from 650 BC and a Mycenaean architectural relief from c. 630 BC. Its demonic aspect is obvious, and perhaps linked to Ker, the Homeric demon of death (*Iliad*: 2.302, 3.454, 11.332, 12.326–327). In the 6th century BC the theme evolved considerably and the sphinx is presented as chasing or abducting young boys, as seen, for example, on a kylix in the Getty Museum (Tsiafakis 2003: 81, fig. 7). The model is taken from Near Eastern art and appears in many Phoenician and Egyptian works of art, as demonstrated in a small ivory statuette dating from 1640–1532 BC, and showing a sphinx holding between its paws a human victim (Cherry 1995: 110).

In Greek art the subject appears in various media starting from 560 BC, including gems, bronze shields, and vases. The theme was particularly popular during the Late Archaic period (500–480 BC) (Tsiafakis 2003: 80). At the beginning of the Classical period depictions begin to appear on vase paintings of sphinxes flanking scenes of battle, or hunting, their role being to transfer the dead to the Underworld (Tsiafakis 2003: 81). Boardman believes that on gems prior to the beginning of the 5th century BC, the sphinx carrying a dead boy was considered to be the 'Sphinx of Thebes', taking its toll before Oedipus solves the riddle (Boardman 1980: 111).

Aeschylus mentions the appearance of the theme on shields (*Seven against Thebes*: 541–545), and Euripides describes a sphinx carrying its victim on the helmet of Achilles (*Electra*: 471). On attic vase paintings, the subject was interpreted as the Athenian *Ephebos* awaiting its inauguration as a *Hoplite* (Tsiafakis 2003: 81). Another proposed interpretation is that the sphinx is capable of being an interlocutor – both erotic and dangerous – for youth, posing them riddles on masculinity, while they are still inexperienced (Vermeule 1979: 171). In some scenes the erotic allusions are clear and explicit, with the sphinx straddling the nude man (Tsiafakis 2003: 81, fig. 7). A series of gems from Zazoff's catalogue features a female sphinx straddling a nude man in a distinctly erotic gesture (Zazoff 1983: Taf. 26, 7–9). Among all the winged lovers and demons of death, the sphinx is the most erotic – when the dead are her victims as well as lovers (Zazoff 1983: Taf. 26, 7–9). Sometimes she is referred to as the 'female hound of Hades', Cerberus' female counterpart (in myth she is his niece) (Vermeule 1979: 171). There is a combination of predator (with its claws and wings) and a beautiful face, made for love, and thus an imprudent young man, boasting of his wisdom, might end his life devoured in her lair, which is a brothel filled with bones (Vermeule 1979: 171). Another example of a sphinx kidnapping a young warrior, armed and naked, although trying to fight back, appears on a gem dating from the beginning of the 5th century BC (Vermeule 1979: 173, fig. 24). A depiction of a young man who is still alive and fighting back, armed and ready to protect himself, was a new concept in that period. An unarmed young man in front of a sphinx appears again only later, during the Classical period, in the group planned by Phidias for the throne of Zeus at Olympia (Boardman 1980: 112). The theme of the abducting sphinx was both a popular and important one among the Greeks, appearing on various media, from Archaic gems to large compositions, such as that which once adorned the throne of Zeus of Phidias at Olympia, and copied in Ephesus, and should be seen as expressing a meditation on death (Pausanias, *Description of Greece*: could be seen as an act of love, despite being painful). The death envoy is always winged and can protect the body, sitting astride her, as a battle comrade, or even to mate with it. The sphinx was regarded as resourceful, and could therefore instruct mortals on how to handle this unknown situation (Vermeule 1979: fig. 23).

Pegasus

A horse's swiftness and grace are reminiscent of flight, and the myth of a winged horse, which existed in many ancient cultures, is a natural step in terms of recognising its great turn of speed. The winged horse first appeared in Mesopotamia in the 2nd millennium BC, and can be seen, for example, on cylinder seals from the Middle Assyrian period (Johns 2006: 168–171). Later, in the New Assyrian period, the horse was associated with the sun-god Shamash. The mythological flying horse is depicted in the visual arts of Greece, from the 7th century BC onward, as a male horse with waved wings, usually appearing in profile, walking proudly or lifting its front hoofs up in an aggressive posture. The winged horse Pegasus emerged, along with his brother Chrysaor, from the neck of the Gorgon Medusa (and fertilised from the seed of Poseidon), when Perseus beheaded her (Hesiod, *Theogonia*: 276–281). Hesiod also indicates that Pegasus was the bearer of Zeus' thunderbolts (*Theogonia*: 285–286). In

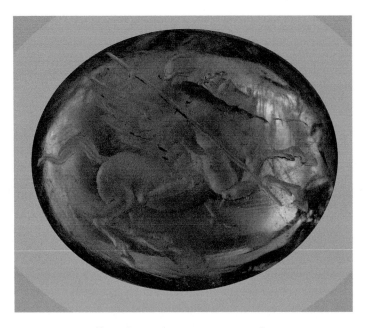

Figure 56a. Bellerophon riding Pegasus, amethyst, 17 x 14 x 5
mm, 1st century BC – 1st century AD.
The Israel Museum Jerusalem, previously in the Bezalel
Collection. IMJ76.42.2425. ©Photo: The Israel Museum,
Jerusalem, by Vladimir Naikhin.

Figure 56b. Impression of the amethyst stone.
©Photo: The Israel Museum, Jerusalem, by Vladimir Naikhin.

Bellerophon, a play by Euripides that did not survive, Pegasus is described as pulling the 'thunder vehicle' (Frag. 314 (Nauck); cf. McCartney 1924: 66). It was also believed in Greece that Pegasus was the storm cloud (Preller, *Griechische Mythologie*: I, 119; cf. McCartney 1924: 66). These functions found their way into the Roman world, and usually explained the depictions on coins, with one side showing Pegasus and on the reverse a thunderbolt (*A Catalogue of the Greek Coins in the British Museum, Corinth, Colonies of Corinth*: 95, nos 9, 10, 14, cf. McCartney 1924: 66). As the son of the sea god, Pegasus was particularly associated with springs and water sources. In Corinth there was a fountain believed to flow from its mouth (Pausanias, *Description of Greece*: II.3.5). When Pegasus struck his hoof into the ground on Mount Helicon, the famous eponymous source burst forth – the Hippocrene spring (Pausanias, *Description of Greece*: II.31.12; IX.31.3).The waters of the Hippocrene issue from the depths of the earth, so that this myth implies that Pegasus is somehow connected to the Underworld. Pegasus served as the horse of Eos, the goddess of dawn, leading souls to the Islands of the Blessed, and finally found its place in the sky as a constellation (Prieur 1988: 16, 142). Plato, speaking of true beauty, the higher soul, describes winged horses lifting their gaze to the sky, like birds, and reaching there (*Phaedrus*: 249 D). But the myths of Pegasus are related mainly to Bellerophon of Corinth, who had the task of killing the Chimera – the fire-breathing monster with the body of a lion, the head of a goat, and a tail that might end in a snake's head. According to the myth, the King Iobates of Lycia ordered Bellerophon to kill the Chimera, and with the help of Pegasus, the winged horse, the hero managed to kill the monster. No one could control the wondrous horse, but Athena came in a dream to Bellerophon, the grandson of Sisyphus, and gave him golden reins (Pausanias, *Description of Greece*: II.4.1). When he found Pegasus, peacefully drinking from a spring, the winged horse stood obediently and responded to the golden reins. Bellerophon took off on the horse, hovered over the Chimera, and shot her with a deadly arrow (Apollodorus, *Bibliotheca*: II.3.2). Similarly, the hero fought the Amazons (Pindar, *The Odes of Pindar, The Olympian Odes*: 13, 84–90). Later he was punished for trying to reach Olympus, beyond man's domain, and thus guilty of the sin of *hybris*. At the command of Zeus, Pegasus threw his rider and Bellerophon fell from on high to the ground (Pindar, *The Isthmian Odes*: 7.41–50). According to another version, when a dispute arose between Bellerophon and the gods, Pegasus threw his rider while in flight (Nonnos, *Dionysiaca*: 11.142; 28.167). Pegasus, however, reached Olympus and found his place within Zeus' stables and becoming immortal.

This mythical animal was very popular among the Greeks and Romans, and its figure decorated many vessels, mosaics, reliefs, coins, gemstones, and metal and stone carvings. As examples, this motif appears on a Carthaginian silver coin dating from 260 BC, on bronze vessels from 325–275 BC (with Bellerophon), as

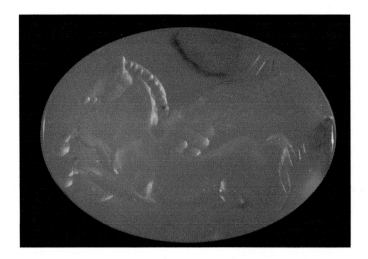

Figure 57a. Pegasus, carnelian, 13 x 9 x 4 mm, 1st century BC.
The Israel Museum Jerusalem, The Harry Stern Collection,
bequeathed by Dr Kurt Stern, London. In memory of
his parents and his brother who perished at Sobibor.
IMJ76.42.2484. © Photo: The Israel Museum, Jerusalem, by
Vladimir Naikhin.

Figure 57b. Impression of the carnelian stone.
©Photo: The Israel Museum, Jerusalem, by Vladimir Naikhin.

well as on the helmet of the statue of Mars Ultor (which copied that of Athena Parthenos), which was decorated with sphinxes and Pegasi (Johns 2006: 168– 172; Zanker 1988: 200, fig. 155). The winged horse usually appears alone, but is also sometimes depicted with other characters, for example when it drinks from the Pierian Spring as Bellerophon put his reins on him, or flies over the Chimera during the struggle (S. Hiller, *Bellerophon: Ein griechischer Mythos in der römischen Kunst*, 1970, cf. Toynbee 1963: 175).

An amethyst intaglio from the Jerusalem museum, dating to the 1st century BC – 1st century AD, depicts Bellerophon riding Pegasus, ready to kill the Chimera with his spear (Figures 56a and b).[28] A similar depiction appears on a 3rd-century BC garnet gem in the British Museum, although here the Chimera also appears (Adams 2011: 11, pl. 3). A 1st-century BC carnelian gem from the Israel Museum features Pegasus galloping to the left (Figures 57a and b). Similar examples are known from Dalmatia (Middleton 1991: no. 136), as well as another from the Caesarea collection (Hamburger 1968: 22, no. 146). Both Jerusalem gems are made in the 'Imperial Classicising Style', inspired by the Classical Greek art of the 5th and 4th centuries BC, especially from famous sculptures and reliefs, but this resuscitation of well-known Classical motifs was mixed with considerable Hellenistic influence (Maaskant-Kleibrink 1978: 195).

Gems depicting Pegasus, the Greek symbol of immortality, alone, or with Bellerophon, are common (Walters 1926: pl. XXIV: 1847–1850; Pegasus, and with Bellerophon pls. XXIV: 1912, XXXII: 3181).

Posidippus, the poet of the 3rd century BC, describes a dark-jasper gem portraying Pegasus rising into the sky while Bellerophon is thrown to the ground (*Posidippi Pellaei quae supersunt omnia*: 35, poem 14). It was believed that a gem engraved with Pegasus was especially beneficial for warriors, inspiring them with courage and speed (Soeda 1987: 186).

Capricorn

A carnelian gem in the Israel Museum bears a representation of a crab under a Capricorn (Figure 58). This gem can be assigned to the 'Small Grooves Style', characterised by rounded wheel grooves used for detailing, hence it can be

---

[28] Scenes on gems showing the killing of the Chimera recall later scenes of Christian saints killing dragons: this similarity is not coincidental. In the 4th century AD, when Christianity had already gained influence in the Roman world, this was one of the pagan scenes adopted by Christians and given a new interpretation. Bellerophon was interpreted as a symbol of Christ, and the Chimera as a symbol of evil. An example of this can be seen in a gold ring from Havering, Essex, dating to the 4th century AD and bearing a depiction of Bellerophon killing the Chimera (Johns 2006: 173).

dated to the 2nd–3rd century AD (see Maaskant-Kleibrink 1978, 251–252, 268, no. 727). These images refer to the zodiac signs of Cancer and Capricorn (Bonner 1950: 36). Sometimes gems were engraved with combinations of constellations that were apparently considered particularly suitable and meaningful for their owners (Henig 1997: 50). Capricorn, a creature with the head and front legs of a goat and the body and tail of fish, originated in the New Sumerian period, from the Mesopotamian hybrid of *suhurmasû*. The identification of the Capricorn with this creature was determined by a *kudurru* capital (a milestone) dating from 1155–1531 BC, and inscriptions set in Assyrian ritual ceremonies for such figurines. Researchers assume that there is a connection to the EA (Enki) deity, as there is an iconographic juxtaposition with the attributes of the antlered god, such as his standards and wands, and in addition the relationship is confirmed by texts. Although the Capricorn, functioning as an amulet, might also have been protective (usually appearing together with a merman in visual depictions), its purpose was to repel evil. For example Assyrian clay figurines of Capricorn and a merman are assumed to have been placed in a box of tiles buried in the foundations of a building to ward off evil. The Capricorn figure enjoyed popularity until the Hellenistic period, and even experienced a revival as Capricornus by the Romans (especially in the art of the Augustan period, as Capricorn was the astrological sign of the Emperor) (Black and Green 1992: 92–93, fig. 70).

This marine Mesopotamian monster evolved in ancient Greece into a friendly animal, which Eros can easily control and ride on, as part of a decorative pattern. According to one version Capricorn was created when Pan was attacked by the Typhon monster and jumped into the Nile: the parts of his body above water remained those of a goat, but those under water became those of a fish. Later on, of course, the Capricorn was to become a heavenly constellation (Hyginus, *L'Astronomie (Poetica astronomica)*: 2.18).

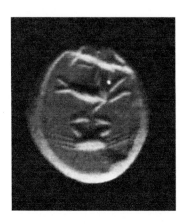

Figure 58. Capricorn and a crab, impression of a carnelian stone, 14 x 10 mm, 2nd–3rd century AD. The Israel Museum Jerusalem. Bequest of Mr. Adolphe Doreen, Paris. IMJ70.62.377. © Photo: The Israel Museum, Jerusalem.

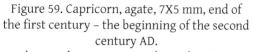

Figure 59. Capricorn, agate, 7X5 mm, end of
the first century – the beginning of the second
century AD.
The Israel Museum Jerusalem, The Harry
Stern Collection, bequeathed by Dr Kurt Stern,
London. In memory of his parents and his
brother who perished at Sobibor. IMJ76.42.2421.
© Photo: The Israel Museum, Jerusalem.

An agate gem from the Israel Museum features a Capricorn galloping to the right,
inlaid in a Roman ring (Figure 59). This gem can be dated to the end of the first
century and the early years of the second century AD because the gold ring is
probably Type III (see: Henig 2007, fig. 1, 9-12). Capricorn is commonly applied on
gems and is considered the astrological sign of Augustus. According to Suetonius,
Octavian met with the astrologer Theogenes in his youth, and the latter fell
to his knees after seeing the star map of his birth day. From that moment on
Octavian began to believe in the fate destined for him, until he publicised his
zodiac sign, and later on minted a silver coin featuring the Capricorn (Suetonius,
De vita caesarum: Augustus: 94). Capricorn does appear quite early on the coins
and glass beads that Augustus' followers wore as rings, as cheap substitutes
for precious gems. Capricorn also appeared on coins minted to perpetuate his
military victories and also as an image of peace, as a reminder that Augustus' role
as the saviour of the Empire was already written in the stars (Zanker 1988: 48,
fig. 36a). From 30 BC his birthday was officially celebrated as a day of good omen
(Zanker 1988: 48, 230–233). Therefore Capricorn on coins is oftenaccompanied by
attributes of Tyche-Fortuna, such as the wheel and the cornucopia – as appearing
on a *cistophorus* of 27–26 BC from Pergamon (Zanker 1988: 48, fig. 36a). Capricorn
also appeared alongside Augustus in works of art, such as the Gemma Augustea,
where the astrological sign appears above his head on the left (Zanker 1988:
231, fig. 182). In the time of Galba (AD 68–69) the sign was still used to honour

Augustus' memory (Hamburger 1968: 20). Another red jasper gem of the same period was discovered in Ribchester Roman bath house and it also features a Capricorn galloping to the left, very similar to the one from the Israel Museum and made in the same style (Henig 1998: 150–151, fig. 16). Also on a gem from the collection of the Fitzwilliam Museum, dating from the 2nd century AD, a galloping Capricorn is depicted (Henig 1994: 176, no. 383), and many other examples are known on gems (Gramatopol 1974: nos 575–577; Richter 1956: nos 400–403; Sena-Chiesa 1966: nos 1230–1244). In the time of Augustus, marine images (such as the Capricorn) alluded to the victory at Actium, such as on a gem from the Staatliche Münzsammlungen in Munich (Zanker 1988: 84, fig. 66) that portrays a Capricorn riding over a ship and above it a star. But in later periods the Capricorn[29] featured simply as one of the zodiac signs, or a marine monster like the hippocamp (Henig 1997: 52). Given the above, it is reasonable to assume that the gem from the Israel Museum, dating to the 2nd–3rd century AD, reflected the zodiacal sign of its owner and is not associated with Augustus.

Hippocamp

Two gems from the Israel Museum bear a similar depiction of Eros on a hippocamp: a red jasper (Figures 60a and b), and a carnelian (Figure 61). Both are dating to the 2nd century AD, the first one from its material and the second on stylistic basis, it being made in the 'Imperial Small Grooves Style' as defined by Maaskant-Kleibrink (1978: 251–252). This motif is also common on Roman engraved gems, as demonstrated by a red jasper example at Bertrand Museum, Châteauroux (Guiraud 1996: fig. 346), and an amethyst in the British Museum (Waltres 1926: fig. 1496).[30] Marine hybrids, such as hippocamps, as well as tritons and nereides, are often also depicted in other media. When shown in funerary art context, they symbolise the journey of the deceased to the Islands of the Blessed. Sea-horses also symbolise continued existence after death, as they embody the journey to the new residence (Henig 1978: 44; Prieur 1988: 64; Toynbee 1963: 46, 265). As noted above, one of these sarcophagi shows the journey to the Underworld, and Erotes riding on hippocamps are also portrayed (Stuveras 1969: fig. 74). Since Eros represents the soul, hippocamps accompanying his journey over the sea to the Islands of the Blessed represent the convoy of the soul to its future dwelling (Henig 1978: 44).

Eros often appears riding a dolphin, or other marine creature such as the hippocamp, as participants in the marine *thiasos*. Poseidon's *thiasos* is similar to

---

[29] When not referring to a military unit, such as Legio II Augusta (Henig 1997: 49; Henig 1978: 43).
[30] Some other examples include a banded agate in the Getty Museum (Spier 1992: fig. 322), a carnelian from Vienna (Zwierlein-Diehl 1973: vol. 2, fig. 1345, pl. 126), and a nicolo ringstone from Norfolk (Henig 1978: fig. 127).

Figure 60a. Eros on a hippocamp, red jasper, 11 x 8 x 1.5 mm, 2nd century AD. The Israel Museum Jerusalem, Bequest of Mr. Adolphe Doreen, Paris. IMJ70.62.343. ©Photo: The Israel Museum, Jerusalem.

Figure 60b. Eros on a hippocamp, drawing. ©Drawing: The Israel Museum, Jerusalem, by Pnina Arad.

Figure 61. Eros on a hippocamp, carnelian, intaglio and impression, 15 x 11 x 2 mm, 2nd century AD. The Israel Museum Jerusalem, Bequest of Mr. Adolphe Doreen, Paris. IMJ70.62.328. ©Photo: The Israel Museum, Jerusalem, by Vladimir Naikhin.

that of Dionysus, but the Dionysian *thiasos* occurs in forests and woods, while Poseidon's takes place in the sea. Instead of satyrs and maenads, the retinue of Poseidon consists of tritons and nereides. In both cases Eros and Erotes are present: marching, riding wild animals, or riding dolphins and other marine creatures (Stuveras 1969: 154–155). This theme can be interpreted as a decorative one, which suits various media compositionally and iconographically, especially floor mosaics, and mosaics from *thermae* in particular, such as the one from Prima Porta (Stuveras 1969: 156, fig. 140). Unlikethe theme of Eros riding a dolphin, the motif of Eros on a hippocamp does not have the loving relationship that unites the dolphin with Venus, the goddess of love (Stuveras 1969: 160). In addition, the motif of Eros on a hippocamp has later visual sources. The hippocamp became a popular motif in Roman art, including engraved gems, only after Octavian's victory at the Battle of Actium, as noted above (Zanker 1988: 82). During this period, the hippocamp is often depicted in art, including gemstones, which enabled people to own a small work of art that reminded them of the victory, like a magical object or amulet. Thus it is clear why hippocamps often appear on magical gems and amulets (Delatte and Derchain 1964). On an agate intaglio from Vienna, Augustus is featured naked, and holding Poseidon's trident, driving a hippocamp-charriot, while underneath the sea-horses an enemy is sinking under the waves: the enemy is identified as either Mark Antony or Sextus Pompey (Lippold 1923: Taf. IV,7; Zanker 1988: 97, fig. 82). On another Imperial gem, a similar motif is represented but excluding the enemy. In both cases, Augustus is depicted as the god Poseidon/Neptune, and therefore the imagery should be interpreted as political propaganda to perpetuate his victory at Actium (Zazoff 1983: 11, 333, Taf. 103).

The Greek god most associated with horses was Poseidon, and he was probably originally a horse himself and even had equine offspring like Pegasus and Areion. In Boeotia, and sometimes in Corinth, Poseidon was worshiped as Poseidon Hippios, with some votive tablets showing him as a rider. Most frequently, however, Poseidon was depicted riding hippocamps: in art works he is seen driving sea-horse-chariots, occasionally a quadriga (Anderson 1961: 10; Johns 2006: 179). This theme is depicted on another carnelian gem in the Israel Museum, on which the god is shown walking on the sea with his trident in his left hand, and in his right he holds the reins, restraining two rampant hippocamps (Figures 62a and b). In the Greek myths Poseidon created horses when he hit the ground with his trident. On many occasions the god would also take the shape of a stallion. In Haliartus in Boeotia there was a sacred pre-Hellenic site where it was believed that a nymph was metamorphosed into a horse when Poseidon chased her, and then the god turned himself into a stallion and abducted her (Brodrick 1972: 107). However, this engraved gem from the Israel Museum was recently recognised to be a post-Antique work, dated to the

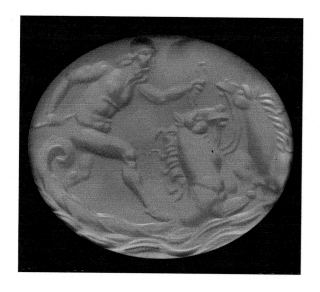

Figure 62a. Poseidon with two hippocamps,
carnelian, 18th century.
The Israel Museum Jerusalem, The Harry Stern
Collection, bequeathed by Dr Kurt Stern, London. In
memory of his parents and his brother who perished
at Sobibor. IMJ76.42.2448. ©Photo: The Israel
Museum, Jerusalem, by Vladimir Naikhin.

Figure 62b. Impression of the carnelian stone.
©Photo: The Israel Museum, Jerusalem, by Vladimir
Naikhin.

18th century on stylistic basis (M. Henig, personal communication, September 2011). These gems of the 18th century were copies of ancient originals as part of a neo-Classical vogue. A close examination of face, muscles and hair depiction, as well as the engraving style, indicates a treatment unknown in the ancient world. On a similar gem from Lippold's catalogue Poseidon is shown walking on the sea, but three hippocamps can be noticed (Lippold 1923: Taf CII, 1).

Gryllos (Hippalectryon)

A carnelian intaglio from the Israel Museum (Figure 63) bears a representation of a horse's head with a wheat sheaf in its mouth, a bearded man (probably a Silenus mask), a ram's head (?), a cornucopia, and a caduceus or palm-branch (?) on rooster legs. It is made in the 'Incoherent Grooves Style', hence is dated to the 2nd century AD (Maaskant-Kleibrink 1978: 326–343).[31]

According to Plutarch, some amuletic devices that could be gems served to neutralise the 'Evil Eye' through the use of alien images that supposedly trapped the harmful gaze and thus distanced the negative forces from the wearer of the gem (Plutarch, *Moralia*, vol. VIII, 'Quaestiones convivales': V.7.681). Such gems were therefore considered apotropaic.[32]

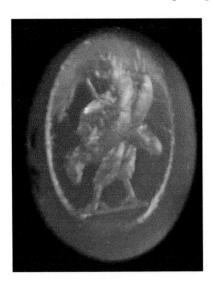

Figure 63. Combination gem (gryllos), carnelian, 2nd century AD. The Israel Museum Jerusalem. Clark Collection (YMCA(purchased by Carmen and Louis Warschaw Fund for Archaeological Acquisition. IMJ90.24.404. © Photo: The Israel Museum, Jerusalem.

---

[31] This style is typified by careless and concise engraving. Details are composed of several grooves made with the head of a rounded drill. It is very difficult to identify the depictions and therefore it can be assumed that these gems were not used as seals. The carving technique of these gems is very reminiscent of that of magical gems.

[32] As Blanchet observes, however, it is very probable that the composite figures of the 'grylloi' had a prophylactic value, and there can be no doubt that many of the elements composing them relate to fertility and wealth (Blanchet 1921: 50. see also Henig 1978: 101).

Some of the apotropaic gems are referred to as 'combination gems', the simplest forms of which are composed of two or more human heads, or a combination of human and animal heads. The human heads usually depicted are those of Silenus, satyrs and masks, while the animals that appear most frequently are eagles, roosters and peacocks. A more complex form of these kinds of gems includes the addition of elements such as the cornucopia, a wheat sheaf, wreath, thyrsus and caduceus. On a red jasper gem from Emory University Museum, Atlanta, a caduceus is depicted as well as an elephant's trunk (Lapatin 2011: 88–90, pls. 1–7). The elephant was closely linked with the victory of Dionysus/ Bacchus, which is why its head and trunk were often combined within those 'combination gem' depictions whose imagery was largely Bacchic (Henig 1980a: 333). The 'combination gems' are also called 'grylloi', following Pliny, who notes a 4th-century BC painting that featured a so-called 'gryllos' figure in a ridiculous costume, and thereafter this kind of ridiculous painting was termed 'gryllos' (*Natural History*: XXXV: 37 (114)). 'Combination gems' began to appear in the 4th century BC and continued until the 3rd century AD.

The carnelian gem from Jerusalem constitutes a specific type of 'gryllos' resembling a *hippalectryon*, consisting of integrated heads, a bearded man (generally identified as Silenus), a ram and a horse with rooster legs. This strange hybrid is a creature whose head and front legs are those of a horse, while its tail, wings and hind legs are those of a rooster. Lapatin mentions that *hippalectrya* appear on Athenian vase paintings (G. Hafner, 'Neue Mischwesen des 4. Jahrhunderts', Wiener Jahreshefte 32 (1940): 25–34, cf. Lapatin 2011: 89, note 5), and especially on Hellenistic and Roman wall-paintings and other decorative arts (Sauron 1990: 36, note 7, 41, note 47). Aristophanes mentions a *hippalectryon* as a symbol painted on ships, adopted from those depicted on Persian rugs (*Frogs*: 930–938). Horace, in the introduction to *Ars Poetica* (1–5), describes a strange painting reminiscent of the *hippalectryon*. Another example of a 'combination gem' representing a specific type of 'gryllos' resembling a *hippalectryon*, is that of a red jasper gem from the Rijksmuseum van Oudheden, Leiden (GS–01089). This features a Silenus mask, a ram with ears of wheat in its mouth on rooster legs, but with the head of a rooster, not a horse. It seems that red jasper, carnelian and sard were the stones most commonly used for 'combination gems', as noted in studies linking the use of red stones to magical gems (Lapatin 2011: 89).

Interactions between animal depictions in various media and their depictions on gems

The parallels between the iconography of animals on gems and other media are naturally numerous, but coins seem to be closest to the engraved gems because of their similar dimensions. In both cases, there is a tendency of reduction and use of clear and concise language, thus enabling the artist to omit excess details (Guiraud 1996: 97). In addition, if we take, for example, the subject of the gods, then both coins and gems were influenced by models of Greek or Roman statues, but the absence of a statue base under the feet of the depicted figures, and the presentation of the face in profile, as is evident from many of the gods' depictions on gems, are features more reminiscent of the representation of the motif on coins than in sculptures (Guiraud 1996: 98).

The surface of the gem is oval, therefore the Greek artist, who aspired to fill the surface of the gem, faced a compositional artistic challenge when depicting, for example, a lion attacking another animal. Compositions suited for friezes or pediments, such as a simple frontal attack, when the animals turn to one another, or follow one another, did not fit into a gem scene on account of their scale. A depiction of two lions attacking two animals was no longer an option, except for singular individual gems such as those from the Cabinet des médailles at the Bibliothèque National in Paris, where the victim is lying on his back, with a lion and a tiger attacking his stomach (Boardman 1968: 381). On painted vases and other objects another lion is usually shown in this scheme (of two lions attacking two animals), whereas such a depiction only seldom appears on gems. From these groups, in which two attacking lions were represented, the frontal lion was omitted, leaving the familiar scheme of the lion attacking and with the hunted animal in its jaws, as illustrated in a 5th-century BC gem from the Museum of Fine Arts in Boston (Boardman 1968: no. 440). Usually, one hind paw of the lion stands on the ground, but sometimes, especially on Late Archaic and Classical gems, the lion attacks the back of the victim (with both hind legs), leaping at its neck, when the bodies of the attacker and victim are almost parallel. In Archaic gems the animals commonly attacked by a lion are boar, goat, bull or deer. Sometimes the hind paw of the victim can be seen dragged behind, as is usually shown in vases. The scheme, especially with another lion attacking from the front, is common on vases and other objects, and in these cases deer are the most popular victims, and tigers are the more common attackers rather than lions, as depicted on most gems.When, on reliefs or vases, two lions are depicted attacking a reclining animal, again one lion is always omitted on the gem, although almost never in other media. Schemes in which the bodies intersect, or climb on each other, were naturally favoured because they were the most concise, as can be seen, for example, on some Archaic gems mentioned by Boardman (1968: 122–123, nos 391, 418).

Among the various works of art on which battles with a lion are shown, the black-figure Athenian vases are the most common, and only a few are from eastern Greece, even though on gems the motif of the attacking lion appears mainly in eastern Greece (Boardman 1968: 137, notes 8, 9).

Another example of adapting a motif from other media to engraved gems is that of clasped hands. Hands clasped in *Dextrarum Iunctio/Dexiôsis* (right handshake between man and woman) are a symbol of harmony, or more specifically, the engagement or the marriage union, and expressing the desired harmony between the couple. Depictions of handshakes appear in Greek tombs, for example on a fragment of a funerary relief dating from the end of the 4th century BC in the Museum of Cycladic Art in Athens, and on a tombstone from 320 BC from the J. Paul Getty Museum in California. Such scenes include the deceased, usually sitting, as well as a standing relative who is separating from them. The handshake was a common symbolic gesture of classical Attic tombstones, which represented the family connection, continuing even after death, namely the continuity of the relationship between the dead and the living, suggesting a belief in immortality and eternity.

Similarly, in Roman funerary representations the handshake symbolised marriage. It was a ceremonial gesture during Roman weddings, when the *dextrarum iunctio* stood for the promise of future loyalty. On funerary art, such as the sarcophagus of 280–270 AD from the Palazzo Massimo alle Terme in Rome, another layer of meaning is added by this symbol: the reunification between spouses in the Afterlife.

However, the representation of the theme of *dextrarum iunctio/dexiôsis* on gems includes only the hands and not the overall depiction with family members appearing in other media. For example, a granite gem of the 1st century BC–

AD 30 from the Israel Museum shows at the bottom a pair of clasped hands and in the centre an ear of corn enclosed between a pair of goats; a leaping goat is seen above (Figure 12). According to Henig, such a depiction has been linked to prosperity, and he mentions a similar carnelian gem which portrays a handshake, but above them both is a krater enclosed between two cornucopias and in the upper part appear three eagles (Henig 1981: 273–275, pl. VIII C).

Of course, the engravers had to reduce the motif because of the small area on which to work. Animal depictions on gems differ from other media, because the small space forced the artist to simplify and reduce the forms, but allowed details to be carved in a manner that could seem naturalistic. Stewart, who wrote on miniatures, argues that the miniature depiction concentrates the object to its significant properties, and this reduction of the physical dimensions actually multiplies the ideological characteristics (Stewart 1993: 47–48).

In addition, it is sometimes possible to see that the subjects seen on gems correspond to those that are popular in a given period in other media as well. A prominent example is the theme of hybrids. The 1st century BC was a turbulent era in the history of Rome, which was marked by civil wars, the decline of the Republic and the emergence of the Principate. The political conflicts were also reflected in an interesting aesthetic phenomenon: hybrid compositions took a prominent place in contemporary art, from wall- paintings to the support of marble and bronze furniture. We know indeed, thanks to Vitruvius, that already in the decorative painting of the Hellenistic period, centaurs were depicted, for example, as supporters for architraves (epistyles) (*De architectura* VII: 5.5), But how can we explain representations of multiple monsters in the Roman decorations of the end of the Republic? The interest in hybrids was not derived from them being mythological creatures, but by being associated with chaos and the creation of the world (Sauron 1990: 35–38). Their depictions in art expressed political propaganda, the essence of which was the beginning of a new era in Rome and the creation of a new world order. Thus, for example, the sphinx was a symbol of the conquest of Egypt, the harbinger of the Golden Age and the guardian of the New World. Sphinxes appear, for example, on both sides of a *trapezophoros* in the Galleria Doria Pamphilj in Rome, and on a pediment from the Gardens of Sallust/Horti Sallustiani in the Palazzo dei Conservatori in Rome, as well as on many contemporary engraved gems (Sauron 1990: 42, figs 2, 7). On an agate gem from the Israel Museum, originally from Chios, Greece, the sphinx is depicted sitting in the foreground in right profile, with its wings drawn back, its tail twisted and its head adorned with a complex hairstyle (Figures 53a and b). Another gem from the Israel Museum, made of carnelian, features a sphinx sitting in the foreground in left profile, its wings also drawn back, tail erect, wearing a headdress (its feathers are seen above the forehead) with diagonal lines across it (Figures 54a and b), probably a remnant of the headdress sometimes used to characterise Egyptian sphinxes. Pegasus is also found among the contemporary representations of hybrids, such as on a capital from the Temple of Mars Ultor in Rome. These mythical winged horses, that led mortals heavenwards, symbolised Augustus' future apotheosis (Sauron 1990: 41, fig. 14). Pegasus also appears on many contemporary gems, for example on a carnelian gem of the 1st century BC from the Israel Museum portraying the winged horse galloping to the left (Figure 57a and b).

However, there are representations that appear exclusively on engraved gems and do not appear in other media. Usually these are symbols that today seem strange and meaningless, or combinations of motifs that do not exist in other media depictions. Often such mysterious themes belong to the category of magical gems. But there are also a number of gems from the collection of the Israel Museum, which are not defined as magical, as they are not inscribed, yet they contain depictions remain undeciphered, such as a heliotrope (bloodstone) that dates to the 2nd–3rd century AD and features an eagle, a goat, and an unidentified animal standing on rocks with plants in the background (Figure 64).[33]

Some other examples can be referenced that appear on engraved gems only:

On an amethyst gem from the Israel Museum, dated by Henig to the 1st century AD, two goats are leaping back-to-back on either side of an amphora, from which grow an ear of corn and another plant, possibly an olive (Figure 13).This depiction is related to the Tree of Life symbolism, and the interpretation is related to prosperity, where the amphora containing wine represents the life fluid.

Figure 64. Eagle, goat, and an unidentified animal standing on rocks, drawing, heliotrope, 13.5 x 11 x 3 mm, 2nd–3rd century AD.
The Israel Museum Jerusalem. Bequest of Mr. Adolphe Doreen, Paris. IMJ70.62.113.
©Drawing: The Israel Museum, Jerusalem, by Pnina Arad.

---

[33] A carnelian gem from Dover, dated by Henig to the mid 2nd – beginning of the 3rd century AD, supports this dating based on stylistic criteria. In this gem, a goat is depicted standing on a rock cliff in a way similar to the one seen on the Israel Museum intaglio, with the rock also shown in the form of a winding coil, from which a plant protrudes (Henig 1985: 463–464, plate CIII.e).

Figure 65. Boar confronting a snake with a radiated
head, impression of a carnelian stone, 12 x 8 x 7 mm, an
Etruscan 'globolo' style scarab, late 3rd century BC.
The Israel Museum Jerusalem, The Harry Stern
Collection, bequeathed by Dr Kurt Stern, London. In
memory of his parents and his brother who perished
at Sobibor. IMJ76.42.2385. © Photo: The Israel Museum,
Jerusalem.

A late 3rd-century BC 'globolo' Etruscan Scarab from the Israel Museum bears
a representation of a boar confronting a snake with a radiated head (Figure
65). Henig identifies this depiction as belonging to the Etruscan culture, and
one intending to symbolise a strong creature defeating an evil one (personal
communication, September 2011).

A nicolo gem in the Israel Museum, and dated to the 2nd century AD, shows
an elephant emerging from a sea-shell (Figure 51). Such depictions of an
elephant and shell probably served an apotropaic function similar to that of
'combination gems' (Henig 1984b: 244). Furthermore, both shells and elephants
had a symbolic significance in Antiquity. The sea-shell represented the *uterus*,
from which arises life, and therefore constituted a powerful symbol of fertility
and rebirth. An elephant emerging from a sea-shell presents an apt symbol of
rebirth, due both to its renowned longevity and to its being favoured by the
sun-god (Henig 1978: 102; Henig 1984b: 244, 246).

A carnelian intaglio of the 2nd century AD from the Israel Museum (Figure
63) bears a representation of a horse's head with a wheat sheaf in its mouth,
a bearded man (probably a Silenus mask), a ram's head (?), a cornucopia
and a caduceus or palm-branch (?) on rooster legs. According to Plutarch,

some amuletic devices that could be gems served to neutralise the 'Evil Eye' through the use of alien imagery that supposedly trapped the harmful gaze and thus distanced the negative forces from the gem wearer (*Moralia*, vol. VIII, 'Quaestiones convivales': V.7.681). Such gems were therefore considered apotropaic.[34] Some apotropaic gems are called 'combination gems', the simplest forms of which are composed of two or more human heads or a combination of human and animal heads. The human heads that are usually depicted are those of Silenus, satyrs and masks, while the animals that appear most frequently are eagles, roosters and peacocks. A more complex form of these types of gems includes the addition of elements such as the cornucopia, a wheat sheaf, wreath, *thyrsus* and *caduceus*. The 'combination gems' are also called 'grylloi', following Pliny, who noted a 4th-century BC painting that featured a so-called 'gryllos' figure in a ridiculous costume, and thereafter this painting style was termed 'gryllos' (*Natural History*: XXXV.37, 114). The carnelian gem from Jerusalem constitutes a specific type of 'gryllos' that resembles a *hippalectryon*, consisting of integrated heads, a bearded man (generally identified as Silenus), a ram and a horse with rooster legs. This strange hybrid is a creature whose head and front legs are those of a horse, while its tail, wings and hind legs are those of a rooster. Lapatin mentions that *hippalectrya* appear on Athenian vase paintings (Hafner 1940: 25–34; cf. Lapatin 2011: 89, note 5) and especially in Hellenistic and Roman wall-paintings and other decorative arts (Sauron 1990: 36, note 7, 41, note 47). Aristophanes mentions a *hippalectryon* as a symbol painted on ships, adopted from those depicted on Persian rugs (*Frogs*: 930–938).

A carnelian gem of the 2nd–3rd century AD from the Israel Museum bears a representation of a crab under a Capricorn (Figure 58). These images refer to the zodiac signs of Cancer and Capricorn (Bonner 1950: 36). Sometimes gems were engraved with combinations of constellations that were apparently considered particularly suitable and meaningful for their owners (Henig 1997: 50). The crab depicted on gems can also have magical significance (Bonner 1950: 36). According to the religious concepts prevalent in Antiquity concerning the human soul, the zodiac was linked to reincarnation and death. It was believed that when the soul returned to earth it had to pass through a gate located at the intersection of the heavenly bodies symbolising Cancer and the Milky Way – which is the human gate; the divine gate, on the other hand, was considered to be located at the intersection of the celestial bodies symbolised through Capricorn and the Milky Way.

---

[34] As Blanchet observes, however, it is very probable that the composite figures of the 'grylloi' had a prophylactic value, and there can be no doubt that many of the elements composing them relate to fertility and wealth (Blanchet 1921: 50; see also Henig 1978: 101).

Two gems from the Israel Museum feature a rooster with a mouse: the first, a red jasper, which dates to the end of the 2nd century AD (Figures 44a and b), portrays a rooster preying upon a mouse; the second is a carnelian of the 3rd century AD (Figure 45), with a representation of a mouse riding a rooster and whipping it. The rooster was associated with daybreak, with light (Bonner 1950: 125–127; Gray 1951: 969; Orth 1913: cols. 2532–2533), while a mouse, in contrast, was considered a chthonic creature (Aelian, *De natura animalium* XII: 5). Consequently, this depiction of a rooster preying upon a mouse was perceived as the victory of good over evil, and of life overcoming darkness (Henig 1997: 47). The second gem, bearing a representation of a mouse riding a rooster, is considered as apotropaic, since, according to Plutarch, anything curious was thought to both attract and neutralise the baleful stare of the 'Evil Eye' away from the wearer (*Moralia*, vol. VIII, 'Quaestiones convivales': V.7.681; see also Henig 1977: 47).

Associations between animal depictions and the type of gemstone and its believed qualities

The Greeks believed that gemstones were given as a gift to mankind by Zeus, providing them with protection against such catastrophes as diseases, wild beasts, aggressors, drowning at sea, as well as constituting talismans for victory, success in love, abundance and fertility, the ability to predict the future, and even as having the power to raise the souls of the dead from the Underworld.

The belief in the magical power of gemstones originated in the kingdoms of Babylon and Assyria: on a cuneiform script tablet from the library of King Ashurbanipal gems and certain plants are associated with certain stars. This belief in the power of stones and minerals penetrated from Babylon into Persia.

Later, in the 6th century BC, it also reached Egypt. In the zodiac on the ceiling of the *pronaos* of the temple at Dendera matching symbols of minerals and metals are listed for each of the 36 first-magnitude stars. In the 5th century BC, following the war with the Persians, this belief also arrived in Greece. The doctrines that penetrated Greece from Babylonia and Persia were of particular importance in their practical application by priests in the field of the occult: it was believed that a destiny that depended on a certain constellation of the stars could be altered, due to the divine powers that apparently dwelt in animals, plants, and gemstones, and the mutual exchange that existed between them and the stars ('*Lithika*' In *RE* (1926): 749–750, 765).

From these Oriental doctrines, each gemstone contains within it certain images of a particular god identified with a group of stars (or their rulers – the sun and the moon), and it is through this gemstone that this god can be influenced.

According to the main Greek book on the magic power of gems, the *Lithika*, which has not survived in its entirety, the power of stones is superior to that of plants, because a stone retains its strength as long as it exists (Hermann (ed.) 1805, *Lithika* in *Orphica*: 363; West 1983: 36). The Greeks attributed to some stones the ability to engender love and ensure fertility. Engraving a divine image on a gem, or a symbol that highlighted a particular divinity, reinforced this stone's inherent identification with this deity, and thus strengthened the stone's potency in terms of possessing magical power. Consequently, stones were carved with the symbols of the seven planets and the twelve signs of the zodiac. Engravings of animals or plants that symbolised deities were also very popular ('*Lithika*' In *RE* (1926): 751–760).

The colour of stones had considerable importance. Theophrastus and Pliny classified precious gemstones according to colour (Pliny, *Natural History*: XXXVII; Theophrastus, *De Lapidibus*). Sometimes the colour of the gemstone dictated its name, i.e. the form of jasper known as '*boria*' or 'north-wind *iaspis*' because it was, according to Pliny, 'like sky on an autumn morning' (Pliny, *Natural History*: XXXVII.xxxvii.116). The colour of a gem (in addition to the depictions engraved on it) gave it the quality of an amulet (Henig 1980: 331). In other words, the colour of the gemstone was the most important quality in terms of the magical purpose of protecting the wearer, along with the depiction carved on it, and/ or the inscription, rather than its material or shape (Platz-Horster 2010: 195).

The type of stone-cutting was also sometimes determined by colour: for example a hexagonal shape was recommended for beryls because that style suited their colour, and, according to Pliny, 'If they are cut in any other way they lack brilliance' (Pliny, *Natural History*: XXXVII.xix.76). There would typically be a match between the colour of the gemstone and the subject represented on it; and thus, for example, the sea-nymph Galene was depicted on Indian beryl, with the blue colour of the stone having been chosen because it suited the portrayal of the personification of a calm sea, as noted by the poet Addaios (*Anthologia Graeca*: 9.544). Aquamarine, in another example, was believed to be good for the eyes and for healing various diseases; and, moreover, if a crab and a raven were to be engraved upon it, and the gemstone then set in a gold ring, the wearer would also be blessed with love (Damigeron, *De virtutibus lapidum*: 52).

Art in the Hellenistic period was characterised by innovation, and was dynamic compared to the Classical era that advocated the Greek concept of *sophrosyne*, which is why the pale chalcedony was no longer desirable, but, rather, more colourful stones, such as garnet, were preferred. During the Hellenistic period a gemstone was chosen not only according to aesthetic considerations, but also in accordance with the growing belief in its supernatural and magical forces.

Orphism, for example, developed a 'science' of its own to classify the benefits of each gem (Boardman and Vollenweider 1978: vol. 1: 69). In the 2nd century BC various agate stones, composed of coloured horizontal layers, gained popularity, in a trend that increased during the Roman period. Agates, with their colourful layers, were favoured for creating cameos, in another innovation of Hellenistic times (Boardman and Vollenweider 1978: vol. 1: 73–74). Red, yellow and green jasper and heliotrope (a derivative of jasper, also known as bloodstone, and of a dark-green colour dotted with red), as well as carnelian and chalcedony, were all considered as amulets and magical properties were ascribed to them (Boardman and Vollenweider 1978: p. 1v; Bonner 1950: 8–9; Middleton 1891: 145–146; Pliny, *Natural History*: XXXVII.118, 169–170; Richter 1956: p. xx). Chalcedony was considered able to bring victory to its owner, while sard (brown carnelian), preferably engraved with vine and ivy intertwined, was believed to make a woman become loved (Damigeron, *De virtutibus lapidum*: 48, 62). Garnet, too, was considered to make its wearer able to attract love and thus was called 'the lid of Venus' (Pliny, *Natural History*: XXXVII.124). Heliotrope was ascribed predictive abilities, as well as conferring protection, detoxification and popularity upon its wearer (Damigeron, *De virtutibus lapidum*: 8; 'Lithika' In *RE* (1926): 764). Various magical and healing properties were attributed to different types of agate: for example, the ability to counter the venom of spiders and scorpions, to heal the eye, to alleviate thirst (if placed in the mouth), as well as making the wearer rich, powerful and loved by God and man, not to mention becoming an invincible athlete (Damigeron, *De virtutibus lapidum*: 30; Pliny, *Natural History*: XXXVII.139–143).

Two Classical Phoenician scarabs now in the Israel Museum are made of green jasper: the first (Figure 31), portraying a lion seated in profile to the right and looking left, its tail arched over its back (Boardman 2003: 115, 38/30); and the second (Figures 1a and b), on which a cow is shown from behind but looking round at its newborn calf; a grasshopper hovers above (Boardman 2003: 122, pl. 40/55). Both date to the first half of the 5th century BC.

Classical Phoenician scarabs were made of green jasper in Phoenicia from the late 6th century to the mid 4th century BC. Most of them were found in the western Phoenician (Punic) cemeteries of Carthage, Sardinia and Ibiza (Spain), but there are many also from the East Mediterranean. The subjects portrayed on the intaglios are the most eclectic of any medium of the period. They include Egyptianising, Levantine and Hellenising (mainly following later Archaic Greek subjects and styles, due to which many have been called Greco-Phoenician). However, there are also many miscellaneous items, and much overlapping of categories. Boardman noted that the two above-mentioned Classical Phoenician scarabs are from the East Mediterranean (Syria-Palestine, Cyprus or Egypt), and feature a miscellany of subjects, with much overlapping of categories (Boardman 2003: 17).

The most important factor in Antiquity, for both the carver and the owner of such objects, was probably the colour. For example, red carnelian was used for Etruscan scarabs and bore significance both for those who prepared the intaglios and those who wore them (Boardman 2003: 6). The colour green was perceived as lucky in the East and in Egypt, being the colour of new vegetation, growing crops and fertility, and hence of new life, youth and wellness, and even resurrection (Boardman 1991: 31). It was, in particular, the colour of the papyrus plant, which when represented in hieroglyphs produced the word 'wadj', meaning 'to flourish' or 'be healthy' (Andrews 1990: 37).

No particular importance appears to have been attributed to the material from which the intaglio was made, and both the material and the shape of the object created from it were determined according to fashion, convenience and availability (although in Rome several other considerations were introduced) (Boardman 1980: 110). In Sardinia, the local stone (verde di Sardegna), which is a serpentine rock (mineral) softer than green jasper, had been used on the island from earliest times. However, in Egypt and the Dead Sea region green jasper was available and hence was used to make the Phoenician seals in the Late Bronze Age, and sometimes also for Egyptian amulets (Collon 1986:57–70; Moorey 1994: 98–99).

A green jasper scarab nonetheless had an amuletic character and, probably together with the depiction of a lion, which had meanings of guarding and protection, there indeed existed an association between the type of gemstone, the qualities attributed to it and the depiction engraved upon it. It is probable that the choice to depict specifically on green jasper a cow with its suckling calf was not random, especially given this mineral's association with fertility, new life and health, as noted above. In addition, these figures identified as Isis and Horus, an image with implications associated with fertility, birth, rebirth, and resurrection is emphasized by the presence of a grasshopper also bearing associations to immortality and resurrection both in Greek and Egyptian mythology.

Two gems, now in the Israel Museum, are made of amethyst: the first (Figures 56a and b), depicting Bellerophon riding Pegasus, dates to the 1st century BC – 1st century AD; and the second (Figure 13), dating to the 1st century AD, features two leaping goats on either side of an amphora from which grow ears of corn.

The degree of effectiveness of magical amulets was measured according to the considered virtue of the gemstone of which they were made (Henig 1994: xxx). Amethyst has a transparent purple colour and had been used from the Minoan era onwards. It was common in the Hellenistic and Roman periods. The meaning of the name Amethyst in Greek is 'not drunk'. According to Pliny, the Greeks believed that since the colour of the gemstone is close to that of wine, it had the ability to absorb the intoxicating effect of wine, thereby preventing drunkenness (Pliny, *Natural History*: XXXVII.121–124). A person wearing it was considered to be protected against intoxication during feasts, and if living beings were depicted on the stone, its value increased ten-fold (Henig 1994: x–xi). Two gems mentioned in the *Anthologia Graeca* refer to amethysts: one portrays Dionysus and the other a representation of Methe, the goddess of intoxication (*Anthologia Graeca*: ix. 748, 752). According to this poem, Cleopatra wore an amethyst ring engraved with an image of Methe. It is conceivable that a beneficial connection was perceived between the type of gemstone and the depiction on it for these two Israel Museum gems. Moreover, the images of Pegasus and an amphora with goats had a connection to the subject of water and wine as symbols of inspiration: the image of the winged Pegasus, capable of soaring skywards, was attributed with inspiration and creative qualities through drinking water from a sacred spring; while the image of a goat and an amphora was associated to the Dionysian world, leading to inspiration through the drinking of wine. Both wine and water were symbols of the power of inspiration in the ancient Greek world (Crowther 1979: 4). Hesiod associated the name of Pegasus with the Greek word for spring; and, indeed, wherever the winged horse stamped with its hooves upon the ground, an abundant spring erupted. Thus was created the sacred Hippocrene spring on Mount Helicon, which was consecrated to the muses. Greek poets wrote about the dispute between wine drinkers and drinkers of water and identified the latter as poets who sought inspiration from the sacred springs. Thus for example, Antipater of Thesalonica, a poet from the Augustan period, condemned abstinent poets, such as Hesiod, who drank from the sacred springs, in favour of Archilochus and Homer, the wine drinkers. Antipater of Sidon preferred to drink one glass of wine rather than a thousand cups from the Hippocrene spring (*Anthologia Graeca*: xi.20, 24).

Three gems now in the Israel Museum are made of heliotrope: the first (Figures 66a and b) is a Phoenician scarab that dates to the 5th century BC and depicts an eagle flying above a bull and a conical rock; the second (Figure 64) is a gem that dates to the 2nd–3rd century AD and portrays an eagle, a goat and another, unidentified, beast standing on rocks, with plants in the background ; and the third 2nd century AD gem bears a representation of Nike/Victory riding a quadriga (Figure 20). As noted above, heliotrope was considered as an amulet and magical properties were ascribed to it. It was thus also used for many Gnostic gems depicting Abraxas (Walters 1926: xiv). Predictability, protection, detoxification and popularity for its wearer were all ascribed to heliotrope (Damigeron, *De virtutibus lapidum*: 8; '*Lithika*' in *RE* (1926): 764).

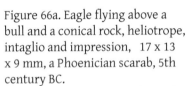

Figure 66a. Eagle flying above a bull and a conical rock, heliotrope, intaglio and impression,   17 x 13 x 9 mm, a Phoenician scarab, 5th century BC.
The Israel Museum Jerusalem, The Harry Stern Collection, bequeathed by Dr Kurt Stern, London. In memory of his parents and his brother who perished at Sobibor. IMJ76.42.2493. ©Photo: The Israel Museum, Jerusalem.

Figure 66b. Eagle flying above a bull and a conical rock, drawing. ©Drawing: The Israel Museum, Jerusalem, by Pnina Arad.

Three gems now in the Israel Museum are made of yellow jasper: the first (Figure 37), bearing a representation of an eagle holding a wreath and placed between two military flags (*vexilla*), dates to the 2nd century AD; the second (Figures 33a and b), featuring a lion attacking a deer with a star above them, also dates to the 2nd century AD; and the third (Figures 34a and b), depicting a lion leaping upon the back of a goat, dates to the 2nd-3rd century AD.

Yellow jasper, which was called 'the gemstone with the colour of the lion's pelt', was ascribed with amuletic and magical qualities, and was also used as a remedy for scorpion bites (Henig 1980: 331; Henig 1994: 168, cat. 358, 175, cat. 381).Yellow jasper was indeed often used for depictions of lions in general and the motif of a lion killing or eating its prey in particular. These gems, made of yellow jasper and engraved with this motif, were designed to protect the wearer, both due to the material from which they were made, and to the depiction on them, a scene that has both chthonic significance and the promise of the eternal Afterlife and a celestial function (Henig 1977: 356–358). In Rome eagles were symbols of victory and power and were attributed with protective abilities (Prieur 1988: 28). They were a symbol of Rome and in particular of its legions, to quote Tacitus: 'Romanae aves, propria legionum numina' (Tacitus, *The Annals of Tacitus*: ii, 17). The military symbol of an eagle between two *vexilla* represented the Roman legions in general, as well as the good fortune of the particular military unit. The eagle was venerated in the military and apparently became a magical symbol (Hamburger 1968: 14; Henig 1997: 49). Thus, yellow jasper combined with the images engraved on it would have enhanced the magical power of this gemstone.

Six gems now in the Israel Museum are made of red jasper, all dated to the 2nd–3rd centuries AD: The first portrays Eros riding a chariot harnessed to two parrots (Figures 40a and b); the second features Eros riding on a galloping lion (Figures 36a and b); the third shows the god of love riding a hippocampus (Figures 60a and b); the fourth has Heracles battling the Nemean Lion (Figure 35); the fifth depicts a peasant driving a pair of oxen harnessed to a plow (Figures 7a and b); and the sixth has an engraving of a rooster preying upon a mouse (Figures 44a and b).

Red jasper, which was popular during the 2nd–3rd centuries AD, was also attributed with magical properties (Pliny, *Natural History*: XXXVII.118). Specific representations, such as cupids, heroes and animals, as well as 'combination gems' (*grylloi*), commonly feature on red jasper. It can be assumed that this preference has a connection to its magical qualities (Henig 1978: 41). However, there are also many gems featuring cupids and *grylloi* made of carnelian or sard, suggesting that the red colour was the significant factor (Dasen 2011: 70–71;

Faraone 2011: 52–53). Red was the colour of blood, with all its connotations of energy, dynamism, power, and even life itself (Andrews 1990: 37). Indeed, in the case of Egyptian funerary jewellery, certain materials were strictly chosen for the magical properties of their colouring. Thus, Chapter 156 of the *Book of the Dead* required that an amulet in the form of Isis's Girdle, placed at the throat of the mummy, be made of red jasper, whose blood-like colouring would intensify the words of the spell: 'You have your blood, Isis; you have your power' (Andrews 1990: 37). Most of the gems known today depicting Heracles battling the Nemean Lion are made of red jasper, which matches the powerful motif. The depiction of a rooster preying upon a mouse also matches the red colour, in addition to the rooster being associated with daybreak, with light, while a mouse, in contrast, was considered a chthonic creature. Consequently, this depiction of a rooster preying upon a mouse was perceived as the victory of good over evil and of light overcoming darkness (Henig 1997: 47). An additional advantage of jasper was that the engraved images stood out against the background, which was particularly valuable since the meaning of particular images on gems became increasingly more significant in the 2nd–3rd centuries AD, when gems were no longer solely used for the purpose of providing seals (Henig 1978: 31).

An examination of the relationship between the colour of a gemstone and its depiction thus illustrates that its colour was the most important factor, in addition to the engraved image, rather than the material from which it was made. Red, for example, was the colour of blood with all its connotations of energy, dynamism, power, even life itself. This is probably why those gems featuring Heracles and the Nemean Lion were usually carved on red jasper. In another example, it seems that amuletic qualities were attributed to the Classical Phoenician scarab made of green jasper, which portrays a seated lion in profile to the right and looking left. The lion was considered to be a symbol of victory in general and of triumph over death in particular. Thus, the engraving of the lion motif upon the green colour symbolizing health, life and rebirth, would have intensified the magical value attributed to the intaglio.

Summary

Engraved gems are precious or semi-precious stones with images featuring on them. During the Greek and Roman periods they were used as seals, jewellery, and amulets. Various images were carved on the gems, such as gods, mythological themes, famous sculptures, astrological signs, and portraits. Many of the images are no longer familiar to us, and research, based on ancient literature sources, is required in order to interpret their meanings. The depictions on the gems were meaningful and often symbolic.

Whereas animals are a frequent depiction on gemstones of the different periods, and play a key role in symbolic representations on these engraved gems, they have generally been overlooked and little studied. Leading archaeologists have suggested that the repetition of seal motifs suggests that the gem-cutters were merely drawing from a stock or repertoire of emblems that had no specific meaning for the client.

While representations of animals on gems have been researched previously, the interest has focused mainly on specific ones, such as Leda and the Swan (Maaskant-Kleibrink 1999: 19–27), or the eagle representing the Roman Empire (Nagy 1992: 99–108). While Henig concentrated on the meaning of animal images on Greek and Roman gems as a whole, and suggested a range of likely explanations (Henig 1997: 45–53), few studies have otherwise dealt specifically with animal representations.

In the present research, a group of about 70 gems (intaglios), comprising part of the collection of the Israel Museum in Jerusalem, was selected as a test case for the wider issue. These gems, first published and discussed in this work, consist of Greek and Roman gems bearing depictions of animals. The gems are presented through a detailed study of the themes described, in an attempt to form a comprehensive approach to the depictions of animals and their significance on Greek and Roman gems. I was able to date the gems approximately, to identify the material of which they were made, and to trace the historical, cultural, and religious perceptions underlying the motifs engraved upon them. The study also discusses the changes in representation of animals on gems compared to other, larger media, and inquires into the significance of these changes.

The primary function of engraved gems (intaglios) lay in their use to create an icon in relief on clay or wax, which could be identified; and whose role was to validate the act of signing. Gems were highly appreciated in ancient times in general and in the Greco-Roman world in particular, and during the early Roman Empire period, aside from their original use as seals, they were also appreciated as jewellery. During the Middle Empire gems became devalued as seals, and were frequently used for decorative purposes only, for example in brooches, and thus unsuited for use as seals. During the Late Roman period, rings were made inlaid with engraved gems, albeit not necessarily used for a specific purpose, but intended from the start to be used as jewellery. Most of them were created as love or marital gifts, thus functioning as miniature objects endowed with personal meanings by their owners, imbued with emotion and human passion.

The great importance attributed to gems is also reflected in the ancient literature. The carved figures on the seals were ascribed meanings of threat and warning, thus acting as a kind of symbolic lock. Whoever dared to break the seal unlawfully risked the threat of terrible punishment for the crime. The 'classic' seal has a parallel in the modern security code, and various means of biometric validation and signature. In ancient times, when much of the population was illiterate, imprinting one's personal seal was the only reliable identification mark. When the need arose to despatch letters by messengers, the seal also became a sign of identification, and consequently, protection against an unauthorised person opening the letter.

The present study demonstrates that images engraved on gems were most probably selected by their owners as a marker of personal identity. The reasons which may have led an individual to choose a specific image as their symbol are no longer known to us. However, we can assume that personal taste, personal interest, and various relationships might have influenced the choice. It seems that a seal was considered as a powerful metaphor for an individual and their relationship with the surrounding world. Indeed, the seal imprint became such a powerful image that the term *tupôsis* (the action of stamping the seal on wax) was used as a philosophical metaphor by Plato, and later on in the Stoic writings, in order to explain the nature of knowledge and the relationship between sensory perception and the soul (Diogenes Laertius, *Lives of Eminent Philosophers* (*Life of Zeno*): 7.177, 7.45–46, 7.50; Plato, *Theaetetus*: 191D, E; 193C;

194C, D). There was a parallel between the seal and its owner, so that the image carved on the gem was perceived as a specific identity marker, and proclaimed an individual's continued presence even during their physical absence.

It is concluded here that the depictions on the gems bore significant and deep meanings. Animals comprised an inexhaustible source of expressing concise messages on the engraved gems. Our inability to fully understand today the comprehensive meanings does not imply that the individuals who ordered a certain engraved gem were not aware of the message they wished to convey to their contemporaries. Therefore, in order to decipher these motifs, it is necessary first to decode the majority of the engraved depictions, which present a combination of motifs, whose significance was undoubtedly recognised in the past. For example, a Greco-Phoenician scarab made of green jasper, dated to the first half of the 5th century BC, depicts a cow suckling a calf near a grasshopper. In the present study I was able to identify the figures as Isis and Horus, an image with implications associated with fertility, birth, rebirth, and resurrection.

The question as to whether meaning should be ascribed to the engraved images on gems recurs throughout this research. It seems that as far as animal motifs are concerned, the gems could be accorded with a deeper symbolism, such as good luck, abundance and fertility, health, success, and victory. All these motifs are perceived as capable of weakening hostile forces. The animals engraved can also symbolise nature's abundance and fertility, especially when represented along with their offspring, pasturing and grazing, or accompanied by such fertility symbols as cornucopia, ears of corn, and wine goblets. Other animals are related to certain gods, and even comprise their attributes, and thus it was believed that the owner of an engraved gem was accorded divine protection. The image of a predatory animal killing its prey, or devouring it, is usually interpreted as an allegory of the triumph over death, such as in a 2nd century AD yellow jasper gem with a lion attacking a deer. It was widely believed that the image of Heracles struggling against the Nemean lion, as depicted on a Roman red jasper gem, helped warriors to defend themselves, and was also believed to cure diseases. A rooster, for example, was associated with daybreak, with light, while the mouse, in contrast, was considered a chthonic creature. Therefore, a depiction of a rooster eating a mouse on a gem from the end of the 1st century AD was conceived as the victory of good over evil, the power of daylight, and of life overcoming darkness.

According to Plutarch, some amuletic devices that could be gems served to neutralise the 'evil-eye' through the use of strange images that supposedly trapped the harmful gaze, and thus distanced the negative forces from the gem wearer (Plutarch, *Moralia*, vol. VIII, 'Quaestiones convivales': V.7.681). These gems were therefore apotropaic, and some of them are called 'combination gems'. The simplest forms are those composed of two human heads or more, or a combination of human-animal heads. The human heads include Sileni, satyrs, and masks, while the most frequent animals are eagles, roosters, and peacocks. Other, more complex patterns on the 'combination gems' might include elements such as cornucopia, ears of corn, a wreath, *thyrsus* and *caduceus*, as seen on a carnelian gem from the 2nd century AD, with a horse's head and a corn ear in its mouth, together with a bearded man, a ram, a cornucopia and a *caduceus* on a rooster's legs. This latter gem is actually a specific type of 'Grylloi' which resembles *hippalektryôn*: this strange hybrid creature has the head and front legs of a horse, and a rooster's tail, wings and hind legs. 'Combination gems' are referred to as 'Grylloi' following Pliny, who relates to one of Antiphilos's (a rival of Apelles) paintings dated to the 4th century BC. According to this citation a person called 'Gryllos' wearing a ridiculous costume was depicted in this painting, following from which these kinds of paintings, considered ridiculous, were called 'Grylloi' (Pliny, *Natural History*: XXXV.37.114). Other gems exhibited at the Israel Museum were intended to protect against evil or to attract love; the latter are interpreted based on the depictions of Eros riding on an animal. This kind of depiction appears on several gems from the collection, such as a carnelian gem from the 1st century AD, with Eros riding a dolphin, and a red jasper gem dated to the 2nd–3rd century AD, engraved with Eros riding a lion.

Another group of gems served for political propaganda. It was customary in the Augustan period to carve gems with sea creatures, such as dolphins and hippocampi, which commemorate and refer to the great victory at Actium.

Several animals were accorded with magical powers that could affect people in a positive or a negative way. It was accepted that certain animals carved on gems could confer desirable traits upon their owners, like courage, strength, and fertility. These beliefs are supported by the ancient literary sources: for example, an image of the proud and brave lion appears in Plato's dialogues (e.g. the *Republic*) as a metaphor of courage (Plato, *Republic* IV: 441 B). The horse was perceived as an emblem of the human spirit, soaring upwards to the realm of the gods, according to Plato's *Phaedrus* (246 A). It can be seen on a garnet gem dated to the 2nd century AD with a torso of a galloping horse. This was meant to imbue the person wearing it with a sense of morality, loyalty and truthfulness.

Certain gemstones, including jasper and agate, were ascribed with the power to cure disease and also as talismanic and possessing protective qualities. Pliny provides a long list of precious and semi-precious stones that possess such qualities, such as the amethyst, which prevents intoxication (probably due to its purple-red colour resembling wine); the emerald, detoxifying when carved with an image of an eagle; and hematite, which is beneficial for eye and liver diseases (Pliny, *Natural History*: XXXVI, XXXVII.169). In light of the present research, regarding the relationship between depictions of animals and the type of gemstone on which they were engraved, it can be concluded that the colour of the gem was perhaps the most important element, rather than the actual material itself. As an illustration, it is reasonable to attribute amuletic powers to a Greco-Phoenician scarab made of green jasper, on which a seated lion is depicted looking at its tail. The lion was considered a symbol of triumph in general and of victory over death in particular. Depictions of a lion on a green gem, considered as symbolizing health, life and resurrection, were probably considered to enhance the magical power of the stone.

The dating of gems from the Israel Museum, which are eclectic in character, is extremely difficult, since no archaeological context is known. The sorting method developed by Maaskant-Kleibrink, who dealt with a similar collection, has therefore been very useful in dating the gems for this study. Maaskant-Kleibrink sorted the gems according to style rather than workshop, since it was obvious that they had been executed in different provinces. In addition, the stones themselves have helped in establishing the correct date, or at least an approximate one, since different materials were typical to different eras. Occasionally the subject matter too has been helpful for the dating, as is the case of pastoral scenes and similar descriptions, which evoke a sense of abundance and prosperity, so common in the Flavian period, and intended to advertise Rome's economic recovery after the Civil War. The green chalcedony gemstone, on which a shepherd wearing an animal skin, a dog, and a goat suckling her offspring are depicted, was dated in this study to the 1st century AD, based on the rural theme and on the material from which it was carved, typical of this time.

Depictions of animals on gems differ from their depictions in other media, partly because of the small size of the medium, which forced the artist to simplify and reduce the forms, or to use the icons in a concise manner in order to convey a complex idea. This is exemplified in the *dextrarum iunctio/dexiôsis* (the right handshake between men and women, which is a symbol of harmony, engagement or marriage) on gems, in which only the hands appear, as can be seen on a granite gem from the 1st century BC, unlike representations of the same subject in other media, which render the entire family.

Every detail, even the smallest one, carved on a gem, can alter its meaning. For instance, on equestrian gems, the presence of a spear enables the identification of the rider as a soldier or a hero; a wreath would indicate triumph in a horse-race, while wings might identify the figure as Eros. For example, a 1st–2nd century AD carnelian gem with a rider holding a spear on a galloping horse can therefore be identified with certainty as a warrior.

It would seem that the owners of these gems had expected to make their impression and mark in the world by the very act of imprinting their signet-ring in wax. They thereby created a chain of signs, a series of replications that related to the 'self', in the most personal sense, as well as to the public and social roles; identifying the 'self' as a rational, moral, and, finally, as a genuine being.

The findings from the current study enable us to more fully grasp the images depicted not only on the gems in the Israel Museum, but also on those preserved in other collections worldwide. It is my hope that this study will facilitate a better understanding of the complex processes that lay behind the choice of specific images to be carved on gems; processes for which almost no written records exist. However, additional questions still remain to be answered, such as whether it is possible to trace the workshops and artists that created certain gems by cross-referencing data from various collections; or whether one can determine from the images depicted on the gems certain sociological aspects, such as rites of passage, various rituals, and social status. Discussion of these issues is beyond the scope of the present work, and further studies will be needed in order to answer these questions.

Abbreviations

DAGR   *Dictionnaire des antiquités greques et romaines*
LIMC   *Lexicon Iconographicum Mythologiae Classicae*
RE   *Pauly's Realencyclopädie der classischen Altertumswissenschaft*

Bibliography

Ancient Sources

Aelian (Translated by A.F. Scholfield 1958-1959). De natura animalium. Cambridge, Mass : Harvard University Press.

Aeschylus (Translated by A.H. Sommerstein 2008). *Agamemnon*. Cambridge, Mass.: Harvard University Press.

Aeschylus (Translated by A.H. Sommerstein 1989). *Eumenides*. Cambridge, Mass.: Harvard University Press.

Aeschylus (Translated by A.H. Sommerstein 2008). *Seven against Thebes*. Cambridge, Mass.: Harvard University Press.

Aesopus (Translated by E. Chambry 1925-1926). *Fables*. Paris, Belles Lettres.

Alexander von Tralles (Translated by T. Puschmann 1963 (1879)). Amsterdam, A.M. Hakkert.

Ammianus Marcellinus (Translated by J.C. Rolfe 1935-1952). *Rerum gestarum libri*. Cambridge, Mass.: Harvard University Press.

Anthologia Graeca (Translated by W.R. Paton 1956 (1918)). Cambridge, Mass.: Harvard University Press.

Apollodorus (Translated by Sir J.G. Frazer 1921). *Bibliotheca*. Cambridge, Mass.: Harvard University Press.

Apuleius (Translated by J.A. Hanson 1989). *Metamorphoses*. Cambridge, Mass.: Harvard University Press.

Aristophanes (Translated by J. Henderson 1998-2007). *Frogs*. Cambridge, Mass.: Harvard University Press.

Aristophanes (Translated by J. Henderson, 1998-2007). *Lysistrata*. Cambridge, Mass.: Harvard University Press.

Aristophanes (Translated by J. Henderson, 1998-2007). *Clouds*. Cambridge, Mass.: Harvard University Press.

Aristophanes (Translated by J. Henderson 2002). *Wealth (The Plutus)*. Cambridge, Mass.: Harvard University Press.

Aristophanes (Translated by J. Henderson 1998-2007). *Women at the Thesmophoria*. Cambridge, Mass.: Harvard University Press.

Aristotle (Translated by A.L. Peck 1965). *Historia animalium*. Cambridge, Mass.: Harvard University Press.

Aristotle (Translated by H. Tredenick and G.C. Armstrong 1933-1935). *Metaphysics*. Cambridge, Mass.: Harvard University Press.

Aristotle (Translated by J.H. Freese 1926). *Rhetorica*. London, W. Heinemann.

Arrian (Translated by A.A Phillips and M.M. Willcock 1999). *Cynegeticus*. Warminster , Aris & Phillips.

Athenaeus of Naucratis (Translated by C.B. Gulick 1930). *The Deipnosophists*. Cambridge, Mass.: Harvard University Press.

Bacchylides (Translated by R.C. Jebb, 1967). *The Poems and Fragments*. Hildesheim, G. Olms.

(The) Book of the Dead (Translated and edited by Budge, E.A. Wallis, 1967 (1895)). The Papyrus of Ani, Egyptian Text: Transliteration and Translation. London: British Museum.

Callimachus (Translated by A.W. Mair 1955(1921)). *Hymns and Epigrams*. Cambridge, Mass.: Harvard University Press.

Cicero (Translated by A.E. Douglas 1990). *Tusculanae Disputationes*. Warminster, Eng.: Aris & Phillips.

Clement of Alexandria (Translated by G.W. Butterworth 1953). *Exhortation to the Greeks*. Cambridge, Mass.: Harvard University Press.

Clement of Alexandria (A. Roberts and E.J. Donaldson (eds) 1885). *Ante Nicene Fathers, vol. II, Exhortation to the Heathen*. Buffalo.

Clement of Alexandria (Translated by S.P. Wood 1954). *Paedagogus*. Washington, D.C.: Catholic University of America Press.

Columella (Translated by E.S. Forster and E.H. Heffner 1941). *De re rustica (On Agriculture)*. Cambridge, Mass.: Harvard University Press.

Damigeron (Translated by P. Tahil and J. Radcliffe (ed.) 2005). *The Virtues of Stones: De virtutibus lapidum*. Ars Obscura Press.

Dio Cassius (Translated by E. Cary 1969(1916)). *Roman History*. Cambridge, Mass.: Harvard University Press.

Diodorus Siculus (Translated by C.H. Oldfather 1933-1967). *Bibliotheca historica*. London, W. Heinemann.

Diogenes Laertius (Translated by R.D. Hicks 1925). *Lives of Eminent Philosophers*. Cambridge, Mass.: Harvard University Press.

Dionysius of Halicarnassus (Translated by E. Cary 1950). *The Roman Antiquities (Antiquitates Romanae)*. Cambridge, Mass.: Harvard University Press.

Dioscorides (Translated by L.Y. Beck 2005). *De materia medica*. Hildesheim: New York: Olms-Weidmann.

Euripides (Translated by D. Kovacs 2002). *Bacchae*. Cambridge, Mass.: Harvard University Press.

Euripides (Translated by J. Lembke and K.J. Reckford 1994). *Electra*. New York: Oxford University Press.

Euripides (Translated by D. Kovacs 2002). *Helen*. Cambridge, Mass.: Harvard University Press.

Euripides (Translated by D. Kovacs 1995). *Hippolytus*. Cambridge, Mass.: Harvard University Press.

Euripides (Translated by D. Kovacs 2002). *Iphigenia in Tauris*. Cambridge, Mass.: Harvard University Press.

Euripides (Translated by D. Kovacs 2002). *Phoenician Women*. Cambridge, Mass.: Harvard University Press.

Eusebius of Caesarea (Translated by E. des Places 1982). *Die praeparatio evangelica*. Berlin: Akademie-Verlag.

Fronto, Marcus Cornelius (Translated by C.R. Haines 1928-1929). *The Correspondence*. Cambridge, Mass.: Harvard University Press.

Gellius, Aulus (Translated by J.C. Rolfe 1946). *Noctes atticae*. Cambridge, Mass.: Harvard University Press.

Geoponica: sive Cassiani Bassi Scholastici De re rustica eclogae (Bibliotheca scriptorum Graecorum et Romanorum Teubneriana), (H. Beckh (ed.) 1895). Leipzig.

Héliodore (Translated by J. Maillon 1960). *Les Éthiopiques*. Paris, Les Belles Lettres.

Herodotus (Translated by R. Waterfield 1998). *Historiae*. Oxford, New York: Oxford University Press.

Hesiodus (Translated by G.W. Most 2006-2007). *Theogonia*. Cambridge, Mass.: Harvard University Press.

Hesiodus (Translated by G.W. Most 2006-2007). *The Shield of Heracles*. Cambridge, Mass.: Harvard University Press.

Homer (Translated by A.T. Murray 1999). *Iliad*. Cambridge, Mass.: Harvard University Press.

Homer (Translated by A.T. Murray 1995). *Odyssey*. Cambridge, Mass.: Harvard University Press.

Homeric Hymns (Translated by M.L. West 2003). Cambridge, Mass.: Harvard University Press.

Horace (Translated by C.E Bennett 1978 (1914)). *The Odes and Epodes*. Cambridge, Mass.: Harvard University Press.

Horace (Translated by H. R. Fairclough 1978 (1926)). *Satires, Epistles and Ars poetica*. Cambridge, Mass.: Harvard University Press.

Horapollo (Translated by G. Boas 1993(1950)). *Hieroglyphica*. Princeton, N.J.: Princeton University Press.

Hyginus (Translated by A. Le Boeuffle 1983). *L'Astronomie (Poetica astronomica)*. Belles Lettres, Paris.

Iamblichus (Translated by E. des Places 1966). *De mysteriis*. Paris: Belles Lettres.

Isidore of Seville (Translated by S.A. Barney, W.J. Lewis, J.A. Beach and O. Berghof 2006). *Etymologies- Book 16: De Lapidibus et Metallis; Stones and Metals*. Cambridge: Cambridge University Press.

Lithika in Orphica (G. Hermann (ed.) 1971(1805)). Lipsiae, reprinted Hildesheim.

Livy (Translated by B.O. Foster et al. 1955-1961). *Ab urbe condita.* Cambridge, Mass.: Harvard University Press.

Lucian of Samosata (Translated by A.M. Harmon 1936). *Alexander of Abonuteichos - the False Prophet.* Cambridge, Mass.: Harvard University Press.

Lucan (Translated by J.W. Joyce 1973). *Pharsalia.* Ithaca, Cornell University Press.

Lucian (Translated by H. Williams 1900). *Lucian's Dialogues.* Bohn's Classical Library, London: George Bell & Sons.

Lucilius (F. Marx (ed.) 1904), *C. Lucili Carminum Reliquiae, vol. I: Prolegomena and Text.* Teubner, Leipzig.

Macrobius (Translated by R.A. Kaster 2011). *Saturnalia.* Cambridge, Mass.: Harvard University Press.

Manilius (Translated by G.P. Goold 1977). *Astronomicon.* Cambridge, Mass.: Harvard University Press.

Marbode of Rennes (Translated by J.M. Riddle 1977). *De Lapidibus.* Franz Steiner Verlag GMBH, Wiesbaden.

Martial (Translated by D.R. Shackleton Bailey 1993). *Epigrams.* Cambridge, Mass.: Harvard University Press.

Martial (Translated by D.R. Shackleton Bailey 1993). *Liber de spectaculis.* Cambridge, Mass.: Harvard University Press.

Nonnus (Translated by W.H.D. Rouse 1968(1940)). *Dionysiaca.* Cambridge, Mass.: Harvard University Press.

Oppian (Translated by A.W. Mair 1928). *Cynegetica, Halieutica.* Cambridge, Mass.: Harvard University Press.

The Orphic Hymns (Translated by A.N. Athanassakis and B.M. Wolkow 2013). Baltimore: The Johns Hopkins University Press.

The Orphic Poems (Translated by M. L. West 1983). Oxford: Clarendon Press.

Ovidius (Translated by G. Showerman 1977). *Amores.* Cambridge, Mass.: Harvard University Press.

Ovidius (Translated by J.G. Frazer 1989 (1976)). *Fasti.* Cambridge, Mass.: Harvard University Press.

Ovidius (Translated by F.J. Miller 1984). *Metamorphoses.* Cambridge, Mass.: Harvard University Press.

Papyri Graecae Magicae (K. Preisendanz and A. Henrichs (eds) 1974). Stuttgart.

Pausanias (Translated by W.H.S. Jones 1918-1955). *Description of Greece.* Cambridge, Mass.: Harvard University Press.

Petronius (Translated by M. Heseltine 1987(1913)). *Satyricon.* Cambridge, Mass.: Harvard University Press.

Phaedrus (Translated by J. Henderson 2001). *Fabulae.* Oxford, Oxford University Press.

Philostratus (Translated by A. Fairbanks 1931). *Imagines.* London, W. Heinemann.

Philostratus (Translated by F.C. Conybeare 1950 (1912)). *The Life of Apollonius of Tyana.* London, W. Heinemann.

Pindar (Translated by Sir J. Sandys 1946 (1915)). *The Odes of Pindar.* Cambridge, Mass.: Harvard University Press.

Pindar (Translated by W.H. Race 1997). *The Isthmian Odes*. Cambridge, Mass.: Harvard University Press.

Pistis Sophia (Translated by V. MacDermot, C. Schmidt (ed.) 1978). Leiden: E.J. Brill.

Plato (Translated by W.R.M. Lamb 1924). *Euthydemus*. Cambridge, Mass.: Harvard University Press.

Plato (Translated by P. Woodruff 1982). *Hippias Major*. Oxford: B. Blackwell.

Plato (Translated by W.R.M. Lamb 1924). *Laches*. Cambridge, Mass.: Harvard University Press.

Plato (Translated by C. J. Rowe 1993). *Phaedo*. Cambridge: University Press.

Plato (Translated by R. Hackforth 1952). *Phaedrus*. Cambridge: University Press.

Plato (Translated by P. Shorey 1935). *Republic*. Cambridge, Mass.: Harvard University Press.

Plato (Translated by H.N. Fowler 1977(1921)). *Theaetetus*. Cambridge, Mass.: Harvard University Press.

Pliny (Translated by D.E. Eichholz 1962). *Natural History*. Cambridge, Mass.: Harvard University Press.

Pliny the Younger (Translated by B. Radice 1969). *Letters*. Cambridge, Mass.: Harvard University Press.

Plutarch (Translated by B. Perrin 1914-1926). *Lives*. Cambridge, Mass.: Harvard University Press.

Plutarch (Translated by F.C. Babbitt 1927). *Moralia, vol. V, Isis and Osiris*. Cambridge, Mass.: Harvard University Press.

Plutarch (Translated by P.A. Clement and H.B. Hoffleit 1969). *Moralia, vol. VIII, Quaestiones convivales*. Cambridge, Mass.: Harvard University Press.

Plutarch (Translated by H. Cherniss and W.C. Helmbold 1984 (1957)). *Moralia, vol. XII, The E at Delphi*. Cambridge, Mass.: Harvard University Press.

Poetarum Lesbiorum Fragmenta (E. Lobel and D. Page (eds), 1955). Oxford: Clarendon Press.

Posidippus of Pella (C. Austin and G. Bastianini (eds) 2002), *poems 1-20. Posidippi Pellaei quae supersunt omnia*. Milano: Edizioni Universitarie di Lettere Economia.

Propertius (Translated by G.P. Goold 1990). *Elegies*. Cambridge, Mass.: Harvard University Press.

Pyramid Texts: The Pyramid of Unas (Translated by A. Piankoff 1968). Princeton, N.J.: Princeton University Press.

Quintus Smyrnaeus (Translated by A.S. Way 1955 (1913)). *The Fall of Troy*. Cambridge, Mass.: Harvard University Press.

Seneca (Translated by T.H. Corcoran 1971-1972). *Quaestiones naturales*. Cambridge, Mass.: Harvard University Press.

Sophocles (Translated by H. Lloyd-Jones 1994). *Electra*. Cambridge, Mass.: Harvard University Press.

Sophocles (Translated by H. Lloyd-Jones 1994). *Oedipus Tyrannus*. Cambridge, Mass.: Harvard University Press.

Sophocles (Translated by Sir R.C. Jebb 1962). *The Trachiniae*. Amsterdam: A.M. Hakkert.

Statius (Translated by D.R. Shackleton Bailey 2003). *Silvae*. Cambridge, Mass.: Harvard University Press.

Strabo (Translated by H.L. Jones 1970 (1917)). *Geography*. Cambridge, Mass.: Harvard University Press.

Suger Abbot of Saint Denis (Translated and edited by E. Panofsky, 2nd ed. by G. Panofsky-Soergel 1979). *Abbot Suger On the Abbey Church of St. Denis and its Art Treasures*. Princeton, N.J.: Princeton University Press.

Suetonius (Translated by J.C. Rolfe 1914). *De vita Caesarum*. London, W. Heinemann.

Suidas (A. Adler (ed.) 1967-1971). *Suidae Lexicon, s.v. ' Orpheus,' vol. III, p. 564*. Stuttgart.

Tacitus (F.R.D. Goodyear (ed.) 1972-1996). *The Annals of Tacitus*. Cambridge: University Press.

Theocritus (Translated by R. Hunter 2003). *Idylls*. Berkeley, Calif.: University of California Press.

Theophrastus (Translated by D.E. Eichholz 1965). *De Lapidibus (On Stones)*. Oxford.

Thucydides (Translated by C. Forster Smith 1977 (1921)). *History of the Peloponnesian War*. Cambridge, Mass.: Harvard University Press.

Varro (Translated by R.G. Kent 1951). *De lingua Latina*. London, W. Heinemann.

Varro (Translated by W.D Hooper 1935). *De re rustica (On Agriculture)*. Cambridge, Mass.: Harvard University Press.

Vergilius (Translated by J. Dryden 1909). *Aeneid*. New York: P.F. Collier, The Harvard Classics.

Vergilius (Translated by H.R. Fairclough 1999(1916)). *Eclogues*. Cambridge, Mass.: Harvard University Press.

Vergilius (Translated by H.R. Fairclough 1999 (1916)). *Georgics*. Cambridge, Mass.: Harvard University Press.

Vitruvius (Translated by F. Granger 1931). *De architectura*. Cambridge, Mass.: Harvard University Press.

Xenophon (Translated by C.L. Brownson 1998). *Anabasis*. Cambridge, Mass.: Harvard University Press.

Xenophon (Translated by E. Delebecque 1978). *De re equestri (On Horsemanship(.* Belles Lettres, Paris.

Modern Sources

Aldington, R. (trans.) 1989 (1968). 'Pan'. *New Larousse Encyclopedia of Mythology*: 161. London: P. Hamlyn.

Amorai-Stark, S. 1999. Gems, Amulets and Seal stones. In R. Gersht (ed.), *The Sdot Yam Museum Book of the Antiquities of Caesarea Maritima*: 87-113. Tel-Aviv: Hakibbutz Hameuchad (in Hebrew with English abstracts).

Adams, N. 2011. The Garnet Millennium: The Role of Seal Stones in Garnet Studies. In N. Adams and C. Entwistle (eds), *Gems of Heaven: Recent Research on Engraved Gemstones in Late Antiquity*: 10-24. London: British Museum Research Publication.

Amorai-Stark, S. 1993. *Engraved Gems and Seals from two Collections in Jerusalem*. Jerusalem: Franciscan Printing Press.

Anderson, J. C. 1979-1980. A Polygonal Ring with Signs of the Zodiac. *Gesta* 18-19: 39-44.

Anderson, J. K. 1961. *Ancient Greek Horsemanship*. Berkeley: University of California Press.

Andreae, B. (ed.) 1998. *Museo Pio Clementino – Cortile Ottagono, Bildkatalog der Skulpturen des vatikanischen Museums, Bd. 2*. Berlin: Walter de Gruyter.

Andrews, C. 1990. *Ancient Egyptian Jewellery*. London, British Museum.

Aurigemma, S. 1960. *L'Italia in Africa, vol. I, Mosaici della Tripolitania*. Rome: Instituto poligrafico dello stato.

Babelon, E. 1897. *Catalogue des camées antiques et modernes de la Bibliothèque Nationale*, 2 vols. Paris: E. Leroux.

Babelon, E. 1899. *Collection Pauvert de la Chapelle, Intailles et Camées*. Paris: E. Leroux.

Babelon, E. 1896. s.v. 'Gemmae' In C. Daremberg and E. Saglio (eds), *DAGR* 2.2: 1460-1488. Paris: Hachette Livre.

Babelon, E. 1901. *Traité des monnaies greques et romaines*. Paris: E. Leroux.

Baird, L. Y. 1981-2. Priapus Gallinaceus: The Role of the Cock in Fertility and Eroticism in Classical Antiquity and the Middle Ages. *Studies in Iconography* 7-8: 81-111.

Barb, A. A. 1964. Three Elusive Amulets. *Journal of the Warburg and Courtauld Institutes*: 1-22.

Basic, R. 2009. Between Paganism and Christianity: Transformation and Symbolism of a Winged Griffin. *Journal of Iconographic Studies* 2: 85-91.

Beazley, J. D. 1986 (1951). *The Development of Attic Black-figure*. Berkeley, California: University of California Press.

Beazley, J. D. and Boardman, J. 2002 (1920). *The Lewes House Collection of Ancient Gems*. Oxford: Archaeopress.

Beer, C. 1994. *Temple-Boys: a Study of Cypriot Votive Sculpture*, Part 1. (Catalogue, Studies in Mediterranean Archaeology vol. 113). Jonsered: Paul Atsröms Förlag.

Bevan, E. 1986. Representations of Animals in Sanctuaries of Artemis and other Olympian Deities. PhD dissertation, University of Edinburgh.

Bing, P. 2005. The Politics and Poetics of Geography in the Milan Posidippus Section One: On Stones (AB 1-20). In K. Gutzwiller (ed.), *The New Posidippus: a Hellenistic Poetry Book*: 119-140. Oxford: Oxford University Press.

Bivar, A. D. H. 1969. *Catalogue of the Western Asiatic Seals of the British Museum*. London: Trustees of the British Museum.

Black, J. and Green, A. 1992. *Gods, Demons and Symbols of Ancient Mesopotamia: An Illustrated Dictionary*. University of Texas Press.

Blanc, N. and Gury, F. 1981. s.v. 'Eros/Amor, Cupido' *LIMC* III: 952-1049. Zürich und München.

Blanchet, J. A. 1921. Recherches sur les 'Grylles', à propos d'une pierre gravée, trouvée en Alsace. *Revue des Études Anciennes* 23(1): 43-51.

Boardman, J. 1997. Classical Gems and Media Interaction. In C. M. Brown (ed.), *Engraved Gems: Survivals and Revivals, Studies in the History of Art* 54: 13-21.

Boardman, J. 1968a. *Archaic Greek Gems: Schools and Artists in the Sixth and Early Fifth Centuries BC.* Evanston: Northwestern University Press.

Boardman, J. 1974. *Athenian Black Figure Vases.* Oxford: Oxford University Press.

Boardman, J. 2003. *Classical Phoenician Scarabs.* Oxford: Beazley Archive and Archaeopress.

Boardman, J. 1991. Colour Questions. *Jewellery Studies* 5: 29-31.

Boardman, J. 1968b. *Engraved Gems: The Ionides Collection.* Evanston: Northwestern University Press.

Boardman, J. 1980. Greek Gem Engravers, Their Subjects and Style. In: E. Porada (ed.), *Ancient Art in Seals:* 101-119. Princeton: Princeton University Press.

Boardman, J. 1970. *Greek Gems and Finger Rings: Early Bronze Age to Late Classical.* London: Thames and Hudson.

Boardman, J. 1999. The Lewes House Gems: Warren and Beazley. In M. Henig (ed.), *Classicism to Neo-Classicism: Essays Dedicated to Gertrud Seidmann:* 217-225. Oxford: Archaeopress.

Boardman, J. and La Rocca, E. 1978. *Eros in Greece.* London: J. Murray.

Boardman, J. and Vollenweider, M. -L. 1978. *Catalogue of the Engraved Gems and Finger Rings in the AshmoleanMuseum, vol.1: Greek and Etruscan.* Oxford: Clarendon Press.

Bodson, L. 1993. *Contributions à l'histoire des connaissances zoologiques.* Liège: Université de Liège.

Bonner, C. 1951. Amulets chiefly in the British Museum. *Hesperia* 20: 301-345.

Bonner, C. 1954. a Miscellany of Engraved Stones. *Hesperia* 23: 138-157.

Bonner, C. 1945. Eros and the Wounded Lion. *American Journal of Archaeology* 49(4): 441-444.

Bonner, C. 1950. *Studies in Magical Amulets: Chiefly Graeco-Egyptian.* Ann Arbor: University of Michigan Press.

Brandt, E. 1972. *Antike Gemmen in deutschen Sammlungen* Bd. I. Staatliche Münzsammlung München. München.

Briant, P. 1991. Chasses royals macedoniennes et chasses royals perses: le theme de la chasse au lion. *Dialogues d'histoire ancienne* 17(1): 211-255.

Brodrick, A. H. 1972. *Animals in* Archaeology. London: Barrie and Jenkins.

Brugnoli, G. 1989. *L'Astronomia a Roma nell'età augustea.* Galatina: Congedo.

Bruneau, P. 1974. *Mosaics on Délos.* Paris: Diffusion de Boccard.

Budge, E. A. Wallis. 2004 (1904). *The Gods of the Egyptians.* London: Methuen.

Caneva, G. 2010. *The Augustus Botanical Code: Rome- Ara Pacis: Speaking to the People through the Images of Nature.* Rome: Gangemi Editore.

Carandini, A., Ricci A. and de Vos, M. 1982. *Filosofiana: The Villa of Piazza Armerina – The Image of a Roman Aristocrat at the Time Of Constantine.* Palermo: S. F. Flaccovio.

Cassin, B. and Labbarière, J.-L. (eds) 1997. *L'animal dans l'antiquité.* Paris: Librarie Philosophique J. Vrin.

Castriota, D. 1995. *The Ara Pacis Augustae and the Imagery of Abundance in Later Greek and Early Roman Imperial Art.* Princeton: Princeton University Press.

Cermanović-Kuzmanović, A. 1992. s.v. 'Heros Equitans" *LIMC* VI: 1019-1081. Zürich.

Charboneaux, J., Martin, R. and Villard, F. 1973 (1970). *Hellenistic Art.* New York: Braziller.

Cherry, J. 1995. *Mythical Beasts.* London: British Museum Press.

Chifflet, J. 1662. *Socrates, sive, De gemmis eius imagine coelatis iudicium.* Antwerp: Balthazar Moretus.

Christou, C. 1968. Potnia theron. PhD dissertation, Rheinische Friedrich Wilhelms Universität in Bonn, Thessaloniki.

Clark, G. 1986. *Symbols of Excellence: Precious Materials as Expressions of Status.* Cambridge and New York: Cambridge University Press.

Clauss, M. 2001. *The Roman Cult of Mithras: The God and his Mysteries.* New York: Routledge.

Collon, D. 1986. Green Jasper Cylinder Seal Workshop. In M. Kelly-Buccellati, P. Matthiae and M. Van Loon (eds), *Insight through Images: Studies in Honor of Edith Porada*: 57-70. Malibu, California: Undena Publications.

Cook, A. B. 1894. Animal Worship in the Mycenaean Age. *Journal of Hellenic Studies* 14: 81-169.

Cook, A. B. 1965. *Zeus, a Study in Ancient Religion.* Cambridge: Cambridge University Press.

Cooper, J. C. 1992. *Symbolic and Mythological Animals.* London, HarperCollins.

Crawford, M. H. 1974. Roman Republican Coinage. Cambridge: Cambridge University Press.

Crowther, N. B. 1979. Water and Wine as Symbols of Inspiration. *Mnemosyne* 32: 1-11.

Cunliffe, B. 1971. *Fishbourne: a Roman Palace and its Garden.* Baltimore: The Johns Hopkins University Press.

Dasen, V. 2011. Magic and Medicine: Gems and the Power of Seals. In N. Adams and C. Entwistle (eds), *Gems of Heaven: Recent Research on Engraved Gemstones in Late Antiquity*: 69-74. London: British Museum Research Publication.

Deiss, J.J. 1989. *Herculaneum, Italy Buried Treasures.* Malibu, California: J. Paul Getty Museum.

Delaporte, L. 1923. *Catalogue des Cylindres, cachets et pierres gravées de style orientale. Musée du Louvre, vol. 2: Acquisitions.* Paris: Librairie Hachette.

Delatte, A. and Derchain, P. 1964. *Les intailles magiques gréco-égyptiennes.* Paris: Bibliothèque nationale de France.

Delivorrias, A., Berger-Dover, G. and Kossatz-Deissmann, A. 1984. s.v. 'Aphrodite', In *LIMC* II (1): 98-101, pls. 947-986. Zürich und München.

Dessenne, A. 1957. *Le sphinx: étude iconographique.* Paris: E. de Boccard.

Devambez, P. 1981. s.v. 'Amazones', In *LIMC* I (2): pls. 168-229. Zürich und München.

Dixon-Kennedy, M. 1998. s.v. 'Pan', In *Encyclopedia of Greco-Roman Mythology*: 235. California, Oxford: ABC-Clio.

Dierichs, A. 1990. Leda-Schwan-Gruppen in der Glyptik und ihre monumentalen Vorbilder. *Boreas* 13: 37-50.

Dodds, E. R. 1965. *Pagan and Christian in an Age of Anxiety*. Cambridge: Cambridge University Press.

Douglas, N. 1972 (1929). *Birds and Beasts of the Greek Anthology*. New York, B. Blom.

Dunbabin, K. M. D. 1999. *Mosaics of the Greek and Roman World*. Cambridge: Cambridge University Press.

Dunbabin, K. M. D. 1978. *The Mosaics of Roman North Africa*. Oxford: Clarendon Press.

Dunbabin, K. M. D. 1982. The Victorious Charioteer on Mosaics and Related Monuments. *American Journal of Archaeology* 86: 71-72.

Dvorzetsky, E. 2007. Animals on the Coins of the Cities of the Land of Israel in the Roman Period: Art and Propaganda. In B. Arbel, J. Terkel and S. Menashe (eds), *Human beings and Other Animals in the Mirror of History*: 99-131 (in Hebrew). Jerusalem: Carmel.

Evans, A. 1925. The Ring of Nestor: a Glimpse into the Minoan After-World and a Sepulchral Treasure of Gold Signet-Rings and Bead-Seals from Thisbê, Boeotia. *The Journal of Hellenic Studies* 45: 1-75.

Faraone, C. A. 1999. *Ancient Greek Love Magic*. Cambridge, MA: Harvard University Press.

Faraone, C. A. 2011. Text, Image and Medium: The Evolution of Graeco-Roman Magical Gemstones. In N. Adams and C. Entwistle (eds), *Gems of Heaven: Recent Research on Engraved Gemstones in Late Antiquity*: 50-61. London: British Museum Research Publication.

Fletcher, B. 1987 (1896). *A History of Architecture*. London: B. T. Batsford.

Foerster, G. 2005. A Modest Aphrodite from Bet Shean. *Israel Museum Studies in Archaeology* 4: 3-14.

Forsdyke, E. J. 1934. An Archaic Greek Gem. *The British Museum Quarterly* 8 (3): 109-110.

Frazer, J. G. 1951 (1890). *The Golden Bough, V - Spirits of the Corn and of the Wild, II*. London: Macmillan.

Frontisi-Ducroux, F. 1997. Actéon, ses chiens et leur maître. In Cassin, B. and J.-L. Labbarière (eds), *L'animal dans l'antiquité*: 435-444. Paris: Librarie Philosophique J. Vrin.

Furtwängler, A. 1896. *Beschreibung der geschnittenen Steine im Antiquarium*. Berlin.

Furtwängler, A. 1900. *Die antiken Gemmen, 3 vols*. Leipzig.

Gargola, D. G. 1995. *Lands, Laws and Gods: Magistrates and Ceremony in the Regulation of Public Lands in Republican Rome*. University of North Carolina Press.

Gasti, F. and Romano, E. (eds). 2002. *Gli animali nel pensiero e nella letteratura dell'antichità*. Pavia.

Gentili, G. V. 1959. *La villa erculia di Piazza Armerina*. Rome.

Gersht, R. 2007. Deities and Animals in Roman Art and Thought. In B. Arbel, J. Terkel and S. Menashe (eds), *Human beings and Other Animals in the Mirror of History*: 79-98 (in Hebrew). Jerusalem: Carmel.

Gersht, R. 1999. Animals in Roman Sculpture. In O. Rimon and R. Shchori (eds), *Depictions of Animals from the Leo Mildenberg Collection*: 41-45. Haifa: Hecht Museum, University of Haifa.

Giebel, M. 2003. *Tiere in der Antike : von Fabelwesen, Opfertieren und treuen Begleitern.* Stuttgart.

Gignoux, P. and Gyselen, R. 1987. *Bulles et sceaux sassanides de diverses collections.* Paris: Association pour l'Avancement des études iraniennes.

Gilhus, I.S. 2006. *Animals, Gods and Humans - Changing Attitudes to Animals in Greek, Roman and Early Christian Ideas.* New York: Routledge.

Gitler, H. and Lorber, C. 2000/02. Small Silver Coins of Ptolemy I. *Israel Numismatic Journal* 14: 34-42.

Goldman, A.L. 2014. The Octagonal Gemstones from Gordion: Observations and Interpretations. *Anatolian Studies* 64: 163-197.

Goldman, B. 1960. The Development of the Lion-Griffin. *American Journal of Archaeology* 64: 319-328.

Goodenough, E.R. 1953-1968. *Jewish Symbols in the Greco-Roman Period.* 13 vols. New York: Pantheon.

Gordon, R. 2011. Archaeologies of Magical Gems,'in N. Adams and C. Entwistle (eds), *Gems of Heaven: Recent Research on Engraved Gemstones in Late Antiquity*: 39-49. London: British Museum Research Publication.

Gordon, R. 2002. Magical Amulets in the British Museum. *Journal of Roman Archaeology* 15: 666-670.

Gorton, A. F. 1996. Egyptian and Egyptianizing Scarabs. Oxford: Oxford University Committee for Archaeology.

Gramatopol, M. 1974. *Les pierres gravées du Cabinet numismatique de l'Académie Roumaine.* vol. 138. Bruxelles: Latomus.

Gray, L. H. 1951. s.v. 'Cock,' In J. Hastings (ed.), *Encyclopedia of Religion and Ethics* VIII: 694-698. New York.

Guiraud, H. 1988. *Intailles et camées romains.* Paris: Editions du CNRS.

Gury, F. 1997. s.v. 'Zodiacus (Capricorne, Lion etc.),' In *LIMC* 8: 490-497, pls. 1-22. Zürich und München.

Gutzwiller, K. (ed.) 2005. *The New Posidippus: a Hellenistic Poetry Book.* Oxford: Oxford University Press.

Gyselen, R. 1978. *Catalogue des sceaux, camées et bulles sassanides de la Bibliothèque Nationale et du Musée du Louvre.* Paris: Bibliothèque nationale.

Hamburger, A. 1968. Gems from Caesarea Maritima. *'Atiqot* 8: 1-31.

Harris, H. A. 1972. *Sport in Greece and Rome.* London.

Head, B. V.1892. *Catalogue of the Greek Coins of Ionia.* London.

Hendrickson, L. M. 1987. Magic, Medicine and the Survival of the Gods. In *Survival of the Gods: Classical Mythology in Medieval Art*: 141-149. Providence, Rhode Island.

Henig, M. 1984a. A Bronze Key Handle from Brampton, Norfolk. *Antiquaries Journal* LXIV: 407-408.

Henig, M. 1973. A Cornelian Intaglio from Aldborough. *The Yorkshire Archaeological Journal* 45: 180.

Henig, M. 1978. *A Corpus of Roman Engraved Gemstones from British Sites.* (British Archaeological Reports 8). Oxford.

Henig, M. 2007 (1978). *A Corpus of Roman Engraved Gemstones from British Sites.* (British Archaeological Reports 8 third edition). Oxford: Archaeopress.

Henig, M. 1980. A New Combination-Gem. *The Antiquaries Journal* 60: Exhibits at Ballots: 332-333.

Henig, M. 2010. A Two-sided Cornelian Intaglio from Thurleigh, Bedfordshire, England. *PALLAS (Revue d'études antiques)*: 155-158.

Henig, M. 1991. Antique Gems in Roman Britain. *Jewellery Studies* 5: 49-54.

Henig, M. 1997a. The Intaglio. In P.M. Booth *Asthall, Oxfordshire: Excavations in a Roman 'Small Town', 1992* (Thames Valley Landscapes Monograph 9): 100. Oxford: Oxford Archaeological Unit.

Henig, M. 1994. *Classical Gems: Ancient and Modern Intaglios and Cameos in the Fitzwilliam Museum.* Cambridge: Cambridge University Press.

Henig, M. 1981. Cornelian Intaglio from Burial XXXV. In C. Partridge (ed.), *Skeleton Green – A late Iron Age and Romano-British Site* (Britannia Monograph Series 2): 273-275, pl. VIII C. London.

Henig, M. 1977. Death and the Maiden: Funerary Symbolism in Daily Life. In J. Munby and M. Henig, *Roman Life and Art in Britain* (British Archaeological Reports 41): 347-366. Oxford, .

Henig, M. 1997b. Et in Arcadia Ego – Satyrs and Maenads in the Ancient World and Beyond. In C. M. Brown (ed.), *Studies in the History of Art, 54 – Engraved Gems: Survivals and Revivals*: 23-31. Washington: National Gallery of Art.

Henig, M. 2000. From Classical Greece to Roman Britain: some Hellenic themes in provincial art and glyptics. In G. R. Tsetskhladze, A.J.N.W. Prag and A.M. Snodgrass (eds), *Periplous – Papers on Classical Art and Archaeology presented to Sir John Boardman*: 124-135. London: Thames and Hudson.

Henig, M. 1988a. Gemstones from the out fall drain. In B. Cunliffe (ed.), *The Temple of Sulis Minerva at Bath, vol.2: The finds from the Sacred Spring*: 32, no. 25. Oxford: Oxford University Committee for Archaeology.

Henig, M. 1999a. One Hundred and Fifty Years of Wroxeter Gems. In M. Henig and D. Plantzos (eds), *Classicism to Neo-Classicism: Essays dedicated to Gertrud Seidmann* (BAR International Series 793): 49-66. Oxford: Archaeopress.

Henig, M. 1985. Roman Gemstones from Dover. (Exhibits at Ballots) *The Antiquaries Journal* LXV: 463-464. part II.

Henig, M. 1997c. Roman Sealstones. In D. Collon (ed.), *7000 Years of Seals.* London: British Museum Press.

Henig, M. 1988b. The Chronology of Roman Engraved Gemstones. *Journal of Roman Archaeology* 1: 142-152.

Henig, M. 1984b. The Elephant and the Sea-Shell. *Oxford Journal of Archaeology* 3 (2): 243-247.

Henig, M. 2006. The Language of Love and Sexual Desire in Roman Britain: Jewellery and the Emotions. In M. Henig (ed.), *Roman Art, Religion and Society: New Studies from the Roman Art Seminar* BAR International Series 1577): 57-66. *Oxford, 2005.* Oxford: Archaeopress.

Henig, M. 1975. *The Lewis Collection of Engraved Gemstones in Corpus Christi College, Cambridge.* Oxford.

Henig, M. 1997d. The Meaning of Animal Images on Greek and Roman Gems. In M.A. Broustet (ed.), *La glyptique des mondes classiques – mélanges en hommage à Marie-Louise Vollenweider*: 45-53. Paris: Bibliothèque National de France.

Henig, M. 2008. The Re-use and Copying of Ancient Intaglios set in Medieval Personal Seals, mainly found in England: An aspect of the Renaissance of the 12th Century. In N. Adams, J. Cherry and J. Robinson (eds), *Good Impressions: Image and Autority in Medieval Seals*: 25-34. London: British Museum.

Henig, M. 1999b. Three Gems in the Society's Collection. *The Antiquities Journal* 79: 389-392.

Henig, M. and MacGregor, A. 2004. *Catalogue of the Engraved Gems and Finger Rings in the Ashmolean Museum, vol. 2: Roman.* Oxford: Archaeopress.

Henig, M. and Whiting, M. 1987. *Engraved Gems from Gadara in Jordan: The Sa'd Collection of Intaglios and Cameos.* Oxford: Oxford University Press.

Hermary, A., Cassimatis, H. and Vollkommer, R. 1981. s.v. 'Eros,' In *LIMC.* III: 850-942. Zürich und München.

Higgins, R. 1974 (1967). *Minoan and Mycenaean Art.* London.

Hill, G. F. 1923. Alexander the Great and the Persian Lion-Gryphon. *The Journal of Hellenic Studies* 43: 156-161.

Hinks, R. P. 1933. *Catalogue of Greek, Etruscan, and Roman Paintings and Mosaics in the British Museum.* London: British Museum.

Hoffmann H. 1974. Hahnenkampf in Athen, Zur Ikonologie einer Attischen Bildformel. *Revue Archéologique* 195-220.

Hopfner, T. 1926. s.v. 'Lithika', In A. F. Pauly and G. Wissowa (eds), *RE*, Bd. 13.1, cols. 747-769. Stuttgart.

Humphrey, J. H. 1986. *Roman Circuses - Arenas for Chariot Racing.* London,:Batsford.

Huskinson, J. 1996. *Roman Children's Sarcophagi: Their Decoration and its Social Significance.* Oxford: Clarendon Press.

Hyland, A. 1990. *Equus: The Horse in the Roman World.* London: Batsford.

Jennison, G. 2005. *Animals for Show and Pleasure in Ancient Rome.* Philadelphia: University of Pennsylvania Press.

Jereb. 1949. s.v. 'Papagei', In A. F. Pauly and G. Wissowa (eds), *RE*, Bd. 18.3, cols. 933, 934. Stuttgart.

Johns, C. 2006. *Horses: History, Myth, Art.* Cambridge: Harvard University Press.

Jouanna, J. 1992. *Hippocrate.* Paris: Fayard.

Kahil, L. 1992. s.v. 'Artemis', In *LIMC* II (1). Zürich und München.

Kahil, L. 1992. s.v. 'Leda', In *LIMC* VI. Zürich und München.

Kawami, T.S. 1986. Greek Art and Persian Taste: Some Animal Sculptures from Persepolis. *American Journal of Archaeology* 90(3): 259-267.

Keller, O. 1963 (1909). *Die antike Tierwelt.* Leipzig.

Keller, O. 1887. *Thiere des classischen Alterthums.* Innsbruck.

Kerenyi, C. 1996 (1976). *Dionysos Archetypal Image of Indestructible Life.* Princeton: Princeton University Press.

Kibaltchitch, T.W. 1910. *Gemmes de La Russie méridionale.* Berlin.

Kinga, C. W. 1887. *The Gnostics and their Remains, Ancient and Mediaeval.* London.

Kinney, D. 2011. Ancient Gems in the Middle Ages: Riches and Ready-mades. In R. Brilliant and D. Kinney (eds), *Reuse value: spolia and appropriation in art and architecture from Constantine to Sherrie Levine*: 97-119. Farnham: Ashgate.

Kleiner, D. E. E. 1992. *Roman Sculpture.* New Haven and London: Yale University Press.

Klingender, F. 1971. *Animals in Art and Thought*. London: Routledge.

Klinger, S. 1999. Animals in Greek Art. In O. Rimon and R. Shchori (eds), *Depictions of Animals from the Leo Mildenberg Collection*: 21-26. Haifa: Hecht Museum, University of Haifa.

Koch-Harnack, G. 1983. *Knabenliebe und Tiergeschenke, ihre Bedeutung im päderastischen Erziehungssystem Athens*. Berlin: Mann.

Kohler, H. 1960. An Etruscan Tomb-Guardian: The Lion. *Expedition* 2 (2): 25-29.

Kourou, N., Komvou, M., Raftopoulou, S., Krauskopf, I., and Katakis, S. E. 1997. s.v. 'Sphinx', In *LIMC* VIII (1): 1149-1174. Zürich und München.

Krauskopf, I. 1994. s.v. 'Oidipous und die Sphinx', In *LIMC* 7: 1-15, pls. 10-81. Zürich und München.

Kunze, M. 1992. *Die Antikensammlung im Pergamonmuseum und in Charlottenburg*. Berlin: Staatliche Museen zu Berlin.

Kurtz, D. C. and Boardman, J. 1971. *Greek Burial Customs*. London: Thames and Hudson.

Kuttner, A. 2005. Cabinet Fit for a Queen: The Lithika as Posidippus' Gem Museum. In K. Gutzwiller (ed.), *The New Posidippus: a Hellenistic Poetry Book*: 141-163. Oxford: Oxford University Press.

La Rocca, E. 1986. *Rilievi Storici Capitolini – Il Restauro dei Pannelli di Adriano e di Marco Aurelio nel Palazzo dei Conservatori*. Roma.

Lambrinudakis, W. 1984. s.v. 'Apollon Mit Maus (Apollon Smintheus)', In *LIMC* II (1): 231-232. Zürich und München.

Lapatin, K. 2011. Grylloi. In N. Adams and C. Entwistle (eds), *Gems of Heaven: Recent Research on Engraved Gemstones in Late Antiquity*: 88-98. London: British Museum Research Publication.

Lawrence, A. W. 1996 (1957). *Greek Architecture*. New Haven: Yale University.

Lehner, M. 1992. Reconstructing the Sphinx. *Cambridge Archaeological Journal*. 2(1): 3-26.

Liapis, V. 2011. The Thracian Cult of Rhesus and the 'Heros Equitans'. *Kernos* 24: 95-104

Lippold, G. 1923. *Gemmen und Kameen des Altertums und der Neuzeit*. Stuttgart.

Lochin, C. 1994. s.v. 'Pegasos,' In *LIMC*. 7: 214-230, pls. 1-242. Zürich und München.

Maaskant-Kleibrink, M. 1978. *Catalogue of the Engraved Gems in the Royal Coin Cabinet, The Hague: The Greek, Etruscan and Roman Collections*. Den Haag, Government Publishing Office/Wiesbaden: Franz Steiner Verlag.

Maaskant-Kleibrink, M. 1975. *Classification of Ancient Engraved Gems: a Study based on the Collection in the Royal Coin Cabinet*. Leiden.

Maaskant-Kleibrink, M. 1999. Leda on Ancient Gems. In M. Henig (ed.), *Classicism to Neo-classicism: Essays Dedicated to Gertrud Seidman*: 19-27. Oxford: Archaeopress.

Maaskant-Kleibrink, M. 1986. *The Engraved Gems – Description of the Collection in the Rijksmuseum G.M. Kam at Nijmegen*. Nijmegen.

Maaskant-Kleibrink, M. 1989. The Microscope and Roman Republican Gem Engraving. Some Preliminary Remarks. In T. Hackens and G. Moucharte (eds), *PACT (Journal of the European Study Group on Physical, Chemical, Biological and Mathematical Techniques Applied to Archaeology) – Technology and Analysis of*

Ancient Gemstones, European Workshop, Ravello, November 13-16th 1987, 23: 189-191. Bruxelles.

Maaskant-Kleibrink, M. 1997. The Style and Technique of the Engraved Gems. In C. Johns (ed.), *The Snettisham Roman Jewller's Hoard*: 25-27. London: British Museum Press.

Maddoli, G. 1965. Le cretule del Nomophylakion di Cirene. *Annuario della Scuola Archeologica di Atene* 41-42: 40-145.

Mariette, P. J. 1750. *Traité des pierres gravées*. Paris.

Markman, S. D. 1969. *The Horse in Greek Art*. New York.

Marshman, I. 2017. All that glitters: Roman signet rings, the senses and the self. In E.M. Betts (ed.) *Senses of the Empire : Multisensory Approaches to Roman Culture*: 136-146. London; New York, NY: Routledge.

Maspero, G. 1901-1904. *History of Egypt*. London: The Grolier Society.

Mastrocinque, A. 2014. *Les intailles magiques du département des Monnaies, Médailles et Antiques*. Paris: Édition de la Bibliothèque nationale de France.

Mastrocinque, A. 2004-2007. *Sylloge gemmarum gnosticarum*. Rome.

McCartney, E. S. 1924. The Symbolism of Pegasus on Aera Signata. *American Journal of Archeology* 66.

Meshorer, Y. 1984. City-Coins of Eretz-Israel and the Decapolis in the Roman Period. Jerusalem (in Hebrew).

Meshorer, Y. 1989. *The Coinage of Aelia* Capitolina. Jerusalem: the Israel Museum.

Michaeli, T. 2007. Funerary Lights in Painted Tombs in Israel: from Paganism to Christianity. In C. Guiral Pelegrin (ed.), *Circulación de temas y sistemas decorativos en la pintura mural Antigua*: 203-208. Calatayud 533.

Michaeli, T. 2006. The Pictorial Program of the Apolophanes Tomb at Maresha. In D. Guergova (ed.), *Helis V: The Getae - Culture and Traditions, 20 Years Research of the Sveshtari Tomb*: 360-376. Sofia.

Michaeli, T. 2009. *Visual Representations of the Afterlife - Six Roman and Early Byzantine Painted Tombs in Israel*. Leiden.

Michaeli, T. 1998. Wall Paintings in Roman and Early Byzantine Tombs in Israel. PhD dissertation, University of Tel-Aviv.

Michel, S. 2004. *Die Magischen Gemmen: Zu Bildern und Zauberformeln auf geschnittenen Steinen der Antike und Neuzeit*. Berlin.

Middleton, J. H. 1891. *The Engraved Gems of Classical Times with a Catalogue of the Gems in the Fitzwilliam Museum*. Cambridge.

Middleton, S. E. H. 1999. Eastern Gems and Classical Prototypes. In M. Henig (ed.), *Classicism to Neo-Classicism: Essays Dedicated to Gertrud Seidman*: 127-141. Oxford: Archaeopress.

Middleton, S. E. H. 1991. *Engraved gems from Dalmatia*. Oxford: Oxford University Committee for Archaeology, Institute of Archaeology.

Mielsch, H. 2005. *Griechische Tiergeschichten in der antiken Kunst, Kulturgeschichte der antiken Welt, Bd. 111*. Mainz.

Molesworth, H. and Henig, M. 2011. Love and Passion: Personal Cameos in Late Antiquity from the Content Collection. In N. Adams and C. Entwistle (eds), *Gems of Heaven: Recent Research on Engraved Gemstones in Late Antiquity*: 179-185. London: British Museum Research Publication.

Mollard-Besques, S. 1963. *Catalogue raisonné des figurines et reliefs en terre-cuite grecs et romains, vol.* II. Paris: Éditions des Musées Nationaux.

Moorey, P. R. S. 1994. *Ancient Mesopotamian Materials and Industries.* Oxford: Clarendon Press.

Mottahedeh, P. 1997. *Out of Noah's Ark: Animals in Ancient Art from the Mildenberg Collection.* Mainz on Rhein: von Zabern.

Mucznik, S. and Ovadiah, A. 2001. The Bronze Statuette of a Mouse from Kedesh and its Significance. *BABesch* 76: 133-138.

Nagy, A. M. 1992. Ein kaiserzeitlicher Talisman. *Archäologischer Anzeiger*: 99-108.

Natter, L. 1754. *Traité de la méthode antique de graver en pierres fines comparés avec la méthode moderne.* Paris.

Neils, J. 1992. Panathenaic Amphoras: Their Meaning, Makers, and Markets. In J. Neils (ed.), *Goddess and Polis: The Panathenaic Festival in Ancient Athens*: 29-51. New Jersey: Hood Museum of Art, Dartmouth College, New Hampshire, Princeton University Press.

Névérov, O. J. 1976. Presentations sur les gemmes-cachets, Bagues en Metal et Amulets des premiers siécles de notre ère. Decouvertes faites sur le littoral Nord de la Mer Noire. In M. M. Kobylina (ed.), *Études préliminaires aux religions orientales dans l'empire romain, vol. 52, Divinités Orientales sur le littoral Nord de la Mer Noire.* Leiden.

Nilsson, M. P. 1957. *Griechische Feste von religiöser Bedeutung.* Stuttgart.

Orth. 1913. s.v. 'Huhn', In A.F. Pauly and G. Wissowa (eds), RE, Bd. 8.2, cols. 2532-2533. Stuttgart.

Otto, W. F. 1993 (1965). *Dionysus – Myth and Cult.* Dallas, Indiana University Press.

Pannuti, U. 1983. *Catalogo della Collezione Glittica.* Roma: Museo Archeologico Nazionale di Napoli.

Pannuti, U. 1994. *La Collezione Glittica.* Roma: Museo Archeologico Nazionale di Napoli.

Petrain, D. 2005. Gems, Metapoetics, and Value: Greek and Roman Responses to a Third-Century Discourse on Precious Stones. *Transactions of the American Philological Association* 135 (2): 329-357.

Petrie, Flinders, W. M. 1914. *Amulets.* London: University College.

Picard, O. 1989. Le lion et le taureau sur les monnaies d'Acanthe. In *Kraay – Mokholm Essays*: 225-231. Louvain-La-Neuve.

Plant, R. 1979. *Greek Coin Types and their Identification.* London.

Plantzos, D. 1999. *Hellenistic Engraved Gems.* Oxford: Clarendon Press.

Platt, V. 2006. Making an Impression: Replication and the Ontology of the Graeco-Roman Seal Stone. *Art History* 29 (2): 233-257.

Platt, V. 2009. Where the Wild Things Are: Locating the Marvellous in Augustan Wall Painting. In P. Hardie (ed.), *Paradox and the Marvellous in Augustan Literature and Culture*: 41-74. Oxford: Oxford University Press.

Porten, B. 1996. *The Elephantine Papyri in English: Three Millennia of Cross-Cultural Continuity and Change*, (Documenta et Monumenta Orientis Antiqui, vol. 22). Leiden, New York and Koln: Brill.

Platz-Horster, G. 1984. *Die antiken Gemmen im Rheinischen Landesmuseum Bonn.* Bonn.

Platz-Horster, G. 2010. Kleine-Praser and Chromium-bearing Chalcedonies: about a Small Group of Engraved Gems. *PALLAS* 83: 179-202.

Pollard, J. 1977. *Birds in Greek Life and Myth*. Plymouth.

Prieur, J. 1988. *Les animaux sacrés dans l'antiquité*. Rennes: Quest-France.

Rahmani, L. 1967. Jason's Tomb. *Israel Exploration Journal* 17: 67-100.

Rea, J. R. 1980. A Gold Ring with a Horoscope of A.D. 327. *Zeitschrift für Papyrologie und Epigraphik* 39: 155-158.

Reinach, S. 1922. *Répertoire de peintures grecques et* romaines. Paris: E. Leroux.

Reitler, R. 1949. Theriomorphic Representation of Hekate-Artemis. *American Journal of Archaeology* 29-31.

Renouf, P. Le Page. 1893. The Myth of Osiris Unnefer. *Transactions of the Society of Biblical Archaeology* IX: 281–294.

Richter, G. M. A. 1930. *Animals in Greek Sculpture*. Oxford: Oxford University Press.

Richter, G. M. A. 1956. *Catalogue of Engraved Gems: Greek, Etruscan and Roman, in the Metropolitan Museum of Art*. Rome: L'Erma di Bretschneider.

Richter, G. M. A. 1971. *Engraved Gems of the Greeks, Etruscans and Romans II: Engraved Gems of the Romans: a Supplement to The History of Roman Art*. London: Phaidon Press.

Richter, G. M. A. 1968a. The Subjects on Roman Engraved Gems, Their Derivation, Style and Meaning. *Revue Archéologique* 63: 279-286.

Richter, G. M. A. 1968b. *The Engraved Gems of the Greeks, Etruscans and Romans*. London: Phaidon.

Robert, C. 1890. *Die antiken Sarkophagreliefs*. Berlin.

Rozenberg, S. 1999. The Depiction of Animals in Wall Paintings of the Second Temple Period. In O. Rimon and R. Shchori (eds), *Depictions of Animals from the Leo Mildenberg Collection*: 27-34. Haifa: Hecht Museum, University of Haifa.

Saglio, E. 1877. s.v. 'Alektryonon agones', In C. Daremberg and E. Saglio (eds), *DAGR* I (1): 180-181. Paris: Hachette Livre.

Sauron, G. 1990. Les monstres, au coeur des conflits esthétiques à Rome au 1er siècle avant J.-C. *Revue de l'Art* 90: 35-45.

Schnapp, A. 1997. *Le chasseur et la cité: chasse et érotique en Grèce ancienne*. Paris: Albin Michel.

Schneider, K. 1912. s.v. 'Hahnenkämpfe', In A.F. Pauly and G. Wissowa (eds), *RE* 7.2: 2210-2215. Stuttgart.

Scullard, H. H. 1974. *The Elephant in the Greek and Roman World*. London.

Sena Chiesa, G. 1966. *Gemme del Museo Nazionale di Aquileia*. Padua.

Simone, M. and Zazoff, P. 2002. Magical Amulets in the British Museum. *Journal of Roman Archaeology* 15 (1): 666-670.

Simpson, M. 1976. *Gods and Heroes of the Greeks: The 'Library' of Apollodorus*. Amherst: University of Massachusetts Press.

Soeda, A. 1987. Gods as Magical Charms: The Use of Ancient Gems in the Medieval Christian West. In *Survival of the Gods: Classical Mythology in Medieval Art*: 185-192. Providence: Rhode Island.

Spier, J. 1992. *Ancient Gems and Finger Rings*. Malibu, California: J. Paul Getty Museum.

Spier, J. 1999. Conyers Middleton's Gems. In M. Henig (ed.), *Classicism to Neo-Classicism: Essays dedicated to Gertrud Seidmann*: 205-215. Oxford: Archaeopress.

Spier, J. 2010. Most Fowl: Athena, Ares, and Hermes Depicted as Birds on Engraved Gems. *PALLAS*: 245-250.

Stebbins, E. B. 1929. *The Dolphin in the Literature and Art of Greece and Rome*. Menasha, Wisconsin.

Stewart, S. 1993. *On Longing: Narratives of the Miniature, the Gigantic, the Suvenir, the Collection*. Durham: Duke University Press.

Stuveras, R. 1969. *Le putto dans l'art romain*. Brussels: Latomus.

Thorndike, L. 1964. *A History of Magic and Experimental Science*. New York: Columbia University Press.

Tiradritti, F. 1998. *Isis, the Egyptian Goddess who Conquered Rome*. Cairo.

Toynbee, J. M. C. 1973. *Animals in Roman Life and Art*. London: Thames and Hudson

Toynbee, J. M. C. 1963. *Art in Roman Britain*. London: Phaidon Press.

Toynbee, J. M. C. 1971. *Death and Burial in the Roman World*. London: Thames and Hudson.

Toynbee, J. M. C. and Ward Perkins, J. B. 1950. Peopled Scrolls: a Hellenistic Motif in Imperial Art. *Papers of the British School at Rome* 18: 1-43.

Toynbee, J. M. C. 1953. *The Ara Pacis Reconsidered and Historical art in Roman Italy*. Proceedings of the British Academy, XXXIX. London: G. Cumberledge

Trendall, A. D. 1967. *The Red-Figured Vases of Lucania, Campania and Sicily*. Oxford: Clarendon Press.

Troy, M. L. 1976. Mummeries of Resurrection, The Cycle of Osiris in Finnegans Wake. PhD dissertation, University of Uppsala.

Tsiafakis, D. 2003. πέλωρα - Fabulous Creatures and/or Demons of Death? In J.M. Padgett (ed.), *The Centaur's Smile: the Human Animal in Early Greek Art*: 73-104. Princeton: Princeton University Art Museum.

Turcan, R. 1966. *Les sarcophages romains à réprésentations dionysiaques*. Paris: E. de Boccard.

Vermeule, E. 1979. *Aspects of Death in Early Greek Art and Poetry*. Berkeley, Los Angeles, London: University of California Press.

Vermeule, C. C. 1957. *Engraved Gems from Sommerville Collection*. Philadelphia: University Museum.

Vollenweider, M.-L. 1967-1983. *Catalogue raisonné des sceaux, cylindres, intailles et camées, Musée d'Art et d'Histoire de Genève, 3 vols*. Mainz.

Vollenweider, M.-L. 1966. *Die Steinschneidekunst und ihre Künstler in spatrepublikanischer und Augusteischer zeit*. Baden Baden.

Wagner, C. and Boardman, J. 2003. *A Collection of Classical and Eastern Intaglios, Rings and Cameos* (BAR International Series 1136). Oxford: Archaeopress.

Walters, H. B. 1926. *Catalogue of the Engraved Gems and Cameos, Greek, Etruscan and Roman, in the British Museum*. London: The British Museum Trustees.

Walters, H. B. 1929. *Corpus Vasorum Antiquorum: Great Britain, British Museum, vol. 4*. London.

Ward, W. A. 1992. A Silver Scarab from Ibiza: The Motif of the Cow Suckling her Calf. *Rivista di studi fenici* 20 (1): 67-81.

Watanabe, C. E. 2002. *Animal Symbolism in Mesopotamia: a Contextual Approach.* Wien: Institut für Orientalistik der Universität Wien.

Waurick, G. 1988. Helme der Hellenistischen Zeit und ihre Vorläufer. In W. D. Heilmeyer et al. (eds), *Antike Helme: Sammlung Lipperheide und andere Bestände des Antikenmuseums Berlin*: 159-163. Mainz.

White, K. D. 1970. *Roman Farming.* London: Thames and Hudson.

Zanker, P. 1988. *The Power of Images in the Age of Augustus.* Ann Arbor: The University of Michigan Press.

Zazoff, P. 1970. *Antike Gemmen in Deutschen Sammlungen.* Wiesbaden.

Zazoff, P. 1970. *Antike Gemmen - Staatliche Kunstsammlungen Kassel.* Wiesbaden.

Zazoff, P. 1983. *Die antiken Gemmen.* München.

Ziegler, K. 1912. s.v 'Gryps', In A. F. Pauly and G. Wissowa (eds), *RE* 1.7 (2): 1902-1929. Stuttgart.

Zwierlein-Diehl, E. 1970. *Antike Gemmen in deutschen Sammlungen, Staaliche Museen Preußischer Kulturbesitz Antikenabteilung, Berlin, Bd. 2.* München.

Zwierlein-Diehl, E. 1973. *Die antiken Gemmen des Kunsthistorischen Museums in Wien, Bd. 1.* München.

Zwierlein-Diehl, E. 1992. *Magische Amulette und andere Gemmen des Instituts für Altertumskunde der Universitität zu Köln.* Opladen.